Black in Latin America

Henry Louis Gates, Jr.

Black in Latin America

New York University Press • *New York and London*

NEW YORK UNIVERSITY PRESS
New York and London
www.nyupress.org

Black in Latin America, with Henry Louis Gates, Jr., is a production
of Inkwell Films, Wall to Wall Television, and THIRTEEN in
association with WNET.org.

Library of Congress Cataloging-in-Publication Data
Gates, Henry Louis.
Black in Latin America / Henry Louis Gates, Jr.
p.   cm.
Includes bibliographical references and index.
ISBN 978-0-8147-3298-4 (cl : alk. paper)
ISBN 978-0-8147-3299-1 (e-book)
ISBN 978-0-8147-3342-4 (e-book)
1. Blacks—Latin America—History. 2. Blacks—Race identity—
Latin America. 3. Slavery—Latin America—History. 4. Latin
America—Civilization—African influences. 5. Latin America—
Race relations.   I. Title.
F1419.N4G38 2011
980'.00496—dc22   2011007759

New York University Press books are printed on acid-free paper,
and their binding materials are chosen for strength and durability.
We strive to use environmentally responsible suppliers and materials
to the greatest extent possible in publishing our books.

Manufactured in the United States of America

10 9 8 7 6 5 4 3 2 1

For Glenn H. Hutchins

Contents

Acknowledgments

This project would not have been possible without the support of a very large group of dedicated people who advised me and supported me at every stage—from the development and production of the four-hour PBS documentary series *Black in Latin America* through the researching, writing, and editing of this book. I cannot thank them enough. The following is simply a modest attempt to acknowledge my enormous debt.

First, I would like to thank the scholars who assisted me throughout the extensive process of researching and scripting the four-hour documentary series. I learned a tremendous amount from each of them. Each is an expert on the history of race and slavery in one of the six countries examined in the series and in this book, and I shall be forever grateful to each for their tolerance and patience with me as I attempted to understand the many ways in which race and racism are configured differently in Latin America than they have been in the United States. They include the following: Carlos Aguirre, Wlamyra R. de Albuquerque, Guy Alexandre, George Reid Andrews, Paul Austerlitz, María del Carmen Barcia, Manuel Barcia, Miguel Barnet, Maribel Arrelucea Barrantes, Celsa Albert Batista, Rachel Beauvoir-Dominique, Herman Bennett, Alexandra Bronfmann, Ginetta E. B. Candelario, Glenda R. Carpio, Mónica Carrillo, Roberto Cassa, Graciela Chailloux, Sagrario Cruz-Carretero, Torres Cuevas, José "Cheche" Campos Dávila, Martha Ellen Davis, Juan Manuel de la Serna, Robin Derby, Laurent Dubois, David Eltis, Sujatha Fernandes, Ada Ferrer, Maria Filomena, Alejandro De La Fuente, Júnia Furtada, Anita González, Raymundo Gonzalez, Frank Guridy, Aline Helg, Judith Hernández, Rafael Figueroa Hernández, Linda Heywood, Juliet Hooker, Laura Lewis, J. Lorand Matory, April Mayes, Elizabeth McAlister, Kathryn McKnight, Robin Moore, Lisa Morales, Arturo Motta, Abdias do Nascimento, Maria Lúcia Pallares-Burke, Franklin Franco Pichardo, Frank Moya Pons, Armando

Rangel, João José Reis, Sabrina María Rivas, Tomás Fernández Robaina, Juan Rodríguez, Marilene Rosa, Mark Q. Sawyer, Julie Sellers, Theresa A. Singleton, Katherine Smith, Carlos Hernández Soto, Edward Telles, John Thornton, Silvio Torres-Saillant, Richard Turits, Marial Iglesias Utset, Bobby Vaughn, Bernardo Vega, María Elisa Velázquez, Chantalle F. Verna, Ben Vinson III, Peter Wade, Paula Moreno Zapata, and Roberto Zurbano.

Second, I would like to thank the following scholars for reading and commenting on several drafts of the manuscript of this book: Carlos Aguirre, Laurent Dubois, Ada Ferrer, Linda Heywood, J. Lorand Matory, Frank Moya Pons, João José Reis, John Thornton, Silvio Torres-Saillant, Marial Iglesias Utset, María Elisa Velázquez, and Ben Vinson III.

In addition, I would like to thank the many individuals outside of academia who gave their time, support, and expertise to this project, including especially Susana Baca, Chebo Ballumbrosio, Max Beauvoir, MV Bill, Frank Cruz, Patrick Delatour, Bernard Diederich, Colonel Víctor Dreke, Soandres Del Rio Ferrer, Mestre Boa Gente, Father Glyn Jemmott, Louis Lesley Marcelin, Román Minier, Marta Moyano, Tato Quiñones, Israel Reyes, José Rijo, and Eduardo Zapata.

I would also like to thank the many colleagues and friends who have provided me with advice and inspiration at various stages and in various ways during this long and sometimes challenging process. These include Charlie Davidson, Anne DeAcetis, Angela De Leon, Liza and Maggie Gates, Sharon Adams, Dr. Paul and Gemina Gates, Bennett Ashley, William Baker, Dr. Barbara Bierer, Lawrence Bobo, Tina Brown, Alvin Carter III, Charles Davidson and his colleagues at the Andover Shop, Brenda Kimmel Davy, Jorge Dominguez, James Early, Caroline Elkins, Richard Foley, Badi Foster, Despina Papazoglou Gimbel, Amy Gosdanian, Bill Grant, Vera Ingrid Grant, Merilee Grindle, Patricia Harrison, Dr. Galen Henderson, Jonathan Hewes, Evelyn Brooks Higginbotham, Glenn H. Hutchins, Dr. Steve Hyman, Paula Kerger, Stephen M. Kosslyn, Paul Lucas, Mark Mamolen, Dyllan McGee and Peter Kunhardt, Ciara McLaughlin, Ingrid Monson, Marcyliena Morgan, Dr. Tom Nash, Donald and Susan Newhouse, Diane Peterson, Evan Pimental, Steven Rattner, Tammy Robinson, Daniel Rose, Dr. Marty Samuels, Stephen Segaller, John Sexton, Neal Shapiro, Graham Smith, Doris

Sommer, Marta Vega, Darren Walker, John Wilson, Abby Wolf, Donald Yacovone, and Eric Zinner.

I would also like to express my deepest appreciation to the production team that helped me to create the four-hour documentary version of this project and stood by me at every point in its development, including Raquel Alvarez, Fernando Continentino, Mario Delatour, Christina Daniels, Paula Garcia, George Hughes, Beth James, Francisco Lewis, Jeanne Marcelino, Francis Martinez Maseda, Deborah McLauchlan, Raul Rodriguez Notario, Verity Oswin, Diene Petterle, Ricardo Pollack, Tricia Power, Minna Sedmakov, Ilana Trachtman, Jemila Twinch, Nelson Rivera Vicente, and Tamsynne Westcott.

I am also very grateful to the researchers who searched through hundreds of hours of interview transcripts to aid me in shaping the scripts for each of the four episodes in the documentary series and the six chapters in this book. They include Jemila Twinch, Donald Yacovone, and especially Sabin Streeter.

Finally, I want to thank the funders of this project for their generosity, notably Darren Walker and Orlando Bagwell and the Ford Foundation, Richard Gilder, Lewis Lehrman, James Basker and the Gilder-Lehrman Foundation, Alphonse Fletcher, Jr., and the Fletcher Foundation, Patricia Harrison, Ernest Wilson III, and the Corporation for Public Broadcasting, Paula Kerger and John Wilson and PBS, Badi Foster, Luis Murillo, and Phelps Stokes, Luis Alberto Moreno and his team at the Inter-American Development Bank, Tammy Robinson, Bill Grant, Neal Shapiro and Channel Thirteen/WNET, as well as all of our nation's PBS stations and its brilliant, devoted viewers.

Introduction

I FIRST LEARNED that there were black people living someplace in the Western Hemisphere other than the United States when my father told me the first thing that he had wanted to be when he grew up. When he was a boy about my age, he said, he had wanted to be an Episcopal priest, because he so admired his priest at St. Philip's Episcopal Church in Cumberland, Maryland, a black man from someplace called Haiti. I knew by this time that there were black people in Africa, of course, because of movies such as *Tarzan* and TV shows such as *Shena, Queen of the Jungle* and *Ramar of the Jungle*. And then, in 1960, when I was ten years old, our fifth-grade class studied "Current Affairs," and we learned about the seventeen African nations that gained their independence that year. I did my best to memorize the names of these countries and their leaders, though I wasn't quite sure why I found these facts so very appealing. But my father's revelation about his earliest childhood ambition introduced me to the fact that there were black people living in other parts of the New World, a fact that I found quite surprising.

It wasn't until my sophomore year at Yale, as a student auditing Robert Farris Thompson's art history class "The Trans-Atlantic Tradition: From Africa to the Black Americas," that I began to understand how "black" the New World really was. Professor Thompson used a methodology that he called the "Tri-Continental Approach"—complete with three slide projectors—to trace visual leitmotifs that recurred among African, African American, and Afro-descended artistic traditions and artifacts in the Caribbean and Latin America, to show, à la Melville Herskovits, the retention of what he called "Africanisms" in the New World. So in a very real sense, I would have to say, my fascination with Afro-descendants in this hemisphere, south of the United States, began in 1969, in Professor Thompson's very popular, and extremely entertaining and rich, art history lecture course. In addition, Sidney Mintz's anthropology courses and his brilliant scholarly work

1

on the history of the role of sugar in plantation slavery in the Caribbean and Latin America also served to awaken my curiosity about another black world, a world both similar to and different from ours, south of our borders. And Roy Bryce-Laporte, the courageous first chair of the Program in Afro-American Studies, introduced me to black culture from his native Panama. I owe so much of what I know about African American culture in the New World to these three wise and generous professors.

But the full weight of the African presence in the Caribbean and Latin America didn't hit me until I became familiar with the Trans-Atlantic Slave Trade Database, conceived by the historians David Eltis and David Richardson and based now at Emory University. Between 1502 and 1866, 11.2 million Africans survived the dreadful Middle Passage and landed as slaves in the New World. And here is where these statistics became riveting to me: of these 11.2 million Africans, according to Eltis and Richardson, only 450,000 arrived in the United States. That is the mind-boggling part to me, and I think to most Americans. All the rest arrived in places south of our border. About 4.8 million Africans went to Brazil alone. So, in one sense, the major "African American Experience," as it were, unfolded not in the United States, as those of us caught in the embrace of what we might think of as "African American Exceptionalism" might have thought, but throughout the Caribbean and South America, if we are thinking of this phenomenon in terms of sheer numbers alone.

About a decade ago, I decided that I would try to make a documentary series about these Afro-descendants, a four-hour series about race and black culture in the Western Hemisphere outside of the United States and Canada. And I filmed this series this past summer, focusing on six countries—Brazil, Cuba, the Dominican Republic, Haiti, Mexico, and Peru—choosing each country as representative of a larger phenomenon. This series is the third in a trilogy that began with *Wonders of the African World*, a six-part series that aired in 1998. That series was followed by *America Behind the Color Line*, a four-part series that aired in 2004. In a sense, I wanted to replicate Robert Farris Thompson's "Tri-Continental" methodology to make, through documentary film, a comparative analysis of these cardinal points of the Black World. Another way to think of it is that I wanted to replicate the points of the Atlantic triangular trade: Africa, the European colonies of the Caribbean and South America, and black America. *Black in Latin America,* another four-hour series, is the third part of this trilogy, and this book expands considerably on what I was able to include in that series. You might say that I have been fortunate enough to find myself over the past decade in a most curious position: to be able to make films about subjects about which I am curious and about which I initially knew very little, with the generous assistance of many scholars in these fields and many more informants I interview in these countries.

The most important question that this book attempts to explore is this: what does it mean to be "black" in these countries? Who is considered "black" and under what circumstances and by whom in these societies? The answers to these questions vary widely across Latin America in ways that will surprise most people in the United States, just as they surprised me. My former colleague, the Duke anthropologist J. Lorand Matory recently explained the complexity of these matters to me in a long and thoughtful email: "Are words for various shades of African descent in Brazil, such as *mulattoes, cafusos, pardos, morenos, pretos, negros,* etc., types of 'black people,' or are *pretos* and *negros* just the most African-looking people in a multidirectional cline of skin color–facial feature–hair texture combinations?" And how do social varables enter the picture? Matory asks: "Suppose two people with highly similar phenotypes are classified differently according to how wealthy and educated they are, or the same person is described differently depending upon how polite, how intimate, or how nationalistic the speaker wants to be? In what contexts does the same word have a pejorative connotation, justifying the translation of *nigger,* and in another context connote affection, such as the word *negrito?*"

How important is the relation of race and class? As Matory told me, "Debates about 'race' are almost always also about class. We debate the relative worth of these *two* terms in describing the structure and history of hierarchy in our two societies. North Americans," he concluded quite pungently, "tend to be as blind about the centrality of class in our society and vigilant about the centrality of race as Latin Americans are vigilant about the reality of class and blind about the reality of race." And what about the term *Latin America?* Though this term lumps together speakers of the Romance languages and ignores the fact that there are millions of speakers of English, Dutch, and various creole languages throughout the Caribbean and South America, for convenience sake, it seemed to be the most suitable and economical term that we could agree on to refer to this huge and richly various set of societies, each with its own unique history of slavery, genetic admixture, and race relations.

The more I learn about the trans-Atlantic slave trade, the more I realize how complex and extensive the cultural contacts among the three points of Robert Farris Thompson's "Tri-Continental" triangle could be, even—or especially—at the individual level, both those of slaves and of black elites, with Europeans and Americans and with other black people. Most of us were taught the history of slavery in school (if we were taught at all) through simple stereotypes of kidnappings by white men, dispersal of related tribal members on the auction block to prevent communication and hence rebellion, and the total separation of New World black communities from each other and from their African origins. The idea that some members of the African elite were active players in the commerce of the slave trade or that they traveled to the New World and to Europe and home again for commercial, diplomatic, or educational purposes is both surprising and can be quite disturbing.

While some scholars of slavery and of African American Studies (and I include myself in this group) may have come late to an understanding of the remarkable extent of contact between Africans on the continent with Africans in Europe and throughout the Americas (as well as, for our purposes in this book, the similarities and differences in the historical experiences and social and cultural institutions Afro-descendants created throughout the Western Hemisphere), intellectuals, writers, musicians, and elites of color have long been keenly aware of each other, starting as early as the seventeenth and eighteenth centuries, if not before. For example, exchanges between African rulers and the courts of Europe started very early in the modern era. We know from the visual archival record, for instance, that emissaries from the monarchs of Ethiopia and the kingdom of Kongo came to the Vatican as early as the fifteenth and sixteenth centuries, respectively, and established formal diplomatic embassies there. An Ethiopian embassy before Pope Eugenius IV at the Council of Florence in 1439 is depicted in bronze at the entrance to St. Peter's. And Antonio Emanuele Funta (or Ne Vunda) was ambassador to the Vatican from Kongo, sent by King Alvaro II to Pope Paul V in 1604, via Brazil and Spain, arriving in

1608, when he died. The role of African elites in the trans-Atlantic slave trade after the early 1500s led to diplomatic and commercial negotiations back and forth between Europe and Africa and Africa and Brazil, for example. And this is a logical development, once we allow Africans the same degree of agency that we presume for Europeans in the exercise of the slave trade, which was, all too often, I am sad to say, first and last, a business. But these commercial contacts were followed by those between scholars and intellectuals as well. "El negro Juan Latino," a former slave who wore his blackness in his name, became the first African professor of grammar at the University of Granada and the first African to publish a book of poetry in Latin, in 1573. Latino is mentioned in the opening section of Cervantes's *Don Quixote* and was sometimes cited in biographical dictionaries in the eighteenth century as evidence of the African's "improvability." The Abbas Gregorius, from Ethiopia, collaborated with a German scholar to create the first grammar of the Amharic language less than a century after Juan Latino thrived. We recall him both through his grammar and through a striking image of him that has survived. But black men and women of letters from across the black world seem to have shared a certain fascination with each other as well and seem to have taken inspiration from the accomplishments of each other, if only through works such as the Abbé Henri Grégoire's *De la littérature des nègres* (The Literature of Negroes), published in 1808. In 1814, the Haitian Emperor Henri Christophe ordered fifty copies of Grégoire's book and invited him to visit his kingdom.

Perhaps in the same way that Latin and the Roman Catholic Church gave men and women of letters in the late Middle Ages—say, in what is now Italy or what is now Germany or France—a certain degree of common culture, even if workers or serfs in those societies did not share access to that common identity, so, too, black writers in Boston and New York, London and Paris, Jamaica and the Gold Coast throughout the eighteenth century could be aware of each other, sometimes commented on each other's existence, read and revised or troped each other's books, sometimes even corresponded about each other, and traveled back and forth either between Africa and Europe, America and Europe, or among Africa, Latin America, America, and Europe. I am thinking of Jacobus Capitein and Anton Wilhelm Amo from the Gold Coast, both of whom attended universities in Europe before returning to Africa; the Jamaican Francis Williams, one of the first black persons to read law at Lincoln's Inn in London (whose writing Hume disparaged in his influential essay "Of National Characters" of 1754), and who returned to Jamaica following his studies to establish a school, just as Capitein did in the Gold Coast; the widely read and commented on poet Phillis Wheatley, the first person of African descent to publish a book of poetry in English, who sailed to London to publish her book and served as inspiration to some of the black abolitionists there; the master of the epistle, Ignatius Sancho, who corresponded with Sterne and who wrote about Wheatley's enormous significance; and the first five authors of a new literary genre called the slave narratives, who revised what I call "the trope of the talking book" in each of their memoirs of their enslavement. One of these, the best-selling author Olaudah Equiano (Gustavus Vassa), who was born in Africa, visited fourteen islands in the West Indies as a slave (including the Bahamas, Barbados, Jamaica, Montserrat, St. Kitts, and the Mosquito Shore) and the United States, before ultimately settling in England as a free man. Many of these people were cited by foes of slavery as prima facie evidence that the African was at least potentially the intellectual equal of Europeans and was therefore an argument for the abolition of slavery. Indeed, Grégoire dedicated his book to Amo, Sancho, Vassa, his friend Cugoano, and Wheatley, among others.

As the free African American community grew in the United States, contacts with the Caribbean and Latin America increased dramatically in the nineteenth century. The black abolitionists Henry Highland Garnet and Frederick Douglass offer two salient examples. Garnet, a militant abolitionist, the first black minister to preach to the House of Representatives and a pioneering figure in the black colonization movement, traveled to Cuba as a cabin boy before he was ten and in 1849 founded the African Civilization Society to advocate for the emigration of free black people to Mexico and the West Indies, as well as to Liberia. Garnet served as a missionary for three years in Jamaica. In 1881, he became the United States minister to Liberia, where he died two months later and where he is buried. Frederick Douglass, between January 24 and March 26, 1871, served by appointment of President Ulysses S. Grant as the assistant secretary to the commission to Santo Domingo, exploring the possibility of annexing the Dominican Republic as a state, the nation's first black state, according to Douglass, who passionately supported this plan for this reason. Between 1889 and 1891, Douglass served as the US consul general to Haiti and chargé d'affaires to the Dominican Republic. During this period, Douglass wrote several essays and speeches about the Haitian Revolution and Toussaint Louverture and the importance of Haiti as "among the foremost civilized nations of the earth," as a speech delivered on January 2, 1893, was entitled. Even in nineteenth-century African American literature, Cuba was a fictive presence, for example, in Martin R. Delany's novel *Blake* (serialized in 1859 and in 1861–1862) and in a short story published by Thomas Detter in 1871 entitled "The Octoroon Slave of Cuba."

In the twentieth century, as we might expect, the contacts only increased in degree and number. Booker T. Washington, as the historian Frank Andre Guridy notes, had extensive interchanges at the beginning of the century with black Cuban intellectuals such as Juan Gualberto Gómez, whose son studied at Tuskegee. His autobiography was published in Spanish in its first Cuban edition in 1903, just two years after it was published in the States. Washington developed programs that trained black Cuban students at his Tuskegee Institute in the vocations and industrial arts and trades. Washington's educational program also influenced the thinking of the black Brazilian intellectual Manuel Querino.

Marcus Garvey's United Negro Improvement Association (UNIA) in the early decades of the twentieth century had more of a presence throughout the Caribbean and Latin America than most of us have realized, again thanks to Frank Guridy's research. Garvey named the ships of his Black Star Line after black heroes such as Phillis Wheatley and Frederick Douglass, as we might expect, but also after Antonio Maceo, the "Bronze Titan," one of the leading generals in the Cuban War of Independence and one of Cuba's founding fathers. The first stop of the *Frederick Douglass*, in fact, on its 1919 Caribbean tour was Cuba; the Cuban branch of the UNIA was founded that year, and Garvey visited Cuba two years later in March 1921, a trip that was covered in the *Heraldo de Cuba* newspaper in Havana. It turns out that Cuba had more branches of the UNIA than did any country other than the United States. The UNIA operated in Cuba until 1929, when it was closed down under the Machado government, using the same law, the Morua law, that had been used to ban the all-black Independent Party of Color and the organization of political parties along racial lines in 1912.

Du Bois—himself of Haitian descent, through his father, who was born in Haiti in 1826—proudly boasted of the many Afro-Latin Americans who attended the Pan-African Conference in London in 1900 and the first Pan-African Congress in Paris in 1919. At the 1900 conference, representatives from St. Kitts, Trinidad, St. Lucia, Jamaica, Antigua, and Haiti attended. In the pages of the *Crisis*, Du Bois reported that thirteen representatives from the French West Indies attended the 1919 congress (just three less than came from the United States), seven from Haiti, two from the Spanish colonies, one from the Portuguese colonies, and one from Santo Domingo. He tells us that Tertullian Guilbaud came from Havana, "Candace" and "Boisneuf" came from Guadeloupe, "Lagrosil" from the French West Indies, and "Grossillere" from Martinique. Du Bois also tells us that Edmund Fitzgerald Fredericks, a "full-blooded Negro," attended from British Guiana.

The historian Rebecca Scott discovered that the Cubans Antonio Maceo and Máximo Gómez not only visited the United States but rented a house together in New Orleans, in the Faubourg Tremé district in 1884. The pivotal role of black officers such as Maceo and black soldiers in the Cuban-Spanish-American War attracted the attention, as you might suspect, of black journalists, intellectuals, and activists throughout the United States. Du Bois, of course, regularly covered events germane to the black communities throughout the Caribbean and South America as well as Africa in the pages of the *Crisis*, and published Arturo Schomburg's (himself a Puerto Rican) account of the massacre of three thousand followers of the Independent Party of Color in Cuba in 1912.

James Weldon Johnson, perhaps truly the Renaissance man of the Harlem Renaissance, had extensive contacts with Afro-Latin America. In 1906, he was made consul to Venezuela; in 1909, he transferred to Nicaragua. In 1920, the NAACP sent Johnson to investigate allegations of abuse by occupying US Marines. He blasted the imperialist intentions of the US occupation of Haiti in a three-part series published in the twenties in the *Nation* magazine, a series he published as the book entitled *Self-Determining Haiti*. In his autobiography, *Along This Way*, Johnson relates the curious and amusing story that, just as he and a companion traveling on a train are about to be booted from a "first-class car," or a white car, and removed to the Jim Crow car, they talk to each other in Spanish. This is what happens when they do:

As soon as the conductor heard us speaking in a foreign language, his attitude changed; he punched our tickets and gave them back, and treated us just as he did the other passengers in the car. . . . This was my first impact against race prejudice as a concrete fact. Fifteen years later, an incident similar to the experience with this conductor drove home to me the conclusion that in such situations any kind of a Negro will do; provided he is not one who is an American citizen.

These levels of contact not only occurred between intellectuals and writers and at the diplomatic level. Stories about black baseball players pretending to be Cuban were part of the lore of black popular culture when I was growing up; teams in the Negro Baseball Leagues played teams in Cuba and even took "Cuban" names as early as the late nineteenth century, names such as the Cuban Giants, the Cuban X-Giants, the Genuine Cuban Giants (one team was named the Columbia Giants). And several "Cuban" teams, which purportedly included white and black Cubans and some African Americans, played in the United States under these rubrics in defiance of the color line, including the All Cubans, the Cuban Stars (West), the Cuban Stars (East), and the New York Cubans. So what we might think of as "transnational black consciousness" has unfolded at many levels of culture, high and low, between African Americans and black people in the Caribbean and Latin America, as extensively in the arts and letters as in popular cultural forms such as sports.

Of course, several musical collaborations come to mind, including "Cubana Be, Cubana Bop," recorded in 1948 as a single by Dizzie Gillespie, Chano Pozo, and George Russell; and the albums *Orgy in Rhythm*, recorded by Art Blakey, Sabu Martinez, and Carlos "Patato" Valdes in 1957, and *Uhuru Afrika*, recorded by Randy Weston and Candido Camero in 1960, to list just a few early notable examples.

Intricate relations obtained among black writers and critics of the Harlem Renaissance, especially Langston Hughes, who lived for a total equivalent of a year and a half with his father in Mexico and who translated the works of Caribbean writers, such as Nicolás Guillén and Jacques Roumain, from Spanish and French into English. Hughes and his colleagues who created the Harlem Renaissance were pivotal as role models in the birth of the Negritude movement in Paris in 1934, for its founders, Aimé Césaire and Léopold Sédar Senghor. Both movements were directly influenced by Jean Price-Mars's pioneering scholarship of black vernacular traditions and the Vodou religion in works such as *So Spoke the Uncle*.

In all, it is clear that, for well over 250 years, in various degrees and at several levels, there has existed a Pan-African intellectual community keenly aware of one another, looking to one another for support and inspiration to combat anti-black racism in Africa, Latin America, the Caribbean, and the United States, in the northern and southern hemispheres. And you might say that now it is the scholars of diaspora studies who are catching up with the creative writers, artists, activists, athletes, and intellectuals who have long seen themselves as sharing a certain special sort of transcontinental New World "black" subject position.

In spite of the unique histories of slavery and persons of African descent in each of the six countries discussed in this book, certain themes recur. In a sense, this book is a study of the growth and demise of the sugar economy in many of these countries, along with that of coffee and tobacco. In most of these societies, a great deal of miscegenation and genetic admixture occurred between masters and their slaves, very early on in the history of slavery there. Several of these countries sponsored official immigration policies of "whitening," aiming to dilute the numbers of its citizens who were black or darker shades of brown by encouraging Europeans to migrate there.

And speaking of skin color, each of these countries had (and continues to have) many categories of color and skin tone, ranging from as few as 12 in the Dominican Republic and 16 in Mexico to 134 in Brazil, making our use of *octoroon* and *quadroon* and *mulatto* pale by comparison. Latin American color categories can seem to an American as if they are on steroids. I realized as I encountered people who still employ these categories in everyday discussions about race in their society that it is extremely difficult for those of us in the United States to see the use of these categories as what they are, the social deconstruction of the binary opposition between "black" and "white," outside of the filter of the "one-drop rule," which we Americans have inherited from racist laws designed to retain the offspring of a white man and a black female slave as property of the slave's owner. Far too many of us as African Americans see the use of these terms as an attempt to "pass" for anything other than "black," rather than as historically and socially specific terms that people of color have invented and continue to employ to describe a complex reality larger than the terms *black, white,* and *mulatto* allow for.

After extended periods of "whitening," many of these same societies then began periods of "browning," as I think of them, celebrating and embracing their transcultural or multicultural roots, declaring themselves unique precisely because of the extent of racial admixture among their citizens. (The abolition of "race" as an official category in the federal censuses of some of the countries I visited has made it extremely difficult for black minorities to demand their rights, as in Mexico and Peru.) The work of José Vasconcelos in Mexico, Jean Price-Mars in Haiti, Gilberto Freyre in Brazil, and Fernando Ortiz in Cuba compose a sort of multicultural quartet, though each approached the subject from different, if related, vantage points. The theories of "browning" espoused by Vasconcelos, Freyre, and Ortiz, however, could be double-edged swords, both valorizing the black roots of their societies yet sometimes implicitly seeming to denigrate the status of black cultural artifacts and practices outside of an ideology of *mestizaje,* or hybridity.

What did all of these societies ultimately share in common? The unfortunate fact that persons of the seemingly "purest" or "unadulterated" African descent disproportionately occupy the very bottom of the economic scale in each of these countries. In other words, the people with the darkest skin, the kinkiest hair, and the thickest lips tend to be overrepresented among the poorest members of society. Poverty in each of these countries, in other words, all too often has been socially constructed around degrees of obvious African ancestry. Whether—or how—this economic fact is a legacy of slavery, and of long, specific histories of anti-black racism, even in societies that proudly boast themselves to be "racial democracies," "racism free," or "postracial," is one of the most important themes explored in this book and cries out to be explored and acted on in the social policies of each of these six countries.

1

Brazil

"May Exú Give Me the Power of Speech"

On the whole emancipation [in Brazil] was peaceful, and whites, Negroes, and Indians are to-day amalgamating into a new race.
—W. E. B. Du Bois, 1915

In South America we have long pretended to see a possible solution in the gradual amalgamation of whites, Indians and Blacks. But this amalgamation does not envisage any decrease of power and prestige among whites as compared with Indians, Negroes, and mixed bloods; but rather an inclusion within the so called white group of a considerable infiltration of dark blood, while at the same time maintaining the social bar, economic exploitation and political disfranchisement of dark blood as such. . . . And despite facts, no Brazilian nor Venezuelan dare boast of his black fathers. Thus, racial amalgamation in Latin-America does not always or even usually carry with it social uplift and planned effort to raise the mulatto and mestizoes to freedom in a democratic polity.
—W. E. B. Du Bois, 1942

FOR A VERY long time, whenever I heard the word *race*, only images of black people in the United States came to mind. As silly as it might sound now, to me, then, *race* was a code word for black people, and for their relations with white people in this country. I think that this is probably some sort of African American exceptionalism for people my age, people who came of age in the Civil Rights Movement of the late fifties and sixties. Even today, in our era of multiculturalism, I still find it necessary sometimes to remember that *race* is not just a black thing, that *race* (by which most of us mean ethnicity) signifies a lot of different kinds of people, representing a full range of ethnicities, in a lot of different places, and that African Americans in this country don't have a patent on the term or the social conditions that have resulted either from slavery or the vexed history of racial relations that followed slavery in the United States.

I should say that African Americans don't have a patent *especially* on slavery, as I much later came to realize, throughout the New World. When I was growing up, I simply assumed that the slave experience in the New World was dominated by our ancestors who came to the United States between 1619 and the Civil War. And I think that many Americans still assume this. But it turns out that the slave ancestors of the African American people were only a tiny fraction—less than 5 percent—of all the Africans imported to the Western Hemisphere to serve as slaves. Over eleven million Africans survived the Middle Passage and disembarked in the New World; and of these, incredibly, only about 450,000 Africans came to the United States. The "real" African American experience, based on numbers alone, then, unfolded in places south of our long southern border, south of Key West, south of Texas, south of California, in the Caribbean islands and throughout Latin America. And no place in our hemisphere received more Africans than Brazil did.

I think that probably the first time that I ever thought about race, integration, segregation, or miscegenation outside of the context of the United States, Jim Crow, and the Civil Rights Movement was the night that I saw the film *Black Orpheus*. I had thought about Africa quite a lot, and the black people who lived in Africa, from the time I was in the fifth grade, in 1960, the great year of African independence, the year that seventeen African nations were born. But thinking about black people and Africa is not the same as thinking about race. No, that came, for the first time, when I was a sophomore at Yale, assigned to watch *Black Orpheus* in the class called "From Africa to the Black Americas," the art history class taught by the great scholar Robert Farris Thompson.

Black Orpheus, directed by Marcel Camus and shot in Brazil, was released in 1959, to rave reviews. In fact, it won the Palme d'Or at the Cannes Film Festival that year and an Academy Award for Best Foreign Language Film and a Golden Globe for Best Foreign Film in 1960. Based on a play written by Vinicius de Moraes entitled *Orfeu da Conceição*, the film adapts the legend of Orpheus and Eurydice. Set mostly in the Morro da Babilônia favela in the Leme neighborhood in Rio de

Janeiro, the film is stunning, even fifty years later, for the fact that it seamlessly transforms a classical Greek tale in black or brown face, as it were, without preaching about race or class and without protest or propaganda. It just assumes its propositions, as it were. The key Greek characters are here, including Hermes, the messenger of the gods, and Cerberus, the three-headed dog that guards the gates of Hades, as well as Orpheus and Eurydice, of course, played by an athletic Breno Mello and the irresistibly beautiful Marpessa Dawn, the goddess of black Brazilian cinema, who turned out to have been born in Pittsburgh of Filipino and African American descent.

Three things grabbed me when I saw the film. First, as I have mentioned, was the seamless translation of the Greek myth to a Brazilian context, with the race of the characters taken for granted and not trumpeted or strained in any way. Second was the use of Umbanda and Candomblé, which some people have called Brazil's national African religions. When Orpheus descends (down a spiral staircase at, cleverly, the Office of Missing Persons) into Hades to find and retrieve Eurydice, "Hades" turns out to be an Umbanda ritual, complete with female worshipers dressed in white and the pivotal Yoruba god Ogun. Eurydice's spirit speaks to Orpheus, in fact, through one of these female worshipers, now possessed by her spirit. Most striking sociologically, perhaps, is the fact that virtually everyone in the film is black or brown; very few "white" people appear in the film, and none appears in a significant role, similar, as I later discovered, to Zora Neale Hurston's novel *Their Eyes Were Watching God*. Watching the film, my friends and I thought that Brazil was that most remarkable of places: a democracy in brown. Brazil, judging from the film, was a mulatto. For us, *Black Orpheus* seemed to be a sort of cinematic analogue to Gilberto Freyre's theory of Brazil as a unique racial democracy. And all that made me want to visit there, but not as much, to be honest, as the vain hope that I'd spot one of the daughters of the beautiful Marpessa Dawn.

I thought about all of this, in flight, high above the Amazon, I supposed, on my way to Brazil for the first time, heading to Carnaval in February 2010. Between 1561 and 1860, Brazil (as we have seen) was the final destination of almost five million African slaves—some of them, perhaps, my distant cousins. But that wasn't where my mind was taking me. Try as I might, I couldn't help dwelling on the Brazil of my imagination: the pageantry and ecstasy of Carnaval; its syncretic mixtures of indigenous, African, and European cultural elements; the dancing to music and song born in Africa; the Yoruba, Fon, and Angolan–based religions blended into Candomblé and Umbanda; the many regional expressions of Afro-Brazilian religions such as Xangô, Batuque, Tambor de Mina. All of these forms of culture were signal aspects of an irresistibly vibrant national culture synthesized from so many strands contributed by its multiethnic people—a sea of beautiful brown faces with brilliant white smiles, at least as shaped in my mind by Carnaval scenes from *Black Orpheus*.

So much of Brazil's syncretic culture manifests itself at Carnaval. And the most "African" of the various manifestations of Carnaval traditions in the country occurs each year in Bahia. As I boarded the packed connecting flight from São Paulo to Salvador—full of Brazilian tourists from other parts of the country, tourists from other countries, and even a few other African Americans, some of whom I learned were regulars —I began to wonder what exactly I would find when my plane touched down. Because about 43 percent of all slaves brought to the Americas ended up in Brazil, today over 97 million Brazilians in a total population of 190 million people have a significant amount of African genetic ancestry, self-identifying as either Brown (*parda*) or Black (*preta*) in the federal census (among five categories, including White (*branca*), Yellow (*amarela*), and Indígenous, Brown, and Black). This makes Brazil in effect the second-largest black country in the world, after Nigeria, if we use definitions of blackness employed in the United States. (Brazil, one might say, is genetically brown, though there are some areas of the country, such as Porto Alegre, that are overwhelmingly white.) And a third of Brazil's slaves—about a million and a half people—landed in Brazil through the port here, in Bahia.

Thanks to the Trans-Atlantic Slave Trade Database, we now know that about 70 percent of them came from Angola, and much of black Brazilian religion is based on two sources: the Yoruba orishas from western Nigeria and Benin and also what the historians Linda Heywood and John Thornton call "Angolan Catholicism," whose roots were in Angola and which the slaves brought with them to Brazil. (Angolan Catholicism was born out of King Afonso's skillful and deliberate blending of Christianity and Central African religions promoted by "Xinguillas" (as the Portuguese called them), a process that was well advanced by 1516, even before there was any significant African presence in Brazil.

And Angolan Catholicism was every bit as much an African religion as was the Yoruba religion of the orishas. When many slaves from other parts of Africa arrived in Brazil, they were converted to Catholicism not as practiced in Portugal but as practiced in Angola, and indeed many were in fact catechized by Angolans informally, if not formally.) And this syncretic combination manifests itself in the religion called Candomblé, one of the most compelling cultural products of Pan-African culture in the New World. Candomblé is at the heart of black Brazilian culture. And if Brazil's black culture has a capital, it is Bahia, without a doubt.

Brazil, I knew, was also a place of contradictions. It was the last country in the Western Hemisphere to abolish slavery, in 1888, just after Cuba abolished slavery in 1886. But it was also the first to claim it was free of anti-black racism, as Gilberto Freyre's doctrine of "racial democracy" became associated with Brazil's official identity. When I studied Brazil in college, at the end of the sixties, it was still generally thought to be a model society of a postracial world—a far cry from the rigidly segregated United States that the Civil Rights Movement was attempting to dismantle—although its racial-democracy ideology had come under fire (Du Bois critiqued it in 1942) and its military dictatorship had forbidden debate about race and racism in the country. And, indeed, Brazil remains one of the most racially mixed countries on earth—a hybrid nation descended from Africans, Europeans, and its original indigenous inhabitants. In the United States, people with African ancestry are all categorized as black; in Brazil, racial categories are on steroids, including at least 134 categories of "blackness." Brazilians, or so I'd been told, believe that color is in the eye of the beholder. But who are the Afro-Brazilians? And what do they think of their history —of their own relation to Africa and to blackness? I wanted to know their story.

Bahia had especially fired my imagination, since so much of the literature about African retentions in the New World refers to rites and cultural practices developed there. Five hundred years ago, the Portuguese established a sugar cane empire in this region, in the present-day states of Bahia and Pernambuco—one of the largest plantation economies on earth. Initially, the Indians were used as field workers, but their numbers proved inadequate. The Portuguese needed slave labor to meet the demand, and so Africans were poured into the region. The first Africans came from the Portuguese Atlantic islands as specialized workers employed in the sugar-making process proper. As the demand for sugar increased, the number of slaves imported to Brazil exploded. Angola was the central source of these slaves.

By 1600, Brazil produced half the world's sugar, and that sugar was produced through the labor of African slaves. I was extremely keen to see this place that so many Africans had first looked on when they disembarked from the slave ships, no doubt terrified and miserably disoriented, awaiting their fates in the New World, some even convinced that they were about to be eaten by white cannibals! But nothing I had dreamed or imagined, nothing I had read or even researched, prepared me for what I experienced in Bahia. I stepped out of my car on a busy street and looked around, and I thought, "My God, I am back *in Africa!*" Seriously. Everywhere I looked, I saw Brazilians with Africa inscribed on their faces and just as deeply on their culture. Across the street, I spotted a woman's headdress I had seen just a few years before in Nigeria. Because of the long history of cultural trade between Bahia and West Africa, going back to the nineteenth century, West African cloths and other cultural objects were part of the trade, along with slaves.

Few of us realize that the traffic of the Yoruba between Brazil and Nigeria has been a two-way street at least since the early nineteenth century, when some freed slaves returned to the mother land in growing numbers after the defeat of the 1835 Muslim rebellion there, creating cross-pollination in Yoruba religious practices, among other things. Today, I learned, there is a great attempt of some culturally conscious black Brazilians to be "authentic," and items such as cloth are still imported, though Brazilian-manufactured cloths make up the majority percentage of those used by Candomblé devotees and middle-class blacks, since imported cloth is very expensive. Bahia celebrates its African roots, its African heritage, and never more so than during Carnaval. The people here are more "African," genetically, than in any other concentrated part of Brazil. The smells in the air, the gait of men in the streets, the way women move, their ways of worshiping and their religious beliefs, the dishes they eat—all remind me so much of things I had seen and smelled and heard in Nigeria and Angola, but transplanted across an ocean, similar and familiar but distinct: Africa, yes, but with a New World difference, Africa with decided twists.

Mesmerized, avidly on the lookout for those daughters of Marpessa

Dawn, I walked the streets for hours before heading off to my first meeting, with João Reis, professor of history at the University of Bahia. I wanted to understand what had happened here, and so I wanted to start with Professor Reis, who has spent his entire professional life studying the history of slavery in Brazil. Straight off, he told me that ten times more Africans had come to Brazil as slaves than had gone to the United States. The reasons, he said, were both economic and geographic. Brazil was closer to Africa than was any other major destination in the New World (far closer than were the Caribbean or the English colonies in North America); in fact, though it is counterintuitive, it was quicker and easier to sail to Europe from certain African ports through Brazil, as it were. Moreover, the land surrounding the magnificent Bay of All Saints, where Salvador, Bahia's capital, was founded in 1549, was a fertile growing ground for one of the era's most desirable and extraordinarily profitable products: sugar. As a result, by the beginning of the seventeenth century, the words *sugar* and *Brazil* were synonyms. And virtually all of it was produced with slave labor. Sugar is a leitmotif of this book; as the center of sugar production shifted, so did the size of the slave trade and the slave population, over a two-hundred-year period from Brazil to Haiti to Cuba. While both Mexico and Peru had sugar mills, and these were worked by slaves, most Afro-Mexicans and Afro-Peruvians labored in urban areas, many worked in the textile industry, and still others produced foodstuffs in towns. In Colombia, or "New Granada" (outside the scope of this book), they worked primarily in mines and not in sugar.

"Salvador, Bahia, was one of the most important Atlantic cities in the sixteenth, seventeenth, and through the eighteenth century," Reis explained to me, with the patience of a great lecturer used to teaching hopelessly unprepared US undergraduates. "In the nineteenth century, it was full of foreigners from Europe, from the United States, from the Caribbean, and from Africa. It was a multicultural society, a cosmopolitan society, maybe even more cosmopolitan than the way we live here today." Reis explained that Brazil was a prime destination for adventurers, and accordingly, many Europeans who came to Bahia were single men. In the British colonies of North America, entire families often emigrated to set up new lives. But in Bahia's early history, Portuguese bachelors were the norm; and they found sexual conquest where they could—brutally, or coercively, and sometimes willingly—first among native women and then among African slaves. The racial blending that later came to define Brazil began.

I asked Professor Reis how these slaves were treated, especially in comparison to the treatment of slaves in the United States. Were they treated better, more humanely, than were their counterparts in the United States? That they were, of course, is part of Freyre's explanation of the origins of Brazil's "racial democracy" and is now part of its national mythology. The national story Brazil likes to tell today about its slave past is highly unusual. According to this story, the country made a more or less seamless transition from slavery to tolerance, from a terribly informal yet terribly effective racism (Brazil had no laws prohibiting blacks from occupying any post in society or politics) to racial democracy, because of the intimacy—specifically, sexual intimacy—between master and slave. How could did this come about? And could any country make such a shift? Was slavery in Brazil somehow fundamentally different than it was in the United States? The answers I got were complex.

Reis told me that the people of Bahia often freed their slaves or allowed them to buy their own freedom. Indeed, citizens of Bahia granted manumission—emancipation—to more slaves than did any other region in the Americas. You'd think that made it a lucky destination, if a slave could ever be considered lucky. But it belied a deeper, more disturbing reality. There were many more slaves in Bahia at a certain point in the slave trade than there were almost anywhere else—and for most of those who had been born in Africa, life in their new country was short and unbearably harsh. (As slavery matured in southern Brazil thanks to mining and, later, coffee, Minas, Rio, and São Paulo came to have larger slave populations. The city of Rio, for example, became in the mid-nineteenth century the largest slave city in the hemisphere ever, with close to one hundred thousand slaves.) Bahia's steady supply of human labor caused many slaves to suffer especially bad treatment, just because they were so easily replaceable, like spare parts for a car. Working conditions were often brutal beyond description.

"American planters did not have such easy access to the source of slave production in Africa," Reis explained to me, "so slaves were treated much better in the US than they were in Brazil. There, they had better housing, better clothes; they were better fed. And from very early in the slave trade, the slave population was self-reproductive there. Nothing of this sort happened in Brazil."

In Brazil, Reis continued, slave owners could always replace dead Africans with living Africans, at minimal cost. Most of us don't realize how close Brazil is to the west coast of Africa, so importing new slaves could be cheaper than the costs of food, medicine, or decent shelter for older slaves. This wasn't the case in the United States, where the transportation costs of slavery were material and the life of an individual slave was, in a perverse way, accordingly highly valued. In Brazil, the Portuguese often effectively worked the slaves to death because it was cheaper to replace them than to care for them.

The slaves who received their freedom were the exceptions, not the rule, given the huge numbers of slaves imported into Brazil. According to Reis, many of those slaves who managed to be manumitted were the offspring—or descendants—of sexual liaisons between female African slaves and their masters, often the result of rapes. In these cases, the Brazilian-born, mixed-race children fared much better in gaining their freedom than did their African-born mothers, or than most of their female contemporaries and virtually all of their male contemporaries. In this way, different classes of black people emerged under slavery and perpetuated their class position, with "class" being signified by color, by degrees of mixture—hence, the birth of the browning of Brazil. But most of the slaves would not have mixed with white Brazilians, of course; if they propagated, they did so with one another.

"I'm not saying that there was no mixing, no reproduction," said Reis quietly. "There was. But that was on the margins. And the slaves who were born in Brazil received manumission much faster and easier than the African-born person, because they could develop relationships with masters which were more intimate, which were easier to manage—completely different to the Africans who came over without knowing the language, who were sent directly to the labor fields. Most domestic slaves, for example, were born in Brazil. They were in the big house. They were closer to the master's family. And so they could get manumission easier. There are statistics showing precisely that in the competition for manumission, the Brazilian-born slave, especially the mixed race, was much more successful than African-born slaves. It was not humane."

After saying goodbye to Reis, I wanted to examine for myself evidence of Bahia's African roots, having read so much about them. So I visited Pai (Portuguese for "Father," in the religious sense) João Luiz

A Candomblé ceremony in Father João's temple in Salvador. (Christina Daniels)

at his nearby Candomblé temple. As we have seen, Candomblé is the religion created in Brazil by slaves looking for a way to stay in contact with their ancestral gods from Angola, Nigeria, and Dahomey (now the Republic of Benin). Brazil nursed, nurtured, re-created, and embraced the rituals of Candomblé. But Africa birthed them.

Father João's temple is one of more than eleven hundred Candomblé shrines in Salvador. I love learning about the Yoruba gods and reading stories about them—stories as rich as the stories we cherish about the Greek and Roman gods—in their various manifestations on both sides of the Atlantic. Whereas Zeus and Jupiter and their compadres live in Western culture through literature, here the gods live through ritual and worship, generally alongside the Holy Trinity and the Christian saints, though the literature of Umbanda and Candomblé, written by initiates, is also very popular in Brazil, as it is in Cuba. I admire Father João, and told him so, for keeping the African gods alive in the New World.

"It's very important to me," he told me, as we sat down to chat, just outside his temple, in a favela, as we waited for his devotees to arrive for a ceremony. "I was born into a religious family. When I was seven years old, the spirit became a part of me. At fourteen it came to me again, and by the age of sixteen I was in charge of a temple. I'm now forty-nine years old, and I never think about stopping. I just think about evolving and growing. We raise our sons in order for them to take over this vivid and true religion from me, when I am no longer able."

Father João explained how Candomblé combined African traditions with certain tenets of Roman Catholicism—teachings that some Africans had come across first in Angola, because the Portuguese often baptized captured slaves before shipping them to Brazil, and that others encountered only after they arrived in Brazil. But Thornton and Heywood pointed out to me, however, Candomblé's African origins are far more complex: "The Portuguese did capture and then baptize African slaves," they explained to me. "In fact, they usually did, but this misses the point. Christianity was indigenous to West Central Africa, not only in the Kingdom of Kongo where it had been the 'national' religion since the early sixteenth century, and where people took immense pride in being Catholic, but in Angola, too, where the colonized population was also Christian and even in places like Matamba and among the Dembos people that weren't under Portuguese control but accepted the religion anyway." Though the roots of Candomblé are multiple, then, its foundation is solidly in Angolan Catholicism, as we have seen, and in the Yoruba and Fon religions of the orishas and voduns, as imported from Nigeria and Dahomey. These religions organized around worship of the Orishas are still actively practiced in West Africa today and, in various forms, throughout the New World, as Candomblé in Brazil, Santería in Cuba, and Vodou (also known as *Sevi Lwa* in Creole) in Haiti. (*Orişa* is the Yoruba word, *orixá* is Portuguese, *oricha* is Spanish, and *orisha* is English. The gods of Vodou are called *iwa*, rather than *orishas*.)

The spread of these religions, and their commonalities, throughout the larger Latin American slave community is one of the great mysteries in the history of religion and one of the most fascinating aspects of the history of African slavery in the New World. How and why the Yoruba gods became the foundation for this truly Pan-African religion is another great mystery, since the Yoruba were not a dominant ethnic group among the slaves. There are many theories about this, including the relative lateness of the influx of Yoruba slaves in certain parts of Latin America, namely, Bahia and Cuba. Despite the considerable geographic, national, and linguistic barriers of Africans living in Brazil, Cuba, and Haiti, for instance, all of the Yoruba-affiliated religions that they created are cousins, as it were, with their gods bearing the same names (save for linguistic differences among French, Spanish, English, and Portuguese) and similar functions and characteristics as deities. It is also true that Candomblé's precedents among the Ewe-Gen-Aja-Fon ethnic cluster are "just about as rich as its precedents among the ancestors of the Yoruba," as the anthropologist J. Lorand Matory pointed out to me. Followers of Candomblé, the Brazilian version of this larger panreligion, pray to the orixás, deities that are different expressions of the complex human experience and the natural world. The supreme god, Olodumaré, does not have a place in the rituals, being too distant from humans. He is not even considered an orixá, properly speaking. The orixás form a pantheon of gods that help their devotees to survive and live fulfilling lives; the orixás belong to a problem-solving religion. Somewhat like the Greek and Roman gods and somewhat, perhaps, like Catholic saints, orixás keep lines of communication open between mortals and the divine—existing in a state of being somewhere between man and God.

Father João described to me his theory of how the slaves' desperation for relief from the horrendous conditions of their enslavement led to their invocation of the orixás and gave birth to Candomblé. "When the slaves arrived here, they arrived like animals," he said. "They had no value. People just wanted work from them. If it wasn't for the orixás that they brought to Brazil in their hearts and in their minds . . . ," his voice trailed off, and he shook his head, seeming to imagine their despair. "I believe that black people here survived, or managed to carry on, because they had a lot of faith in the orixás. The churches could never have replaced African gods. It was a way they had to worship because they didn't have the liberty to express their religion. The Catholic religion did not provide a path for them. So they used Candomblé in order to communicate with the orixás and ask for protection. This was how they survived."

I asked Father João how this unique mixture of faiths had changed over the centuries—and what he saw in its future. "There was a time when Candomblé faced much discrimination," he said, beaming, referring to opposition from Brazil's white, elite establishment. "But today the people of Brazil are beginning to give it the respect it's due. Back then, Candomblé had no way of evolving because black people were not allowed to study. They were oppressed. Today we live in a more civilized society, where people try to understand the religion. I believe Candomblé has everything in its power to grow." He went on, though, to say that devotees of Candomblé are increasingly subjected to vicious verbal attacks and even physical violence by members of evangelical Christian churches today.

Following a religious ceremony, which struck me as very similar to ceremonies I had seen in Nigeria and ones I was to see in Cuba and Haiti, I left Father João's temple reflecting on the fact that as much as the people of Africa were oppressed under slavery, their culture, their energy, and their ways of life and worship could not be extinguished. They took powerful new forms that still endure across Brazil (and, indeed, wherever slaves were taken in the New World). Candomblé is one manifestation of this process. The next stop on my journey was designed to consider another of these Pan-African cultural forms: capoeira.

Like many art forms, capoeira can be hard to describe in words. It is an extraordinary physical discipline, combining martial arts, dance, and rhythms. Today, its elegance and power can be seen all over the world. But its roots are believed to be traced to urban, nineteenth-century Rio de Janeiro. In the neighborhood of Vale das Pedrinhas, I sat down with renowned capoeira master Mestre Boa Gente, to be interviewed live on his community radio program. He began to talk about how slaves developed capoeira. "The masters of the house, the barons and the colonels,

The author with Mestre Boa Gente and his capoeira group. (Christina Daniels)

did not want the black people to organize themselves," he said, his eyes bright, his entire body engaged in his story. "On coffee plantations, on sugar plantations, weapons were not allowed. But the black people were being tortured. They discovered, in capoeira, a way to strengthen and defend themselves."

According to Mestre Boa Gente, slaves began conditioning their bodies through movements and exercises that became capoeira in preparation for self-defense or rebellion (though there's no evidence that it was ever used for any actual fighting). They couldn't be caught readying for battle, he said, so they disguised their regimen as a kind of ceremonial, even celebratory, dancing, consisting of well-coordinated and syncopated, almost balletic movements and movements characteristic of the martial arts.

"They would be there, training," he explained, "and then they'd hear the cavalry coming. There would be a lookout, a capoeirista, watching, and when he saw them, he'd start playing to the sound of the cavalry. And everything would change from a fight to a dance." Scholars believe that capoeira has its roots in different African martial arts traditions, but no one knows for sure. One version of capoeira is called "Capoeira

Angola," but it originated in Brazil; the reference to Angola no doubt stems from the fact that so very many of the slaves in Brazil hailed from Angola. Capoeira Angola is less popular than Capoeira Regional. As Africans' lives were transformed by slavery, they transformed African traditions and created entirely new ones. They created a new culture in their new world, and capoeira is one such form.

"The cavalry would turn up, and they would see all the black people doing their samba," Mestre Boa Gente went on, laughing. "And the cavalry would say, 'Oh, the blacks, they are playing around, they are dancing.' And they'd start clapping. When the cavalry left, they'd continue training." Today, Mestre Boa Gente helps to keep Bahia's young people off the dangerous streets of the favela by teaching them capoeira. He gives them a proud black tradition to carry forward—an energy and passion that cannot be denied (indeed, he has more energy than any sixty-five-year-old I've ever met).

Not every historian agrees with Mestre Boa Gente's story of how capoeira was born. In 1890, two years after the abolition of slavery in 1888, the Republican criminal code introduced capoeira as a specific crime and repressed, persecuted, and exiled its practitioners in Rio. Gradually, capoeira—always vibrantly alive underground—came out of the shadows and was performed as a ceremonial dance in parades and marches. Its military applications, however, are believed by many scholars to be folklore. Still it is hard, in this vibrant man's presence, not to respect the authority of Brazil's black oral traditions and accept every word he says. Capoeira certainly has no greater champion. "If everyone did capoeira, there would be no wars," he proclaimed. "Capoeira is not a sport. It's something that enters you. With every practice, with every day, you get stronger and stronger."

Having caught some of Mestre Boa Gente's seemingly boundless energy, I hit the streets once again, eager to learn about Bahia's famous version of Carnaval. Like so many public celebrations, Carnaval combines a great number of traditions. The ancient Greeks staged Saturnalias and Bacchanalias, wild parties that included masters and slaves alike. The Catholic Church later absorbed these sorts of celebrations to create what we now recognize as Carnaval, even before the slave trade to the New World began. In Mardi Gras celebrations in New Orleans —and in the liturgical traditions of Catholic, Episcopal, and a few other churches—Fat Tuesday (or Shrove Tuesday) is the culmination

A female member of Ile Aiye, during a Carnaval procession. (Toninho Muricy)

of these celebrations, the day before Ash Wednesday, which marks the beginning of Lent.

Carnaval, like its cousin Mardi Gras, is essentially a joyous annual festival marking the beginning of Lent—one last chance to live it up before embarking on the forty days of this somber fasting period, ending with the feast of Easter. Traditionally, many Catholics and other Christians give up meat or other indulgences for forty days. (In fact, the word *carnival* derives from the Old Italian *carnelevare*, "to remove meat.") In Brazil, Africans added their own traditions to the European traditions. The parades for Carnaval in Rio and São Paulo consist of various samba schools and Blocos Afro and other groups with their respective costumes, bands, and floats. These are akin to "krewes" in New Orleans's Mardi Gras. At the start of the processions of one of the leading Blocos Afro, Ile Aiye, a figure called the "Mãe de Santo" (the mother of the saints) tosses popcorn to the crowds as a symbolic propitiation to the lord of pestilence, Omolu, asking him to intervene to ensure a peaceful celebration.

Carnaval: Bahianas in the parade. (Toninho Muricy)

For a long time, what we might think of as Afro-Carnaval, though
joyously celebrated, was a relatively simple street party in Bahia, heavily influenced by Yoruba traditions, compared to the national and well-
orchestrated event it is today. Indeed, black brotherhoods were banned
from participating in the official Rio Carnaval at the turn of the twentieth century because they were so "African," or "primitive." In the earliest colonial periods, these brotherhoods played a key role in promoting
Afro-Brazilian participation in all of Brazil's religious festivals, well before the Yoruba became a significant presence in the slave trade there.
Though they weren't banned at this point, there were complaints made
that some of their practices were "heathenish." This ban occurred when
Brazil was engaging in an official policy of "whitening," by encouraging the immigration of millions of European migrants. (In fact, between
1872 and 1975, just over 5.4 million Europeans and Middle Eastern
immigrants came to Brazil.) But in the latter half of the twentieth century, black samba groups were welcomed back into official celebrations;
later, in the seventies, influenced by the Black Power movement in the
United States, reggae, and Pan-African movements on the continent, a
variation of these samba groups called Blocos Afro came into being, a
testament to black pride and consciousness.

I traveled to meet with João Jorge, founder of Olodum, one of several principal Blocos Afro. While some of these Afro-Brazilian cultural organizations have a strong cultural-nationalist and activist bent, Olodum is more multicultural than nationalist or traditionally African, as is the Blocos Afro called Ile Aiye ("the world is my house," in the Yoruba language), headed by the magisterial leader named Antônio Carlos Vovo, a man strikingly regal, with a noble bearing reminiscent of a Benin bronze bust (*vovo* means "grandfather"). He explained to me that Ile Aiye is dedicated to preserving the traditional forms of Candomblé and is restricted to black members. When I asked him how in the world one determines who is "black" among the rainbow of browns and blacks that is the face of Brazil, he laughed and said that it is up to prospective members to self-identity.

J. Lorand Matory informed me that "the original entry test in Ile Aiye involved scratching the applicant's skin with a fingernail. Only if it blanched with 'ash' would the applicant be admitted." With good humor, Vovo added, "We know the difference." I got the feeling that Vovo's was a most cosmopolitan definition of blackness: if you say you are black, then you are black. And in Brazil, a huge percentage of the

The author and Olodum's João Jorge. (Toninho Muricy)

population, through its DNA, would most probably satisfy the US law of hypodescent, reaffirmed by the Supreme Court as recently as 1986 (as James Davis points out in a fascinating book about color classification in the United States entitled *Who Is Black? One Nation's Definition*).

I marched along behind Ile Aiye's remarkably stunning procession, starting from its headquarters in Curuzu, a section of the Libertade district, or barrio, at about 9:00 p.m. and converging on the Campo Grande in the center of the city at about 3:00 a.m. The members were all dressed in crisp white, red, and yellow dresses and robes (the official colors of Ile Aiye) and singing hauntingly beautiful songs. I could just as easily have been in Yorubaland, it seemed. Vovo's Ile Aiye represents one stream in the politics of culture of the Blocos Afro; João Jorge's Olodum represents another. Both understand full well the enormous political potential of black culture in Brazil; they just pursue their goals in different ways.

"Olodum was founded as a Carnaval group, to create art and culture from the black-consciousness movement," João Jorge explained. "Before, Carnaval was a celebration, purely and simply for fun. The black population participated, but without a black *consciousness*. The change —the rupture—came when Olodum and other organizations affirmed themselves as black, affirmed that these identities serve political roles. Today, Carnaval in Bahia is an instrument of the black population, a means of social promotion—entertainment through raising awareness."

This is a street party and an expertly choreographed parade with a purpose, I thought. But I also recognized the tension between the Carnaval of yesterday and the Carnaval of today. While African religions, ideas, art, and exuberance had found ways to persist and flourish, it was clear that the stamp of "slave" had never quite disappeared from the Afro-Brazilian experience, and connotations of inferiority associated with slavery shadowed the darkest and "most African" of the Brazilian people. Ile Aiye and Olodum and the other Blocos Afro had to be born, I recognized, as part of a larger effort to restore the legacy of Africa to a place of honor from which it had fallen during Brazil's period of whitening, the long period following the abolition of slavery in which it was in denial about its black roots.

As much as I hated to leave this magical center of African culture in the New World, I now felt that it was time for me to travel beyond Bahia. I knew that further inland an even greater genetic mixing of

The procession of Ile Aiye to the Campo Grande. (Toninho Muricy)

Africans, indigenous peoples, and Europeans had been common. And understanding the many complexities of this mix, I realized, was the only way to begin to understand the complexities of race and racism in contemporary Brazil.

As I drove into the hills of the interior, watching the landscape steadily elevate as we approached the mining region, it occurred to me that this was the journey many slaves had taken in the eighteenth century. The sugar empire in Brazil was fading then, as global prices fell. But gold and diamonds were discovered in the high sierra. Portuguese investors brought slaves to perform more labor there, in a place called Minas Gerais, meaning "general mines."

I soon arrived in the town of Diamantina, where Júnia Furtado, a professor of history, had agreed to meet with me. I was immediately struck by my new surroundings. Diamantina was a Portuguese colonial town, built in 1710, and is preserved to near perfection. You can see drawings of it from three hundred years ago that look almost exactly the same as it does today (though back in the eighteenth century the place

Diamantina: the author and Professor Júnia Furtado. (Toninho Muricy)

would have been buzzing, whereas now it is a rural university town and a tourist destination).

Anyone could tell Diamantina was different from Bahia—and a long way from Africa—just by looking at it for a moment. But Professor Furtado told me something right off the bat that set the two of them even further apart. In Diamantina, she said, blacks and whites had lived together, side by side, throughout the age of slavery. Indeed, she said, many freed slaves owned property, just as they did in Bahia, Pernambuco, and São Paulo. (Bahia also had a class of urban slaves who could move about freely, earn a living, and pay the owner a regular fee; they were called *negros de ganho*.) Furtado explained to me, "Sometimes they even came to own their own slaves. We know that white people, freed black people, and freed mulattoes lived on the same streets, all over the city," she continued. "There were freed black people living on the larger streets in nice houses, with two stories."

After hearing about the brutal working conditions of Bahia's sugar plantations and Minas's plantations and mining fields, this was rather surprising to me. I asked Furtado how this could have occurred at a time when Europeans considered Africans barbaric, uncivilized, and inferior. In the United States, after all, we had communities of free blacks in both the North and the South; about 10 percent of the black population in 1860 was free. But they generally didn't live in integrated communities with whites.

"This place was very distant from everywhere else," she explained, referring to the urban context in contrast to the life of a slave on a plantation or in a mine. "In the eighteenth century, it took months to travel here, so these people were pretty much apart from the rest of the world." In other words, in Diamantina, blacks and whites could live outside social norms. What happened in Diamantina, it seemed, stayed in Diamantina. And quite a lot happened, especially at night. I asked Furtado how free blacks came to be free in the first place. She explained that many of these freed blacks were women, that white men in Diamantina frequently took African women as concubines and then freed them in their wills or on their deathbeds, while others allowed the women to work in the mines or as prostitutes, saving their money to buy their own freedom. "They had to live amongst themselves," Furtado explained. "White men were the majority of the free population, and they needed women to have sex."

The bachelor factor again, I thought, realizing that while, in some ways, Diamantina sounded downright progressive, hadn't slave women always been forced to be concubines for white men throughout the slave trade and across continents in the New World? I asked Furtado what made the women of Diamantina so different.

"Women really achieved a superior social status here," she asserted. "In 1774, around 50 percent of the houses were owned by black women. They possessed slaves. They were able to have a status very similar to the men they were living with."

I found it hard to believe the church would put up with any of this. Furtado nodded with a mischievous smile. "Of course the church disapproved completely of this situation," she chuckled, "but what we saw here was a kind of silence from the church. There were some visits from bishops, and all this sin was denounced. People would pay some amount of money and say, 'I won't do it anymore.' But when the bishop left the city, everybody started living together again!"

The line, according to Furtado, was drawn at marriage. While couples could live together and trust everyone around them to look the other way, only "equals" received the sanctification of the church to marry. "White married white, freed people married freed people, black people married black people," she stated flatly.

Furtado then offered to take me to the house once owned by the most famous black woman in Brazilian history, a woman named Chica da Silva, one of Diamantina's most successful women in the eighteenth century. She's an icon in Brazil. In the 1970s, her story was even made into a film starring the country's first black female superstar, Zezé Motta. Few slaves in the history of the United States could imagine a life as complex as Chica's. And the difference between slavery in Brazil and slavery in the United States lay in the essence of her story: Chica da Silva could *almost* escape her blackness.

Furtado told me that Chica da Silva was born in Brazil and came to Diamantina as a slave. Her master, a white diamond merchant, fell in love with her. "When he met her," said Furtado, "he'd just arrived from Portugal. She had already one small boy with her former owner, a doctor, and he bought her from him. And I think it was a case of love—an immediate case of love, because he arrived in August, in December she already belonged to him, and he freed her on Christmas Day."

"They stayed together for fifteen years," Furtado continued, as we wandered through Chica's impressive home. "They had thirteen children together, one after another. And she was buried in São Francisco Church, a very exclusive church for the white brotherhood."

The thought of an African woman rising to such a height within a slave-owning culture seemed miraculous. But Furtado explained that this ascendance did not come without cost. Chica da Silva was black, yet her rise to power within the community was part of a conscious "whitening" effort. "She acted like she was a white woman," Furtado explained. "She dressed like one; she was buried in the white church. What can I say? It was a way of integration."

The consequences of Chica's choice—the shedding of most vestiges of her black identity—echoed for generations in the lives of her children and grandchildren. "They really embraced the white," Furtado said. "Because it was the way of social climbing in this society. The goal was to become white people." Indeed, Furtado's research shows that many of Chica's sons moved with their father to his homeland of Portugal, settling in Lisbon and presenting themselves as whites in Portuguese society. There are even records that suggest that some of Chica's descendants in Lisbon paid money to the Crown officially to erase their black heritage.

"We have the registers," said Furtado, "of investigations of her blood

Idealized image of Chica da Silva. (Toninho Muricy)

because her sons and grandsons who wanted to take any position in the Portuguese society had to have their lineage investigated, their gene-alogy. Because having someone who was black or Moor or Jewish— they're all problems. It was forbidden for them to enter in the Order of Christ or to enter in the university to apply for a job or a position. So they had to apply this way in Lisbon, and then they had to ask for for-giveness to the queen for having a grandmother or a mother who was black. They had to pay money. And because of the money they had, in fact these children got good positions, good jobs, good places, even in Portugal." They managed to erase their blackness bureaucratically.

This points to something crucial in Chica's story. We shouldn't think of hers as a case of a mixed person "passing," which is the analogy that we, as Americans, generally come to right away. It was much more complicated than that. Chica was definitely African descended, and no amount of European clothing or mimicked behavior could change that. But she wasn't simply trying to hide that. Rather, she was doing something fundamentally different: she was advancing by class. After all, lower-class Portuguese who achieved wealth did much the same thing: they abandoned their country customs and took on the airs of the aristocracy, if they were able to. In the United States, in contrast, no amount of wealth or behavior would ever make a black-skinned person "white," and that is a fundamental difference between the two societies. Class was fluid in Brazil, in a way that it was not for black people in the United States. The process, in other words, was always about class status first and much less about race per se, something very difficult for us to grasp in the United States.

I thought about this as we left the house. Chica da Silva's transformation from a slave to a wealthy matriarch included a whitening process. Her star wouldn't have risen if she had practiced Candomblé, worn traditional garments, and, well, stayed black. And her decision had an effect on her family for generations. I found this capacity of a female slave for social mobility fascinating, since it was so unlike the experience that this same person would have had in the United States, but I also have to say that I found it somewhat disturbing. And the more I thought about it, the more confusing the story seemed to me. I realized, with a start, that I was thinking about Chica da Silva in terms of "passing" for white in the United States, not in the way race was socially constructed in Brazil. Everyone in Brazil knew that Chica was black; money and manners "whitened" her socially only. In the United States, a drop of blood is all it takes to make a person "black"—and the history of passing is replete with tragedy, from the descendants of the abolitionist writer and physician James McCune Smith to the Harlem Renaissance novelist Jean Toomer to the *New York Times* book critic Anatole Broyard. But could blacks in Brazil choose a more nuanced racial identity than we can in the United States? Were the scores of racial classifications that Brazilians of color used to describe themselves neutral descriptors, or were these ways to separate from the darkest, most "Negroid" aspects of the African experience in Brazil, and their connotations as base, inferior, and degenerate? Was I imposing a US interpretive framework on the subtleties of a society I was ill prepared to understand? Had Brazil's long history of miscegenation created a complexly shaded social structure, from white, on one end, to black, on the other, which had managed, somehow, to escape the negrophobia that remains so much a part of US society? In other words, should we be celebrating the social fluidity that Chica da Silva enacted for herself and her progeny, rather than critiquing it? If so, should we, in the era of multiculturalism and mixed-race identities, look at Chica and people like her as prophets of the social construction of race, as harbingers of a new era in race relations?

Questions like this can quickly become abstract, academic, and impossible to answer. I've often found that the place to go for a reality check is the barbershop or the beauty shop. After all, black hair is a big deal—whether you embrace it, tame it, or straighten it with a hot comb or chemicals. I wanted to know how Brazil's mixed-race culture dealt with black hair; I wanted to know what was hiding in "the kitchen."

I headed to Belo Horizonte, capital of the state of Minas Gerais. I knew there were concentrated Afro-Brazilian communities in the favelas there—the poorest areas. And that's where, in the blackest part of Minas Gerais, I stepped into the beauty shop of Dora Álves to find out just how beautiful black is in Brazil. Álves does hair, but she also does politics, as a cultural activist. She told me that her customers often ask her to make their hair look straighter, less frizzy, less kinky . . . more white. Álves teaches them to take pride in their black hair and their black heritage.

"Sometimes, we'll have someone arriving at the salon," she told me, "and she is so depressed, with such low self-esteem. She thinks her hair is ugly, that her hair is terrible. Sometimes the mother still has her baby in a stroller, and she arrives asking me, 'Oh, my God, is there any way to solve this hair?' Sometimes we go into schools, and the teacher will come up with a child—he'll whisper, just like this, into my ear, 'Do you think there's anything that can be done?' "

I shook my head, astonished at the idea of exposing the skull of a baby in a stroller to the torture of hair-straightening chemicals.

"I'll say, 'No, let's have a chat!'" Álves went on, emphatically. "I sit down, I put the child on my knee, and I say, 'Your hair is beautiful. You are beautiful. I'm organizing a fashion show, and you can be in it.' And the child starts to relax, and the next thing you know, the child is strutting around. She's all happy, all joyful, walking around like Gisele," referring to Brazilian Gisele Bündchen, whom *Forbes* magazine recently said was the highest-paid model in the world.

Álves wants to reach kids early, so she regularly visits schools and community centers to promote black pride. It's a big commitment, especially for a woman who runs her own business. But it drives her to distraction to see Afro-Brazilians trying to leave their blackness behind the way Chica da Silva did.

"Why do so many black women have low self-esteem here in Brazil if they have Afro hair?" I asked. Why would black people be so alarmed at having black hair in the world's second-largest black nation?

"It's a question of history," Álves explained, shaking her head. "It's also a question of the media, too. You see it in the advertisements, in magazines, on TV—you see that most of the women are white. If you go and count, there might be one black girl, just one. And the rest are white, with their hair straightened out. So black women can't see themselves at all."

They can't see themselves at all, I thought, stepping out of the shop. I turned back to wave at Álves and thank her again. But my mind was spinning with questions. Black people were everywhere, but had they absorbed Brazil's urge to whiten itself? And their history included characters like Chica da Silva, who had walked away from her blackness —and been idolized for it. In the United States, everyone just sees me as black, and that's how I think of myself. But in Brazil, racial mixing had made things far more complicated, more graduated, more nuanced, perhaps?

So what is blackness in Brazil? And just how beautiful is white? As someone with a mixed-race heritage myself, I decided to ask passersby on the street what they thought of me. And I learned, quickly, that my color was in the eye of the beholder.

"If I lived in Brazil," I asked one man, "what color would I be?"

"*Caboclo*," he answered.

I asked another man, "What race am I, what color?"

"*Pardo*," he said.

The answers kept coming, all different. "Light *moreno.*" "*Mulatto.*" "*Cafuso.*" Each was specific, as if describing a different color of the rainbow. It seemed objective—to a point.

"We're all black, even though we're different colors," one man argued.

"I'm black," another piped in. "He's light *moreno.*"

"Black. He'd be black," a woman said. "I'm not a racist, no."

Her answer rung in my head. I couldn't help noticing that those who called themselves black and identified me as black did so with a certain defiance, or apologetically. Many people wanted to be one of Brazil's seemingly endless shades of brown, not black, and to assure me that I was brown, too. Were these categories, these many names for degrees of blackness, a shield against blackness? The mixing in Bahia, Minas Gerais, and other areas in slavery times and replicating itself since had produced Brazilians of a brown blend. But these many shades of black and brown clearly weren't equal.

I called my friend Professor Reis and described my experience to him. He reminded me that there are in fact well over a hundred different words to describe degrees of blackness in Brazil: 134, in fact—a word for every shade. Very dark blacks are *preto* or *negro azul* (blue black). Medium-dark blacks are *escuro. Preto desbotado* refers to light-skinned blacks. If you're light enough to pass for white and you seem to be trying, then you're *mulatto disfarçado. Sarará* means white-skinned with kinky hair. The country's focus on color, it struck me, bordered on obsession. The list went on, and on, and on, dizzyingly.

I decided to return to Salvador, Brazil's black capital, to find out what in this country's past made attitudes toward blackness so problematic—to learn more about Brazil after slavery, when degrees of blackness were already spread across the country. I met with Wlamyra Albuquerque, another historian who teaches at the Federal University of Bahia. We settled in the library at the Geographical and Historical Institute, carefully drinking cool glasses of water so as not to damage the fragile works in the archives. I asked her what the white ruling class had thought about African culture in Brazil after the abolition of slavery in 1888. "The elite reacted very badly to the end of slavery," she replied. "What bothered them was how to deal with the large population of color. Various ministers who were a part of the government believed that in order for Brazil to become a civilized country, it had to undergo a process of whitening. The government invested a great deal in European immigration to the country."

Abolition may have ended slavery, Albuquerque said, but it didn't transform Brazil into the tolerant multicultural nation that so many blacks and white abolitionists must have hoped it would become. Between about 1884 and 1939, four million Europeans and 185,000 Japanese were subsidized to immigrate to Brazil and work as indentured servants. The process, a formal government program, was called *branqueamento*—which translates, literally, as "whitening." Obviously, the white elite hoped to increase the number of whites reproducing among blacks to lighten the national complexion. But the effort was also aimed sharply at eradicating vestiges of African culture.

"The government told Brazilians that to be black was something close to savagery," Albuquerque explained. "From that moment, they began to persecute practices that were seen as black—like Candomblé and capoeira—trying to convince people that these practices were barbarous and that it was a civilizing act to stop them."

As I silently cheered for Candomblé and capoeira—African creations that survived the era of *branqueamento*—Albuquerque began to tell me about one black man, a pioneering intellectual, who had taken a bold, brave stand against the government's racist ideologies. His name was Manuel Querino. He's still little known even inside Brazil. His story is rarely taught in universities, much less in high schools. But he is an important figure nonetheless: a historian, artist, labor unionist, and black activist who deserves to be better known. You might think of Querino as a Brazilian mixture of Booker T. Washington and W. E. B. Du Bois: he pushed for technical education for blacks and was a teacher at a trade institute, like Washington; but at the same time, he was a member of the exclusive Instituto Geográfico e Histórico (where I was talking to Albuquerque), as Du Bois would have been. But unlike Washington and Du Bois, he was also involved in trade unionism and local politics (he was an alderman), and he often allied himself with oligarchical politicians. Querino, in other words, was a rather complex man.

"Querino emphasized the role of the African as a civilizer," Albuquerque told me. "He thought there was no need for the white immigrants, as Brazil had already been civilized by the Africans. He said the Brazilian worker was much more capable than the foreign worker of dealing with the challenges of Brazilian society."

"Querino was also an artist and spoke about this population's artistic abilities," she continued. "He was concerned with showing African customs and traditions in Bahia. So he was a dissonant voice when everyone else was saying that those who came over as slaves were not capable of a more sophisticated style of work."

I was stunned that I had never heard of this man. (I later learned that the hero of the novel *Tent of Miracles*, by Jorge Amado, is partially based on Querino. Amado can be thought of as the Gilberto Freyre of Brazilian literature.) Slaves were acknowledged as essential in many quarters. But Querino had argued that Africans were integral to Brazil's cultural identity. For me, hearing about his life was like learning for the first time about W. E. B. Du Bois or Carter G. Woodson—two of my great personal heroes in African American history. I was absolutely riveted as Albuquerque began searching the archives' copy of one of Querino's essays for her favorite passages.

"Here it is," she said, thumbing through a journal. " 'Whoever re-reads history will see the way in which the nation always has glory in the African that it imported.' It's about how we should have pride in being the descendants of these Africans. Querino is the father of black history here—and also of black mobilization and of racial positivity within the black movement."

Querino was a seminal figure in the black intellectual history of Brazil. And yet, as I learned from Professor Albuquerque, Querino's pioneering ideas about race and racism largely died with him in 1923. Instead, the creation of Brazil's official identity—as one of the world's few truly mixed, supposedly racist-free nations—is credited to the work of one man: Gilberto Freyre.

Unlike his unsung counterpart Querino, Freyre is taught widely in schools, even in the United States, and is celebrated for recognizing the value and significance of Africans within Brazilian culture (I read his work when I was in college). But also unlike Querino, Freyre was white. He was born into a middle-class family in 1900, only twelve years after abolition. His father was a public employee, and his mother's family owned a sugar plantation. Freyre spent his youth on plantations owned by his mother's relatives. And plantation life served as the inspiration for Freyre's most celebrated work, published in 1933: *Casa Grande e Senzala* (*The Masters and the Slaves*; a better translation would be "The Big House and the Slave Quarters"). In that book, he argued that race relations in Brazil were quite fluid during slavery, in spite of the violence at the heart of the system. But slavery, he argued, was not solely defined by violence. He described Brazil, the last country in the Western Hemisphere to abolish slavery, as the first place most likely to eliminate racism, because it was not a mainstream mentality of normal Brazilian citizens. Racial democracy was in process of being constructed.

Freyre argued that because blacks, whites, and indigenous peoples were all having sexual relationships and reproducing with each other—a mixing traditionally called *miscegenation*, a term of some baggage and controversy today—race relations were better in Brazil than they were in slave-owning cultures that were more rigidly segregated. I'd brought my copy of Freyre's book with me and, as I traveled across Brazil, frequently looked over some of the key passages that had stuck with me all these years later. I found that they still troubled me, like this one:

> The truth is that in Brazil, contrary to what is to be observed in other American countries and in those parts of Africa that have been recently colonized by Europeans, the primitive culture—the Amerindian as well as the African—has not been isolated into hard, dry, indigestible lumps incapable of being assimilated by the European social system. . . . Neither did the social relations between the two races, the conquering and the indigenous one, ever reach that point of sharp antipathy or hatred, the grating sound of which reaches our ears from all the countries that have been colonized by Anglo-Saxon Protestants. The friction here was smoothed by the lubricating oil of a deep-going miscegenation.

Freyre claimed that whites and blacks not only had sex but sometimes married, with the church's blessing (though live-in arrangements were suitably "damned by the clergy"). He argued that this racial mixing constituted the core of Brazil's identity. Like Querino, he maintained that Brazil wasn't Brazil without Africans and their culture. But his work lacks any real sympathy or understanding of what it actually means to be a Brazilian of African descent.

I realized then that Freyre had, in many ways, taken Querino's place in Brazilian history. He's credited with the first view of Brazil as a nation that should take pride in its mixed-race heritage. But did he articulate anything beyond an essentially primitivist or romantic view of race relations during slavery?

> Every Brazilian, even the light-skinned fair-haired one, carries out in him on his soul, when not on soul and body alike . . . the shadow, or at least the birthmark, of the aborigine or the Negro. . . . In our affections, our excessive mimicry, our Catholicism, which so delights the senses, our music, our gait, our speech, our cradle songs —in everything that is a sincere expression of our lives, we almost all of us bear the mark of that influence.

When Freyre wrote these words, in 1933, US blacks were under the boot of Jim Crow. Segregation was the order of the day, and many whites in the United States were fighting to keep it permanent. And yet Freyre asserted that black Brazilians and white Brazilians were bound together by blood and destiny. He argued that they had created each other, that they mutually constituted each other. Many people who read Freyre in the United States—he was actually educated at Baylor and at Columbia—during these years of Jim Crow must have thought he was either dangerously radical or else insane. Who alive here then would ever have dared claim that the United States could be the world's model racial democracy?

When I first read Freyre, I remember faulting him for being overly romantic, even naïve. Masters raped slaves. Many long-term sexual relationships were the result of coercion at best. Respect between peoples comes with social equality. And, obviously, when one person owns another, there can be no equality. Period. But I had to acknowledge the impact that Freyre's writing is said to have had on Brazil. Some scholars argue that it changed the way whites looked at blacks, and it also changed the way blacks thought about themselves, though it is difficult to imagine a work of scholarship having this much social impact. Freyre, drawing on mid-nineteenth-century Brazil legend, was nevertheless one of the first scholars to argue more or less cogently that Brazil—its culture and its identity—was created by the blending of three equal races: Europeans, indigenous peoples, and Africans. We cannot overestimate how novel this idea was in its time, or how eagerly liberal and progressive academics, such as W. E. B. Du Bois, seized on it—at least for a time—in their attempt to undermine de jure segregation in the United States.

Traveling north from Salvador, I was greeted warmly by Gilberto Freyre Neto, the grandson of the writer, at the writer's home in Recife, the capital of the state of Pernambuco and the fourth-largest metropolitan area in Brazil. After Bahia, Pernambuco was Brazil's second-largest center of sugar-plantation slavery in colonial Brazil. Recife's airport is named for Freyre, surely a first, or at least one of the very few times that an airport has been named for an intellectual! I told him I was honored to meet him after having studied his grandfather at Yale. And I relished my personal tour of Freyre's house, where he lived from 1940 until his death in 1987. Neto showed me his grandfather's medals of honor, the desk at which he sat and wrote his books, and even a first-edition copy of *Casa Grande e Senzala*.

Neto's life is dedicated to keeping his grandfather's work alive, so he was happy to sit with me and dig into Freyre's writings. I started by asking him how attitudes toward black people changed after his grandfather's 1933 masterpiece was published.

"I think the book was a real turning point in the 1930s," he told me. "Gilberto raised the Brazilian blacks to the same cultural standing as the Portuguese. He equated them. He said Brazil only became Brazil when African culture, which was often superior to Portuguese, became culturally miscegenated. From that moment on, we had a 'complementariness.' We became an ideal meta-race."

At the time *Casa Grande e Senzala* was published, Germans were rallying behind Hitler and his calls for Aryan purity. Freyre took the completely opposite view, arguing that its racial mix was essential to bringing Brazil to the height of its cultural and societal potential. Whitening had been a mistake.

"His studies were based very heavily on experiences that my grandfather lived through and information that he was able to gather from sources that were curiously trivial," Neto explained. "A lot of the time, they were not even considered academic. He drew from newspaper cuttings, interviews with elderly people, knowledge that was gathered mostly from interactions. So my grandfather inhabits the dichotomy of either 'Love Gilberto Freyre' or 'Hate Gilberto Freyre.' Some academics think of him as a novelist, while others think of him as one of the most profound analyzers of Brazilian society."

The Redemption of Cain, by Modesto Brocos (1852–1936). Three generations of a Brazilian family, each successively whiter (black grandmother, mulatto mother, and white baby). (Museu Nacional de Belas Artes)

Novelist, sociologist, neither, or both, Freyre's impact really can't be overstated. His writings changed attitudes about race across the entire nation. Many of Brazil's leaders, no matter what their politics were, sooner or later embraced his ideas. They overturned institutionalized policies that overtly discriminated against blacks. Brazil's official whitening process came to an end. And Freyre fixed, in its place, the concept of "racial democracy"—the idea that Brazil was so racially mixed that it was beyond racism.

Beyond racism. I sat back for a moment. I was beginning to feel something romantic toward Brazil—as Freyre had always felt. Even today, Brazil boasts of its racial harmony and its multicultural identity.

And I could almost see it. While the United States was busy policing the racial boundaries with Jim Crow, Freyre was arguing, Brazilians were busy embracing one another! The joyous celebration of Carnaval became a globally recognized symbol of Brazilian brotherhood across racial lines. Racial democracy certainly seemed to lie at the heart of Brazilian identity.

But could it be real? What about Brazil's extensive poverty, especially among blacks? What about Ile Aiye and Olodum, which rose in the seventies from a need to reassure blacks (and to educate whites) that it is glorious to be descended from Africa? Like any reasonable person—black or white—I want to believe we live in a world where a society beyond racism can exist, not just in theory. But I need to see evidence of this progress to believe it. And in the restaurants where I ate and in the hotels where I stayed, in upper-class residential neighborhoods, on the covers of magazines at city newsstands—virtually everyone in a position of power looked white.

Neto was adamant in response to my questions. If racial democracy isn't real already, he assured me, it is becoming real. He read once more from his grandfather's works: "I think we are more advanced in solving the racial question," he quoted, "than any other community in the world that I know."

I left Neto with as many questions as answers and headed south to Rio de Janeiro, Brazil's most famous city—and its cultural and intellectual capital. I'd managed to secure a meeting with Zezé Motta, the actress who played Chica da Silva in Brazil's famous film, which premiered in 1976. As a black actress, I thought, she must have had strong feelings about playing this character, and I was hoping she could help me clarify my feelings about this so-called racial democracy.

What I didn't expect—and what I got—was a meeting with a most thoughtful, articulate artist. Chica da Silva may have personified racial democracy, but life for Zezé Motta has been quite different. "Before I became successful," she said, "I took pictures for advertisements, and the client did not approve them, saying, 'This client is middle class and wouldn't take suggestions from a black woman.' And on TV, I played various roles which were actually always the same one: the maid."

"I was always defending Chica da Silva," she explained. "I would say, 'Chica da Silva did what she had to do. Don't demand Angela Davis attitude from her.' Her merit lies in the fact that she was born a slave, but she could not accept this. She turned the game around and became a queen."

Perhaps paradoxically, at the same time she defended Chica da Silva for being complicit in her own whitening, Motta discovered how connected she was to her own blackness.

"It's very hard for a black person in Brazil to have a career as an actress," she confided, "but in the case of Chica da Silva, it had to be a black woman. The producer didn't want me because I was too ugly—until very recently, in Brazil, the black people were considered ugly. The producer preferred her to be a mulatta, a lighter actress. But the director didn't budge. It had to be a black woman."

Who wouldn't want Chica da Silva—a black woman—played by this great, and stunningly beautiful, black actress? I kept listening.

"After the film, I was considered a Brazilian sex symbol," she laughed, "because the character became very present in the male imagination. At that time, there would never be a black person on the cover of the big magazines, because they'd say, 'The cover sells.' But as I had become the queen, the sex symbol, an important magazine put me on the cover. And someone high up in the magazine said that if it didn't sell, the person who signed off on it would be fired!"

Motta's portrayal of Chica da Silva made her a star, overnight. She enjoyed the recognition that came with her fame, and she was certainly proud of her work. But her new status brought her new experiences along Brazil's ever-moving color line. And those experiences revealed to her Brazil's anti-black racism—a racism that her country claimed did not exist.

"I traveled to sixteen countries promoting the film, including the United States," Motta continued. "And I started to think, 'There are so few black actors in the Brazil media. Where is everybody?' This country has a debt toward its black people."

I thought about Motta's words as I traveled to my next meeting. I'd arranged to sit down with one of my heroes, a truly great man who has spent his life advocating for Afro-Brazilians: Abdias do Nascimento. I had wanted to meet him for a very long time; Nascimento is one of the gods of the international black-intellectual tradition. He is now ninety-six years old, but the grip of his handshake is still firm and his mind razor sharp. He's been fighting the good fight for three-quarters of a century, as a senator, a university professor, and a writer. Nominated for the Nobel Peace Prize, he founded the Institute of Afro-Brazilian Studies in Rio and is widely recognized as the country's greatest black activist. Some people even call him the Nelson Mandela of Brazil.

I was honored to be in his presence, and I told him so. He accepted me graciously, with the calm and dignity of a leader naturally born. An exquisite gold statue of Exú, the messenger of the gods, stood on a china cabinet near Nascimento's dining table. I asked him about the status of black people, politically and socially, in all aspects of contemporary Brazil. Was racial democracy an ideal or a reality? Had it ever existed? Could it ever blossom?

"This is a joke, which has been built up since Brazil was discovered," Nascimento replied with conviction. "And Brazil likes to spread this around the world. But it's a huge lie. And the black people know that. The black people feel in their flesh the lie that is racial democracy. You just have to look at the black families. Where do they live? The black children—how are they educated? You'll see that it's all a lie."

He listened patiently while I recounted my recent visit with Gilberto Freyre's grandson. Nascimento didn't buy plantation life as whites and blacks holding hands in the sunshine, either. He told me he found the idea "sentimental." And if you don't accept that picture, he pointed out, you can't accept racial democracy. Interestingly enough, in the late forties, Nascimento published a short-lived magazine called *Quilombo*, in which Freyre and other white intellectuals published essays in a column entitled "Racial Democracy."

"There is the myth that slavery in Brazil was very gentle, very friendly, even," he said. "These are all fabrications. Slavery here was violent, bloody. Please understand, I am saying this with profound hatred, profound bitterness for the way black people are treated in Brazil—because it's shameful that Brazil has a majority of blacks, a majority that built this country, that remain second-class citizens to this day."

He spoke so passionately but without bombast, his convictions firm, well considered, strong. In his eloquence, he reminded me of the Nigerian Nobel laureate for literature Wole Soyinka. As I continued to listen, somewhat in awe, Nascimento explained how formal racism in Brazil had been replaced by an equally dangerous informal racism. Racial democracy was a mask, a public face that Brazil put on for the world, he explained. Day-to-day, real-life Brazil was still hostile to blacks, still trying to "whiten away" vestiges of African culture.

"My parents never talked about African gods," he lamented. "I researched them, but the African gods were hidden. The only gods that appeared in public were the Christian gods, the Catholic ones. But the gods of those who lived in little huts, who were ashamed or afraid to reveal their true beliefs?" He shrugged his shoulders and held out empty hands. "It was not a law. It was an unwritten law that one shouldn't really talk about African gods. It's only now that African gods are talked about openly."

"I was the first black senator who was conscious of being black," he said, proudly. "And I ripped the fantasy of the Senate apart. Every single session, I would start by declaring, 'I invoke the orixás! I invoke Olorum! I call Exú! May Exú give me the power of speech! Give me the right words to get at these racists who have been in power for five hundred years! The right words to tell Brazil, to tell the world that the black people are aware, that the black people are awake!' " I could only imagine that scene, the horror on the faces of his fellow senators as he declaimed about the Yoruba gods, invoking my favorite of the lot, Exú, messenger of the gods, the god of interpretation, rather like Hermes in Greek mythology. I glanced at his statue. It was almost as if the lovely, nine-inch gold statue of the trickster broke into a smile. We both burst into laughter.

I asked him what he saw in Brazil's future. Was he optimistic that the situation might improve? I was curious to see how he'd respond to the question. I was expecting, I think, some kind of visceral explosion. Instead, Nascimento was very calm and seemed to have long ago formed his answer.

"If I weren't an optimist, I would have hung myself," he told me. "This action is so repetitive—this thing that has been going on for five hundred years. So if I weren't an optimist, I would have hung myself."

Everything Nascimento said made me more eager to see more of Brazil as it truly is. The Brazil of my imagination had its place. Brazil's vision of itself has its own life. But for this journey to have meaning, I needed to witness the Brazil of the real world. And there could be no better place than Rio de Janeiro. I roamed widely through the wealthy neighborhoods, Copacabana and Ipanema, walking the beaches and driving around the lovely homes. I began to recognize the wisdom in Nascimento's words. There were very few black people anywhere. I stopped at a newsstand and looked at the magazine covers, slowly taking in what I was seeing: rows upon rows of white faces, white models, a white Brazil. I could have been in Switzerland. As I looked for even one brown face among these pictures, I thought of Zezé Motta's story. If someone asked me for proof that we were standing in a majority-black country, I couldn't have produced it at that newsstand.

I asked myself what black Brazilian I could remember having seen consistently in the media in the United States. Pele, the Albert Einstein of soccer, came to mind first, but then so did Ronaldo, Robinho, Ronaldinho, Neymar, and other soccer players. Maybe a musician or two, such as Milton Nascimento, and a model or two. That was it.

I went on, looking for black Brazil. And I found it—not at Ipanema or Copacabana but in Rio's famous slums, the favelas. I arrived in the particularly infamous neighborhood called the City of God, one of Brazil's most famous favelas, if only because it was the title of a very popular and well-made film released in 2002. Here, among some of the world's worst slums, Afro-Brazilian life was vibrant, visible, omnipresent, and distressfully poor.

The City of God is where Brazil's most famous rapper, MV Bill, was born and raised. I knew he still lived there—even though his fame made it more than possible to leave. He was happy to talk to me about what life is really like for Afro-Brazilians. I started by asking him why he still lives in the same poverty-stricken favela. In the United States, hip-hop stars tend to move to Beverly Hills or a comparable neighborhood when they make it, no matter where they came from.

"I don't condemn those who make money, leave the ghetto, and go to live somewhere else," he replied. "But my thing with the City of God is different, independent of whatever money I make. Living here is part of my identity."

The City of God looked like the opposite of wealthy Rio—here, all the faces were different shades of the darker browns. I asked MV Bill if everyone in the neighborhood is black.

"The majority," he answered, nodding his head. "The City of God is considered one of the blackest neighborhoods in Rio de Janeiro. But even here in a black neighborhood, it is the smaller population of lighter people that have the best opportunities in life."

The remains of whitening, I thought immediately. Those who appear to fit the European dream of *branqueamento* are doing better than their darker neighbors, even after all this time.

The author with MV Bill, Brazilian rapper. (Christina Daniels)

"But in Brazil, we're not allowed to talk like this," MV Bill said, interrupting my thoughts. "We have to live in a racial democracy that doesn't exist. There is no equality."

I told MV Bill that my own experience had reflected that. During my travels, I was fortunate to stay in nice hotels and to eat at good restaurants, but I had often been the only black person who was not serving. MV Bill only seemed surprised to hear I'd been treated so well.

"It's because of your social standing," he explained. "But there will still be many places where you'd be the only black man and you'd still be treated badly."

I had assumed that MV Bill would be treated well wherever he went. After all, the man is a star. But now I asked him if he had ever suffered poor treatment just for being black.

"Of course," he answered readily, "before, during, and after my fame."

"Why is Brazil so racist?" I finally said, for the first time on my journey. "It's the second-largest black nation in the world."

MV Bill nodded. He knew what I was asking, even if he didn't have an answer. "We have lived under the myth of racial democracy," he replied. "But this is exposed as a lie when we look at the color of the people who live in favelas, the color of the people who are in prison, the color of the people who survive by committing crimes. People will tell you that our problem in Brazil is an economic problem or a social problem, anything but a racial problem—it can never be racial. But it is."

His words struck an emotional chord. In the United States, too, blacks are often accused of being at fault for their own poverty.

"There are a lot of people who don't have jobs because they have not had access to education," he went on. "And without access to education, they have not been able to get any professional qualifications. And without any qualifications—on top of all the prejudices against those who live in a place like this—it is very hard to get good jobs. We have a lot of people who are not criminals, who are not drug addicts, but who don't have an occupation, who are not doing anything."

I sat back, trying to process his comments. While it is true that racial segregation was outlawed in Brazil, the legacies of slavery—so recently abolished, relatively speaking—persist, as does color prejudice. Although segregation had never been legal, as it had been in the United States, it manifests itself throughout Brazilian society. As I would find to be true throughout Latin America, the darkest people in these societies tend to be at the bottom of the social scale. Racial democracy was a beautiful and alluring ideal, but had it ever been more than a romantic white worldview, designed to keep Afro-Brazilians in their place? After all, a black-pride movement is not needed, is it, in a society in which racial democracy obtains? As Abdias do Nascimento explained to me quite perceptively, because of this ideology of the country as blessedly free of racism, Brazil never had a civil rights movement, like the one we had in the United States, because it did not have de jure segregation to rail against. Brazil's racism was informal—devastatingly effective, but informal nonetheless. And this meant that blacker Brazilians never

"A Brazilian Sedan Chair and a Person Begging for the Church, 1821," engraving. (Getty Images)

have had a chance to demand redress for the racism that they still feel they suffer.

I turned to watch children playing in the street, young lives full of potential. I asked MV Bill if he thought any of these children might one day become the Barack Obama of Brazil.

"I think so, yes," he said, smiling. "But there is only one way: through education. And education in Brazil is a luxury item. I think our greatest revolution will be to have young people like these becoming lawyers, having political power, influencing the judicial system. Those are the signs we hope for."

I left MV Bill, and his inspiring spirit of hope, in the City of God. But our conversation lingered in my mind. The cycle of poverty is inevitably vicious—no money means no education, no education means no job, no job means no money. And the cause for this cycle, most scholars and activists agree, is the legacy of slavery and a function of the lingering remnants of anti-black racism. What was Brazil doing to right this wrong, to begin, systematically, to put an end to the inequality that slavery visited on persons of African descent and their descendants?

The answer won't surprise Americans, but it has taken hold only recently in Brazil: affirmative action. The future, the hopes, and the very lifeblood of Afro-Brazilians lie in the hands of the country's university system. But unlike affirmative-action programs in the United States, Brazil has embarked on a most radical, and extremely controversial, form, one destined to stir even more controversy in many quarters of Brazilian society than affirmative action has done in the United States.

The first program designed to offer poor blacks a road out of poverty was launched in 2003 at the State University of Rio de Janeiro. It set aside 20 percent of the university's admissions for black students, and it was the only program of its kind anywhere in the country. Now, similar programs have spread through Brazil, leading to often fierce debates. The goal? To help achieve the dreams articulated so eloquently by MV Bill and Abdias do Nascimento: to integrate the middle class, in the same way that affirmative-action programs did in the United States starting in the late sixties, so that black children could grow up to become engineers, lawyers, and doctors in relative proportion to their percentage in the population.

I knew the introduction of affirmative action had been very controversial in Brazil. So I scheduled an appointment to hold a debate with a class taught by Professor Marilene Rosa at the State University of Rio de Janeiro. She offered to speak with me about what affirmative action means for her country and how both blacks and whites feel about it.

"I started teaching at this university in 1995," she told me. "There was already a debate surrounding affirmative action at that time, although it took until 2003 for any laws to be passed."

But then, virtually overnight, the student body at this traditionally white university began to reflect the cultural diversity of Brazil as a nation. I asked her what happened when the program went into effect and what the reaction of the community had been. Rosa shook her head.

"It suffered criticism from all sides," she said, "criticism that said the level would fall, saying the university would fall behind other universities, and it didn't happen. On the contrary, at present I'm coordinating a study group, and my best students are the quota students."

Supporters argued that without affirmative action, Afro-Brazilian children had no chance to achieve equality, much less become leaders who could represent their communities in society and government. Slavery and racism left blacks at a disadvantage, keeping generation after generation of black youth trapped in poverty. Only through affirmative action, and through quotas, they argued, could blacks succeed in

numbers proportionate to their share of the population. And then, perhaps, social equality could follow.

Critics of the policy were just as vocal. They argued that affirmative
action would only increase interracial friction—by forcing Brazilians to
focus on race rather than to dismiss it as irrelevant. Brazil's many categories of blackness didn't help soothe any tensions. After all, who was
"black"? Rosa spent a fair amount of time directing students toward different resources that they needed to thrive. Defining blackness, she explained, was defining who got into the university.

"There was even a debate at one point between the students, who
created a sort of court to determine who the quota students would be by
looking at them," she explained. Ultimately, however, who was "black"
was left to self-identification—a very good thing, too, since I couldn't
imagine the judgments of such a court dictating young people's futures!
But Rosa laughed at my indignation. She saw young people fighting for
their blackness, their identity, and it gave her hope for the future.

"I used to say, 'How good when someone declares themselves black
to get somewhere,'" she said, smiling broadly. "The idea of declaring
yourself black is already a victory."

Many public universities followed the lead of Rosa's school, and
some have put even higher quotas in place. (The Federal University of
Bahia, perhaps fittingly, reserves 40 percent of its spaces for poor and
black students.) But these were wrenching changes, she stressed to me,
and her students continue to argue about affirmative action among
themselves, to this day. As a professor, I know that a debate among students can be quite enlightening. So I asked her to set up a debate, and
she graciously obliged. What I saw did not disappoint.

"Are we not perhaps camouflaging a much deeper problem?" one
student asked urgently. "If the aim is to end racism, aren't we just re-
inforcing it in reverse?"

"It's not a way of camouflaging racism," another answered. "It's a
way of showing that we're trying to readdress it. Because for four hundred years, blacks were enslaved, and when it was abolished, they were
excluded."

"What we are doing is attacking the consequence," a young woman
countered, "and not the cause."

"Whoever benefits from it is in favor, and whoever doesn't is against
it," another student said wearily.

"There are 130 million active voters today," said a young, Afro-coiffed man (one of half a dozen students who belonged to the black student union, who had come to the debate wearing identical T-shirts), whose tone and attitude reminded me of black students in the United States in the late sixties. "Out of these 130 million, only 3 percent hold a university diploma. There are 40 million illiterate people in the country today. The university is already an oligarchic space, an aristocratic space. All of us here are in a privileged position. This is a privilege, do you understand? This is not debatable."

"The role of the public university is to educate all parts of society," one young man piped in. "The public university is not there to cater to the elite."

"I'd like him to itemize the privileges he says the elites get," another student shot back, "because I don't see whites being privileged but, instead, blacks or lower-income people being privileged when they're able to opt for the quota system."

This is getting good, I thought.

"You don't know what the privileges are?" another student asked, incredulous. "In higher education, 1 percent of professors are black. In the health system, black women get less anesthesia in labor than whites. This is official data. Black people with the same education as white people get paid 35 percent less while doing the same job."

I watched these passionate young people, the black nationalists among them growing ever more vocal, more adamant, taking pride in displaying contempt for foes of affirmative action, and thought about scenes like this from the late sixties back at Yale, when ours was the first affirmative-action generation and many of us acted out our political convictions and our anxieties in similarly offensive, impatient ways. I also thought about the privileges of my own life, privileges enabled by my inclusion among that pioneering generation. In 1966, Yale University graduated six black men. The class of 1973, which entered three years later, consisted of ninety-six black men and women.

I wanted to let these students speak and argue and hash it out for themselves, but I also wanted them to know that I would never have gone to Yale without affirmative action. Barack Obama would not have attended Columbia University, and it's likely he would not have attended Harvard Law School. Affirmative action—by which I mean taking into account ethnicity, class, religion, and gender as criteria for college admission—is not a perfect remedy for a history of discrimination, by any means; but it is the best system we have in the United States to address a past that can't be altered. "Not even God can change the past," Shimon Peres is fond of saying. But equal access to elite college education can help to change the effects of structural inequities we inherit from the past. And ultimately, I believe, in Brazil or in the United States, education will be the only way to redress the most pernicious effects of centuries of race-based slavery and a century of anti-black racism, formal and informal. Diversifying the middle class—changing the ratio of black Brazilians to white Brazilians in the upper economic classes, aiming for some sort of curve of class more reflective of Brazil's ethnic composition—is the only way to achieve the "racial democracy" of which Brazil so proudly boasts. Even with the quite drastic form of affirmative action that some of its universities have decided to implement (and Brazil's Supreme Court is soon to weigh in on the legality of these rigid quotas, just as the US Supreme Court did in our country), this sort of class redistribution among Brazil's large black population is going to take a very long time.

I have to say that I found myself somewhat sad to learn from the black people I interviewed that "racial democracy" was at best a philosophical concept, perhaps a dream or a goal, and at worst an often bandied about slogan, rather than a revolutionary anomaly that had been piercing itself across centuries of racial discrimination in Brazil. I remember my excitement when I first encountered this idea in the late sixties, hoping that someplace existed in the Western Hemisphere in which black people in a mixed-race society had been accorded their due as full and equal citizens—a place in which white people didn't discriminate against black people because they were black. There is so much that I love about Brazil, the largest African outpost in the whole of the New World: Candomblé, Carnaval, capoeira; its astonishing menagerie of classifications of brown skin; languidly sensual music forms such as samba and bossa nova; films such as *Black Orpheus* and *City of God* that startle with their bold innovations in the representation of blackness; *feijoada*, its national comfort food of pork and beans; the enticing sensuality more or less openly on display on its beaches; the seamless manner in which practitioners of Roman Catholicism marry this religion to Candomblé; and, always, its soccer teams, among many other things.

Nevertheless, Gilberto's Freyre's "racial democracy" is a very long way from being realized—so far away today, it occurs to me, that I wonder if he meant it to be a sort of call to arms, a rallying cry, an ideal to which Brazilians should aspire. How much farther away must it have been in 1933, when he formulated it? I had expected to find an immense, beautiful, rich landscape, occupied by one of the world's most ethnically diverse people, whose identity has been informed over half a millennium by a rich and intimate interplay among indigenous peoples, Africans, and Portuguese. I certainly found those things. I discovered an Afro-Brazilian experience that is vibrantly alive, evolving, impatient, engaged—right now, today.

At the same time, I encountered a social and economic reality that is deeply troubled, deeply conflicted, by race, a reality in which race codes for class. Perhaps Nascimento is right that for decades, Afro-Brazilians of every hue have lived, and perhaps suffered, in the shadow of a myth. Their country told them that racial democracy had made, or would make, everything racial all right and that there was no need to fight for equal rights. But today's Brazil is a very long way from becoming a racial paradise, and any sensible black Brazilian—and white Brazilian—knows that. Half a millennium of slavery and anti-black racism can't be wiped away with a slogan, no matter how eloquently wrought that slogan is. Nevertheless, I had seen a great deal that made me hopeful, most notably the fact that black consciousness is clearly establishing itself as a political force throughout the society in various ways, ways that compel the larger society to listen. And perhaps Brazil's experiment with affirmative action in higher education—no matter how it is modified, as it will be—will begin to accomplish in the twenty-first century the sort of equality of opportunity that has proved to be so elusive in Brazil for so very long, a Brazil richly and impressively "African" and black in its cultural diversity yet always already economically dominated by the white descendants of the masters and the descendants of post-emancipation white immigrants. I hoped, as my plane took off, that I was witnessing the realization of Abdias do Nascimento's invocation to the god Exú that Brazil's black community at long last find its political voice as forcefully and as resonantly as it had long before found its artistic voice and that, in so doing, Brazil might experience a new kind of social revolution, a revolution that could lead to the creation of the world's first racial democracy.

2

Mexico

"The Black Grandma in the Closet"

Afro-Mexicans are like sugar in coffee; you can't see them, but they make the whole thing taste much better.

—Sagrario Cruz-Carretero

The days of pure whites, victors of today, are as numbered as were the days of their predecessors. . . . [We are entering] the period of fusion and mixing of all peoples.

. . . The *mestizo* will produce a civilization more universal in its tendency than any other race in the past.

—José María Vasconcelos, 1925

ON THE WALL in my dining room hangs a work of art entitled "Lucky," one of the collages or works of found art created by the African American artist Suesan Stovall. "Lucky" is a dapper black man. He is standing, supported by a cane, one ankle crossing the other, wearing a bow tie, an elegant Panama hat, and brown and white leather shoes. The figure "26" sits in the frame of his portrait. He is the subject of a drawing, not the center of a portrait; nevertheless, he is not a type of racist caricature. I have always liked this image of Lucky; in fact, it makes me feel lucky myself, which is one reason why I keep this dapper black man in view of the dining table, where I try to write each day. It was several years after acquiring this image that I learned (from Pablo Gonzalez, a framer visiting my house to hang new Stovall collages) that "Lucky" was actually one of fifty-four figures in a very popular Mexican card game, La Lotería Mexicana, or "Mexican Bingo." What in the world was a black man—known affectionately as "El negrito"—doing functioning almost at the center of an array of fifty-four images in one of Mexico's most popular board games, among images entitled "The Rooster," "The Little Devil," "The Lady," "The Dandy," "The Watermelon," "The Apache," "The Skull," "The Rose," "The Scorpion," and "Death," sandwiched between number 25, "El borracho" (The Drunk), and number 27, "El corazón" (The Heart)? And while a literal English translation for *el negrito* is "little black man," in standard reference works on La Lotería, the term can be used within families, for example, in a kind and loving way, sometimes independent of race, a term of endearment, without irony. But various sources also gloss *el negrito* as "the slave, the Negro."

Each of the fifty-four figures in the game is assigned a short motto or description. And what is Lucky's? "The one that ate the sugar." What was this riddle about? What was a black man—not a mulatto in any way but a man with demonstrably Negroid features—doing at the center of a popular Mexican parlor game? Lucky, or El negrito, is a trace of Mexico's long-buried African past. You might say that solving the riddle of the origins of this black man set in motion my desire to explore the African presence in Mexico.

I set out on my journey, nearly overwhelmed by the implications of the research about the slave trade in Mexico that I had just received from the historian David Eltis. Eltis directs the Trans-Atlantic Slave Trade Database, an Internet site freely accessible to all, which consists of a vast database of about thirty-five thousand voyages of slave ships to the New World, between 1502 and 1866. In the earliest years of the slave trade—up until about 1600—the database indicates that Mexico would have had the largest slave population in the New World. Moreover, according to the most recent estimates from Eltis, approximately seven hundred thousand Africans were brought to Mexico and Peru combined over the course of the slave trade, an estimate much higher than previously thought. That is a quarter million more black people than came to the United States in the entire course of the slave trade! If this is so, where are their descendants? Why don't we think of Mexico as an Afro-Latin American country?

Hernán Cortés was the first conquistador to arrive in Mexican territory in 1519. The final conquest of Mexico-Tenochtitlan took place in 1521. Soon after, the Spanish started to settle there, as they would do in Peru, and a surprisingly large slave trade began. By 1580, Spanish people had been living in Mexico for sixty years. By the beginning of the seventeenth century, although the slave trade had hardly begun, Mexico had one of the biggest slave populations in Latin America, and I would venture that very few Americans realize this. Before 1550, most of the slaves were taken to the island of Hispaniola. The sixteenth-century historian Gonzalo Fernández de Oviedo y Valdés described Hispaniola as a "new Guinea" at about this time. To put this in perspective, by 1550, the island of Hispaniola—the home of Haiti and the Dominican Republic today—was in the midst of its sugar boom, which lasted until 1580. But Mexico was itself beginning to boom economically, thanks to silver-mining discoveries in the 1540s. Mexico was in its early stages of colonization, but it took off quickly and was getting to be quite prominent by the mid- to late-sixteenth century. In other words, Mexico and Hispaniola were both experiencing a form of economic boom between 1550 and 1580; and Mexico surpassed Hispaniola in economic importance before the end of the sixteenth century.

Where are the descendants of these slaves today? Do they hope for racial democracy, as Afro-Brazilians do? What do Afro-Mexican children know of their heritage, and how do the descendants of Mexico's slaves see their future? Do they exist as a distinct class or ethnic group, or is the black presence buried deep in the admixture of Mexico's collective DNA?

I started my search for answers in the great port city of Veracruz. I knew that beginning in the mid-sixteenth century, this was the main portal of arrival for Mexico's slave trade, as well as for almost every other commodity. I'd been lucky to get in touch with two local scholars: Judith Hernández, an archaeologist, and Sagrario Cruz-Carretero, professor of anthropology at the University of Veracruz. We met at the port, the very place all those slaves would have entered the country.

Hernández and Cruz-Carretero told me that historical records indicate that it could have taken as long as two months for ships to reach Veracruz from the ports of West and Central Africa—far longer than it took to reach Brazil. Of course, the slave ships were hot and humid like steam baths. Slaves capable of retaining salt in their system, they said, were actually more likely to survive because they retained more water, which enabled them to avoid dehydration through the torturous journey. (This theory, known as the "Salt Thesis," goes on to speculate that this is why so many descendants of slaves in the United States suffer from hypertension.) Nonetheless, about 15 percent of the Africans died during the Middle Passage.

Veracruz, Mexico. (Jemila Twinch)

"What would happen when the slaves arrived?" I asked. "Would they be checked, medically?"

"There were paid surgeons to review the blacks," Hernández told me, "and the check-up consisted of licking the beard. Because sweat contains salt. If the beard was salty, that meant the slave had good blood pressure."

Once slaves passed their physical exam, they were sold in the city's Central Plaza. Some slaves stayed in Veracruz and were sold in this port. But most of them were then taken to Mexico City and from there were sold to different regions in the territories dominated by New Spain. Cruz-Carretero and Hernández explained that most slaves were bought by hacienda owners who needed labor to farm sugarcane or to raise cattle. Indigenous Mexicans, they said, had no gift for minding cattle because, of course, they never had any indigenously, but some of the Africans knew about livestock and how to care for it, so they quickly became preferred cattle hands—and were prized as such. Other slaves were bought to work in mines, to work the fields, or to take care of lavish homes as house servants.

"How much did a slave cost?" I asked.

"From 150 to 400 pesos," Cruz-Carretero answered. "Let me compare: a house costs 400 pesos. It was a luxury." So a house and a slave to work the fields to pay for the house could cost about the same amount of money, though prices of houses could vary widely, ranging from 200 pesos to 5,000 pesos. And this variation reveals why, for some hacienda owners, slaves were not always considered a luxury.

I took a moment to think about that. Even among scholars who spend their careers researching the slave trade, it's sobering to talk about the price of a person. "These walls are covered with African blood," Cruz-Carretero said, waving her hand at the many historic structures lining the waterfront. "The indigenous population decreased because of illness, so Africans were the ones who constructed these gorgeous buildings. And many of them died in the process. All these walls have the fingerprints of all these Africans. This is the fingerprint of black history in Mexico. It's a history of death and a history of invisibility."

Death and invisibility—those words struck me. They were powerful, ominous. I wondered if I would find them to be true. I wondered if, as in Brazil, Mexican slavery was also a history of creation, cultural contributions, and miscegenation.

Soon after, Hernández had to leave us, so Cruz-Carretero and I went off to have lunch. At the table, she pulled out a small bundle of

Port of San Juan de Ullúa, Veracruz. (Jemila Twinch)

Port of San Juan de Lua, Veracruz. (Jemila Twinch)

family photos to show me. We pored over images of her grandfather, her parents, and her aunts and cousins. Many of them looked indigenous. But in one photo after another, Cruz-Carretero pointed out the black physical features—broad noses, thick lips, kinky hair—the traces of Africa on the very faces of her family. Her family's gene pool was mixed, she explained, with a demonstrable dose of Africa in the mix. And then she told me that she hadn't known about her black genetic heritage until she was nineteen years old.

"How did you find out you were part black?" I asked her.

"I traveled to Cuba," she explained. "When I arrived there, they started talking about African heritage and culture. And I suddenly realized my family was black—because they looked like my grandfather, like my father. I started tasting the food, and I said, 'Oh, my God—this is the food my grandmother prepares at home.'"

I asked Cruz-Carretero how it felt to find out that she had this strain of black ancestry in a country where black people don't officially exist. Cruz-Carretero was nineteen. Was it a positive discovery, or was being of African slave ancestry somehow a badge of shame, which might explain why it took her nineteen years to learn this about her ancestry?

Cruz-Carretero understood the strangeness of her experience. When I asked her about it, she clasped her hands in front of her, thoughtfully cocking her head. "It was weird," she said finally, "very weird. It was like discovering you were adopted and had never known. I came back to Mexico and asked my grandpa why he never told me we were black. And he told me, holding my hand, 'We are not black; we're *morenos.*'"

This was fascinating to me. *Morenos* is a word for a person of mixed race popularly used in parts of Mexico such as Oaxaca and Guerrero. It's a regional term, but it illuminates a much larger national discourse. For centuries, Mexico had sixteen categories of racial mixture, or shades of blackness and brownness, called the *castas,* or ideal types, into which the offspring of mixed sexual unions in Mexico were assigned. Some historians have maintained that the images of these types, which in the eighteenth century were frequently painted in sets, were designed for visiting tourists from Spain, but other historians argue these four-inch-by-four-inch paradigms for race mixture were done in the context of and derived from Enlightenment theories about the diversity and classification of plants, nature, fruits, works, and people—in other words, that they were the result of a "scientific" thrust. Still others argue that they were produced for domestic consumption, not for visitors. Regardless of their target audience, think *octoroon* or *quadroon,* times eight.

Morenos are not depicted in the *casta* paintings as one of the sixteen official shades, perhaps because the term is of regional origin. But this may not be the whole story. As the historian Ben Vinson III explained to me, "Actually, there are probably more categories of blackness. The *casta* paintings were typically done in sets of sixteen images showing the progression of racial mixture as different 'types' intermarried with 'whites.' This may be where the number sixteen comes from. Also, some argue that the *casta* paintings were actually shipped abroad for consumption by Europeans (especially Spaniards)—giving them a sense of what life was like (including flora and fauna) in the New World. Hence, many think that the paintings were oriented for export. With this said, there was a domestic market as well. There were variances between the audiences in Peru and Mexico for the paintings. Despite the paintings, *casta* nomenclature was alive and well, and there may have been at least eighteen different racial categories used semiconsistently in what we know to be colonial Mexico."

As Cruz-Carretero explained the history of racial classification within her own family, I nodded in recognition of a larger phenomenon, one that I encountered throughout my research in Latin America. Just as I had in Brazil, I was encountering here in Mexico a society in which traces of black roots were buried in brownness. Blackness was okay, if it was part of a blend, an ingredient that doesn't exactly disappear but that is only rendered present through a trace, a hint, a telltale sign. Few people in Latin America, it seemed, wanted to be called "*negro*," or "black." Like so many people who would be defined as "black" or "African American" in the United States, Cruz-Carretero's grandfather, according to her, was declaring that his family's mixed-race heritage was a shield against being defined as "black," as a "*negro*." Was this a case of the pernicious American phenomenon, "If you are black, get back. If you are brown, stick around. If you are white, you are all right"? I was determined to find out, eager to avoid imposing my value system on a foreign people.

Cruz-Carretero said about her grandfather, "He was aware that he was a black man, but he rejected that identity. And I think this is something that happens in most families—but you can't talk about it. You hide the black grandma in the closet."

The black grandma in the closet. What an apt turn of phrase. The genetic outlier, that telltale recessive gene, popping up out of nowhere, seemingly, as in the category in the *casta* painting named "*torna atrás*," meaning "go back" and signifying the moment in a family's line when black features show up from less black parents. (As we shall see, the similar phrase in the Dominican Republic is that all of its seemingly white or "Indio" citizens are, in fact, "black behind the ears.") Except that "nowhere," we now know, consisted of more than half of the seven hundred thousand Africans dragged to Mexico and Peru to create colonial economies. I turned my head to watch the steady stream of Mexicans passing our table. Some faces looked brown, some a little red, some a light tan, some almost white. Others were very dark. But as much as the races had clearly mixed, I wondered if they were equal, if color was class, as it seemed to be in Brazil.

"Why, in every mixed-race society, is black always on the bottom?" I asked Cruz-Carretero.

"It's part of human nature," she replied, shrugging, referring to the "color as class" systems that arose in slave societies in the United States, throughout the Caribbean, and in Latin America. "There's a system of 'pigmentocracy,' locating you within social parameters according to the color of your skin. Being lighter skinned puts you in good social position." This was certainly true according to the unconscious classification system in Mexico and throughout the New World. But it is also true that in some periods and regions in Mexico, black people were in a better social position than were the indigenous peoples, and that reality persists in some regions even today. Also, of course, as we shall see, not all black people remained slaves. Racial theories that devalued the blackest colors of human skin arose to justify the New World's economic order based on the exploitation of the labor of people whose faces wore this very skin.

I told Cruz-Carretero that I thought she was absolutely right. In mixed-race societies, color is used, in part, to mark class. You see it in Africa, in India, in Asia, throughout the Americas. And this fact contains another—something I've also seen over and over again: it is very tempting to hide one's blackness in a mixed-race culture. Cruz-Carretero nodded her head in agreement and explained that most of her family members can easily pass for being indigenous, so they choose to do that. Lighter-skinned Mexican women, she continued, bleach their hair to look more European. From inside a culture that actively works to whiten itself—as Brazil had done and as I learned Mexico had done—claiming African heritage isn't always easy, especially when your skin color and physical characteristics don't look African to others. Those who don't think you look black, she said, feel free to tell you you're not. After all, it is supposed, why would anyone want to be that?

"But who owns the negrometer?" she asked me, with a slight smile masking a serious purpose. "Who owns the records and can say who is black and who is not? It's our duty to try to change the idea that being black means being ugly and the idea that the name is derogatory. Otherwise, you're going to be denigrated if you accept your blackness."

I told her it was a great question, that I'd been thinking about this for a very long time, but I didn't know the answer. It's tempting to think that the upper classes—those with the most to gain and lose—are the ones who invent and enforce color distinctions. But history suggests otherwise. The blame, I told Cruz-Carretero, needs to be widely distributed. The "negrometer" lies, to some extent, in all of us.

At the end of the day, I left Cruz-Carretero and Veracruz, impressed that a person not obviously black had so enthusiastically embraced her African heritage, and I began a long drive to the inland city of Tlacotalpan. On my way, I leafed through my sheaf of notes. Tlacotalpan was a major colonial trading post. Sugar, cotton, cattle, horses, and slaves all came through it—commodities that were produced by indigenous and African slaves, along with their offspring, who were often the mixed-race children of European settlers. When slaves were moved deeper into Mexico from Veracruz, this is one of the places they went.

Walking through the streets, I saw a quaint, historic city that probably hasn't changed much since the early seventeenth century. At a little square surrounded by cafés, I met Rafael Figueroa, an ethnomusicologist. Figueroa studies cultures by analyzing their music. He was eager to talk with me about—or, rather, to show me—how African and Mexican and indigenous influences had combined to create new musical forms. Following lunch, he told me that I was in luck because the town would be performing a traditional fandango later that night. I could scarcely stand the anticipation.

We headed for the town square, just after the sun had set, in the cool of the evening. Just about everybody in the town seemed to be there. Chairs had been assembled around an elevated wooden platform, and they were quickly filling up. Figueroa led me across the street to an area where musicians were playing and females and males in various combinations and ranging over a lifespan of ages were dancing with great energy. They took turns dancing on the elevated platform, and the sound of the girls' stamping feet reverberated through the square. I was entranced. The passionate movements of the dance reminded me of Spanish flamenco, but the polyrhythms in the music were African. And there was another influence too, one that I learned came from indigenous tradition. This blend, Figueroa said, was fandango.

I had always thought that fandango was a European musical form. I associated it with Argentina and Brazil, of course, but only as a residue of Spanish and Portuguese colonial rule. I'd never thought of it as African. Figueroa set me straight. "Fandango—it's a mix of Hispanic and African, mainly," he explained. "Even though the instruments are Hispanic, they are played in a really percussive way, and they are played against each other in aggressive polyrhythms. The platform, we call it the *tarima*. And it's a musical instrument by itself."

"Fandango is a regular party for us," he said, smiling. "You can do

An American Indian Man and His Negro Wife, from the sixteen *casta* paintings depicting the color of offspring of various interracial combinations in Mexico. (Museo de America, Madrid, Spain/Giraudon/Bridgeman Art Library)

a fandango at your birthday, if you are going to get married, or just for the sake of it. There are private fandangos in the backyard, and there are public fandangos like this one. It's always just a celebration of music and dance. It's just to have a good time."

"That's definitely black," I laughed.

"Exactly," he laughed back.

"Those girls are great," I marveled. "Now, do the boys dance or just the girls?"

"Well, they always say that the first dance is to watch the girls," Figueroa explained, winking, "so you can see if you want to dance with one of them later. I've seen fandangos still going around 6:00 or 7:00 a.m."

"A.m.?" I responded. "I love this town!"

Figueroa pointed out the African rhythms in the music, the Mexican guitar flourishes, and the strong influences of Spain. Like Carnaval in Brazil, I realized, fandango was born out of a complex mix of cultures. And as we chatted, I learned that many songs and forms that I considered Mexican actually had mixed-race histories. The complicated dance steps known as *zapateo* combine Spanish and African traditions. Even "La Bamba," arguably the best-known Mexican song, had African roots, Figueroa told me. Slaves from Angola and the Congo first sang that tune in Mexico as early as 1683.

This country has blackness all over it, I thought. So why can't we see it? I asked Figueroa why most Mexicans don't look black and why the nation's African heritage isn't more prominent in its cultural identity.

"They mixed, from the beginning," Figueroa answered, referring to indigenous people, slaves, and Europeans. "That's why you can't see it —but it's here." Blackness in Mexico had become diluted, he explained. In some areas, like the Costa Chica on the West Coast and Veracruz on the East Coast, the people still look a little African. But even when Mexicans don't look black, they sometimes reveal their African lineage in the way they speak, he explained. Since I have written about African American spoken language, I wanted to learn more about this idea.

"We have a specific accent," he continued. "When we say '*helado*,' which means 'ice cream,' we drop the *d*, so it's '*hela'o*.' Sometimes we drop the final *s* from words. It's really common among people of African origin." It was also a common usage of the old form of speaking Spanish during the colonial period.

"Hey, I've noticed that," I said, realizing I'd discovered one key to unlocking Mexico's hidden blackness. "I've noticed that some people say '*Buenos día*' instead of '*Buenos días*,' and I wondered what was wrong with them!" "Precisely," he replied, ever the good professor, trying to encourage an eager pupil. (I noticed this accent, too, in the Dominican Republic; even when the *s* is intervocal, it is almost a silent letter, as in "*hablo e'pañol*"—rather than "*hablo español*.")

I asked Figueroa about his own black ancestry. He told me that his mother's hair was very curly and that she knew she had African blood. Remembering Cruz-Carretero's story, I asked Figueroa how his mother felt about that hair. He said she was proud of her heritage—but that pride in blackness has its limits. "For a lot of people, dark skin is a symbol of beauty," he explained. "But it's a little of a love-hate relationship. You don't like it in your kids. If your kid is born lighter than you, you'll say that you're 'improving the race.'"

I have heard that phrase so often in the black community in the United States, though more in the fifties and sixties, of course, than today. And my sister-in-law, Gemina Pena Gates, once told me that her aunt used to say it all the time back home in Puerto Rico. I told Figueroa that I recognized the expression, that they used to say that back home, too, and that I'd heard it myself, many times.

Late that night, as the music of the fandango slowly receded, I retreated to my hotel room, alone with my thoughts. If half a million slaves had come through Veracruz and, to a lesser extent, Acapulco, how did they become black grandmas in the closet, five hundred years later? Why had ethnic mixing here so very effectively pulverized African physical characteristics? What had happened?

The next morning, I traveled to the town of Yanga, hoping to find some clues. It's a place with a fascinating history. In 1553, the Spanish viceroy Luís de Velasco pleaded with King Charles of Spain to limit the number of slaves traveling to Mexico. Velasco was concerned that Mexico already had too many Africans—and he feared what they might do if they were organized. It turned out he had good reason. In 1570, a slave named Gasper Yanga escaped and led a group of his fellow Africans to freedom here in the mountains of Veracruz. Not only did he escape slavery fifty years before the *Mayflower* landed on Plymouth Rock, but he launched guerrilla attacks on the Spanish, tormenting them from the mountains for three decades. The Spanish could never catch him, never put him back in bondage. So in 1609, they gave up and offered him a town of his own in exchange for peace, as long as he refused to give sanction to fugitive slaves. The town of Yanga became one of the first communities founded by free blacks in North or South America —quite possibly, according to some historians, the very first.

I was excited to see Yanga. Let's face it, I was crazy to see it. I barely waited for the car to stop before popping out in the main square. Above me towered a magnificent statue of the man himself, and I paused just a moment to admire his image.

I wanted to know what the residents of this town knew and felt about their history. So I started looking for people to talk to in a nearby park. I immediately encountered a girl named Carmen, and soon others started to gather. They were, I think, drawn by my camera crew, rather than my endless questions. But they were eager to talk.

"Carmen, who is Yanga?" I asked.

"A hero," she replied. "He made Yanga people free."

"A black slave," a man piped in. "Supposedly, he was a slave of the Spanish who broke the chains."

"He freed himself from the oppression of the Spanish," the man's girlfriend added. "He liberated the slaves."

"That's why they call Yanga the first free town in the Americas!" exclaimed a young boy. I couldn't wipe the smile off my face. This was great.

"Is everyone in this town black?" I asked.

"No, the people I know of are brown," the woman answered.

I asked the people around me what color they considered themselves. The answers were familiar: *moreno, mulatto,* other shades of brown. I came back around to my new friend Carmen. She looked indigenous to me, so I asked if she was Indian. "*Negro,*" she said shyly, her eyes shining up at me. Now that's what I am talking about!

It was hard not to enjoy the people of Yanga. They certainly indulged me. And I spent hours exploring the town. But, in the end, I have to admit that it just wasn't the nucleus of black pride I expected. I imagined I'd find museums celebrating African culture, schools dedicated to keeping African music and art alive. I thought I'd find another place like Brazil's Bahia—a thriving black community that trumpeted its African history. Instead, Yanga was something else. It had started black, but like so much of Mexico, it had evolved into a blended brown.

My next stop was the center of the nation: Mexico City, the largest city in the Americas today—a modern, vibrant, bustling metropolis with twenty-one million residents, a magisterial and diverse place since ancient times. The Aztecs called it Tenochtitlan—and made it the seat of their empire. When Spanish conquistador Hernán Cortés first came to Mexico in 1519, he visited Tenochtitlan with another conquistador, Juan Garrido—a free black man. They were both amazed by what they found. The Aztecs had built a complex irrigation system. The city was stunningly beautiful, and of course, it was full of gold. Cortés soon conquered Tenochtitlan, cruelly, along with one hundred thousand soldiers from Tlaxcala, which remains a semi-independent region to this day because of it. (The indigenous Tlaxcalans never get any credit for being the real conquerors of Tenochtitlan, even though they wrote about it and illustrated it for centuries in their own language. But this doesn't fit in neatly with our story of European conquest of the New World.) And

over centuries, modern Mexico City was built in the place of Tenochtitlan—ancient Aztec ruins lie in its center.

I went to meet with María Elisa Velázquez at the National Museum
of Mexico. Velázquez does research and teaches history, and I was eager to get her take on what had shaped Mexico's black experience. She
greeted me warmly at the imposing, impressive museum, and we soon
got down to business. She told me she'd been looking forward to showing me a collection of the *casta* paintings—painted by local artists in
the eighteenth century basically to show Europeans the cultural and racial diversity of the people of Mexico (or New Spain, as it was called).

I was quite intrigued, to say the least. These paintings were created
in the Enlightenment, during years of intense racial mixing, Velázquez
told me—hence the impulse to catalogue racial types. They were the
product of a unique set of historical circumstances. From the start of
the slave trade, white masters had produced children with African and
indigenous slaves (Spanish men born in the New World, known as
"*criollos*," frequently impregnated black women, often by force). In addition, Africans and the indigenous population had intermingled and
had their own children together. Blessings from the church increased
this racial mixing—as the Catholic Church began to recognize mixed
marriages (there were no civil marriages), and the government granted
freedom to slaves born of African and indigenous women.

Mexico, very early on in its colonial history, was becoming a true
melting pot, and its colonial masters were very curious about this. Europeans and Mexicans commissioned the *casta* paintings, Velázquez
explained, almost like a theoretical guide book or encyclopedia to the
diversity of the New World. They wanted these images to serve as a
sort of catalogue or typology of the new categories or ideal types of
black and brown and white genetic combinations that had been created in the New World by all that mixing. But despite the temptation
to see them in this way, she continued, they were not an anthropological cookbook—actual recipes—for lightening the Mexican race;
they did not perform a prescriptive function. Nor were these categories, unlike as in Brazil, used in documents or in daily life, except for
a few, such as *negro, mulata, mestizo,* and *zambo.* Still, I was struck by
how many times I would hear people employing these words today, all
these centuries after they were first coined. So perhaps their descrip-
tive function had had a certain sort of prescriptive one as well. And,

of course, I remembered Ben Vinson's advice that there were quite possibly more than sixteen categories of blackness that were achievable, since the number sixteen seems to have derived from the series typically making up a *casta* painting "set." While many of these mixtures depicted in the *casta* series had no black in them at all, Vinson explained, "I think that there were more than sixteen categories in use during colonial times."

Looking at the *casta* paintings, I saw small portraits organized in a grid, four images across and four down. Tidily and clinically, they detail one artist's conception of the sixteen *castas* in Mexico, though these designations and categories could change in each region and time period, and though a priest's own subjective perspective influenced the way a person might be described. Sixteen is a lot of categories, but, again, it is not nearly as many formal categories of blackness, certainly, as we saw in Brazil but far more than we ever dreamed of employing in the United States.

Velázquez explained them to me, one by one. Spanish and Indian makes *mestizo*. *Mestizo* and Spanish makes *castizo*. And as I was tickled to learn, *castizo* and Spanish makes . . . Spanish again.

"What about me?" I asked. "Which one of the sixteen would I be?"

"You would be here," she said, pointing again: "a mulatto." A mulatto in Mexico but not a mulatto in Brazil.

I asked about Barack Obama and Beyoncé. They'd be mulatto too, Velázquez told me. But Tiger Woods, he'd be *lobo*, because he is a mix of African and indigenous, or "Indio." (Mexico had a lot of "*chinos*," in fact, people from all over East Asia who were brought in through Acapulco from the Manila fleet. They were quite common on the Pacific side of Mexico, though they did indeed tend to blend in as "Indios" in time.) Why did the intermixing of African genes with European ones seem to lead to this intense fascination with exact degrees of color? "These people were crazy," I blurted out, before looking sideways at Velázquez to see how she'd take it. She smiled in return.

"They needed pseudoscientific reasons to explain why some races were inferior," she said, and therefore could be exploited as free or cheap labor. The ruling classes also were seeking to justify their elite status through an appeal to a biological or "natural" white-skin privilege, something that was just an aspect of the larger order of things.

"And they found it," I responded: "sixteen shades of blackness and brownness," remembering that the indigenous people are in the genetic mix as well. Upon a moment's reflection, however, I had to admit that I was surprised by the freedom to mix so much in the first place. In the United States, a single drop of black blood can define you, no matter what you look like. In Mexico, even though some races were oppressed as slaves, sexual relationships between races clearly weren't rare.

"Why were your white people more willing to sleep with black people than my white people?" I asked. It sounds a bit silly, but that's really the question, isn't it?

"Because the church allowed the marriages," Velázquez said, "and because Spanish people have a heritage of being more open to mixture due to the Arabic presence in Spain."

"The Moors were in Spain for eight hundred years," I reminded myself aloud. I'd never really thought about what that meant for Spanish bloodlines.

"Exactly," she responded. "So it was kind of easy to have these kinds of mixtures."

"So there wasn't color prejudice in colonial Mexico?" I asked. I was fascinated but confused. This culture wasn't so easy to pin down.

"Yes, there was," she said slowly, trying to think of the best way to explain it. "But it wasn't as important as it became in the eighteenth century. Before that, African people had some opportunities in certain trades, and they could marry indigenous people and Spanish people. They could improve their conditions in life. But then the slave trade became more important. The Spanish needed to have proof that some cultures were inferior. All these words describing races were created at that moment."

I looked back at the *casta* paintings, and I realized I was looking at the birth of a new kind of racism in Mexico. Before the eighteenth century, Africans were kept as slaves because, well, someone had enslaved them. But after the period when we saw the creation of the *casta* paintings (though not because of them, certainly), when people were drawing on pseudoscience to justify economic exploitation, Africans were kept as slaves because they were deemed "scientifically" inferior. This wasn't human nature, as my lunch companion Cruz-Carretero had generously described it. This was a conscious effort to diminish another people, to draw on "science" to justify an economic order, an economic order that was brutal, harsh, and meant to be eternal. Relatively few of

Mexico's total slave population arrived in the sixteenth century before 1580, but then a big wave began to arrive. That wave petered out in about 1650 or so, and very few more slaves were imported. That means that about a century of mixing took place before the *casta* paintings were created.

Velázquez asked if I'd like to see the museum's exhibit on the Mexican revolution, and I realized I was happy to move on. As a scholar of race, I was deeply satisfied to see the *casta* paintings with my own eyes. But as a black man, I needed some time to digest all that they stood for.

We ambled toward another part of the museum, and Velázquez explained that a priest named Father Hidalgo had launched Mexico's War of Independence in 1810, calling for an end to the entire *casta* system and of slavery. He urged all Mexicans, whatever their color or ancestry, to think of themselves as equals. And he found his country eager for such a message. The people of Mexico were tired of being ruled by Spain, and the American Revolution and the French Revolution inspired them to fight for their own independence.

The war was difficult, bloody, and long, Velázquez explained. It lasted more than a decade, and Father Hidalgo himself did not live to see the end. He was captured and executed by the Spanish in 1811. But his fight was taken up by two generals: José María Morelos y Pavón and Vicente Ramón Guerrero Saldaña. They were great heroes in the war, she told me, and they were both descended from Africans.

That stopped me in my tracks.

"Wait a minute, wait a minute," I said, waving my hands. "Two black people were generals in the Mexican War of Independence? This is like George Washington being black. That's astonishing."

Velázquez led me straight to a portrait of Morelos, looking majestic in full military dress. This was one resplendent black man.

"Morelos definitely is a brother," I said, chuckling. "He would not have been riding in the front of the bus in Mississippi!"

Spanish forces killed Morelos in 1815. But his compatriot, mockingly called "the Negro Guerrero" by his enemies, continued to fight, with the help of thousands of black and white and mixed and indigenous Mexicans. At one point, Guerrero's father, fearing for his son's life, begged him to surrender to the Spanish. Guerrero gave his answer in front of all his men, saying, "You are my father, but the country comes first." A shortened version of this answer, "*La patria es primero*" (the country comes first), is now a famous Mexican phrase.

Allegiances in the war did not strictly break down along racial lines. Many Afro-Mexicans in the Costa Chica, Velázquez said, also supported the Spanish government. Nonetheless, it is inspiring to realize that there was such strong black leadership in the independence movement—and that it proved successful. Guerrero, in alliance with Agustín de Iturbide, finally won independence for Mexico in 1821, after ten years of resistance. And in 1829, he abolished slavery once and for all —thirty-three years before Abraham Lincoln signed the Emancipation Proclamation in the United States. (Morelos tried to abolish it by decree in 1815, but of course that decree didn't apply everywhere in the country.) And that wasn't the end of his accomplishments.

"The important thing about Guerrero," Velázquez told me, "is that he was the second president in Mexico."

The Negro Guerrero—president? "So you had your Barack Obama in 1829!" I blurted out.

"That's right, before the United States," she said, nodding emphatically. I actually sent a text message back home to my friend Larry Bobo, the Du Bois Professor of the Social Sciences at Harvard. *Bing* came his reply. "How come we don't know this!" How come, indeed? Did Mexicans know this? I wondered. On the other hand, how many Americans know anything about Mexican history, anything at all, except maybe the name Pancho Villa?

I also had to wonder what such a figure might have meant for the United States. What if George Washington had been black? Or John Adams? Perhaps a more relevant question is this one: Could George Washington or John Adams have been black? Would we have needed a Civil Rights Movement? My brain was on fire imagining alternative pasts for my own country.

What Velázquez told me next, though, made me pause in my ecstatic thinking. Guerrero had indeed abolished slavery. But in 1822, in the service of an ideal of equality, he and his colleagues also removed racial categories from all certificates of birth, marriage, and death. If race didn't exist, they reasoned, then racism couldn't exist. I had encountered this logic in Brazil and would in Peru as well. The idea about abolishing the recording of color differences, as we might expect, was intended to facilitate the elimination of privileges tied to these color differences. But there were unintended consequences, which Guerrero and his compatriots could not anticipate.

I recognized the well-meaning spirit behind Guerrero's actions. He had yearned to create a society beyond race, to act as if race didn't matter. This same spirit gave birth to the idea of racial democracy in Brazil. But denying roots is different from respecting them equally. Guerrero, with the best of intentions, inadvertently took an action that helped, over time, to bury his own African ancestry and that aspect of the genetic heritage of every Afro-Mexican who followed him.

I asked Velázquez if most Mexicans today know that Morelos and Guerrero were black and that they owed their independence, in part, to the leadership of these two Afro-Mexicans. I was disappointed, but not surprised, by her answer. They don't. These men have towns and states named after them. Morelos even appears on the fifty-peso bill. But their blackness has effectively been buried for far too many Mexicans.

"Many people thought that if we erased the categories of blackness, we would erase racism," I said. "Do you see any merit in that argument?"

"I don't agree," Velázquez answered, shaking her head. "I think we have the right and the need to know about who we are. We have to be proud about it, proud to share a heritage with such important cultures in Africa."

She explained that Mexican culture is like a braid with three strands: indigenous, African, and Spanish. The strands may be equal in length, but they're different in color, character, and texture. She made an eloquent argument for accepting racial differences as part of the fight for equality.

I thanked Velázquez for all she'd taught me and left the museum. Our conversation had me running late, so I hustled along the sidewalk, checking my watch. I was leaving Mexico City shortly—indeed, I had only a few hours to spare. But I wanted to review an essay that I knew was critically important to understanding just about everything I'd seen here thus far.

Those who wanted to obliterate race and racial categories in order to eliminate racism possibly could not anticipate the creation of systematic attempts to whiten the image, and genetic admixture, of Mexico. But those who would whiten Mexico didn't get the last word on the country's collective ethnic self-identity. Mexico might have followed this lead for a century, denying its multicultural past and whitening its story, even encouraging European immigration, just as Brazil had done, to lighten its collective complexion. But I remembered from my research on the black Harlem Renaissance writer Jean Toomer that in the early twentieth century, the philosopher José María Vasconcelos wrote a groundbreaking paper that changed all that. In his essay "The Cosmic Race," Vasconcelos argued—boldly and counterintuitively—that Mexico's distinct mix of indigenous, European, and African "blood," in fact, made it a superior culture, an augury of the world's genetic future. He described Mexico's racial mixing as a unique, ideal destiny, one that prepared the nation for a glorious future. After rummaging through my bags, I sat down with this essay in my hotel room, high above the noise and mayhem of Mexico City's traffic, and read passages like this:

> Perhaps there is nothing useless in historical developments. Our own physical isolation . . . together with the original mixture of bloods, has served to keep us from the Anglo-Saxon limitation of constituting castes of pure races. . . . Never have they been seen to surpass other men, neither in talent, or goodness, or in strength. The road we have initiated is much more daring. It breaks away from ancient prejudices, and it would be almost unexplainable if it were not grounded on a sort of clamor that reaches from a remote distance, a distance which is not that of the present, but that mysterious distance from where the presage of the future comes.

When Vasconcelos's essay was published in 1925, it was an overnight sensation. Mexicans loved this idea. And what today we would call a "brown pride" movement sprang up, practically overnight. It was surely an improvement over massive, systematic efforts at whitening. But what did this movement cost Mexico's black roots? Did the nationalistic usefulness and popularity of Vasconcelos's theory have the effect of valorizing the history and heritage of Mexico's Afro-descendants or of burying them? I had to wonder. When parents celebrate the birth of infants who look lighter than they do, how can this be pride? And what about those whose blackness is visible, indisputable? Those whose black grandma is out of the closet? Does their complexion exclude them from being "cosmic." I couldn't help thinking again of Brazil's Gilberto Freyre and the questionable accomplishments and claims of

Brazil's "racial democracy." Indeed, since Vasconcelos preceded Freyre by eight years, I had to presume a measure of influence. Mexicans were much more willing to embrace "*indigenismo*," the idea that they were descended from the Aztecs, and Aztec civilization's valorization as a world-class, great civilization, than they were to embrace African history, of course, since few of us tend to think of Africa as having as magnificent a civilization as the Aztecs—an erroneous assumption but one still rather difficult to alter.

I was now very eager to see black Mexico. I needed to see it. So I made the arrangements I needed to make and set out for the Costa Chica on Mexico's West Coast. The Costa Chica is known as the blackest part of Mexico. It's south of Acapulco but doesn't resemble a resort in the slightest. It is extremely remote—you couldn't even get there by highway until the mid-1950s. The land is swampy. And the people are desperately poor. Most of them are descended from slaves who toiled there. Other slaves came across the Pacific Ocean and through Acapulco, with the galleons that came from the Philippines. And some of them were runaway slaves or slaves who once labored in Acapulco. There was little racial mixing because the community remained isolated for so long. The Costa Chica started black, and—more than any other part of Mexico that I visited—it has stayed that way.

When we arrived, I asked my driver to take me to San Juan de la Cruz, the Church of St. John of the Cross. I was looking for a particular priest, Father Glyn Jemmott, a Trinidadian Roman Catholic who has lived and worked in the Costa Chica for twenty-five years. We moved slowly through the streets, passing crowds of thin, ragged, desperately impoverished people. Here, finally, were the Afro-Mexicans.

We located the church. And I found Father Glyn, elegant, tall, and thin, who was even more devoted and committed both to his parishioners and to their appreciation of their black heritage than I had hoped he would be. He grasped my hands and welcomed me to his ministry with a loving smile. He led me into the sanctuary and brought me to stand before a statue of a black Christ, the centerpiece of his rural church's altar. It was a sublime moment for me. The famous Peruvian painting of *El Señor de los Milagros* was its own marvel, but it was a painting of a white Jesus created by an Angolan slave. But a life-sized sculpture of a crucified black savior, here, in the middle of nowhere? I had never seen a black crucifix close up before.

San Juan de la Cruz in Oaxaca, Mexico. (Jemila Twinch)

As Father Glyn fussed over me, making sure I was comfortable, we talked about his life in the Costa Chica. He started out as a simple priest, he told me. But over the years, he'd become an activist. Today, he runs an annual conference of black towns in the region and works tirelessly to raise black awareness. He said that his goal is to help people to become comfortable in their skin, to see in themselves beauty in their black features, to regard them with pride or at least neutrality, rather than as traces of a past and an identity about which to be embarrassed.

"On the first occasion that I said mass," he told me, "a grown black man came, and he said, 'Who are you?' And I said, 'Well, I am a priest.' And for about ten minutes he went on, saying, 'You're not a priest— you can't be a priest. I've never seen a black priest. We black people only work the land, we load trucks with bricks.' He grew quite adamant, quite angry. He was insistent." Welcome to black Mexico.

"You can't be the head man," I said, imagining the stranger's thoughts.

"Exactly," Father Glyn answered. "He was really talking about himself."

I asked Father Glyn what it was like to be Afro-descendant in Mexico—and to be really black, someone who couldn't "pass" for brown or "cosmic." His face spread in a wise smile. "Everything is against an Afro-Mexican seeing himself as someone who can lift his head and take his place in Mexican society as an equal," he said. "The black Mexican who cannot claim Latino status is excluded by his lighter-skinned Mexican brother, and if he goes to the US, he's ostracized by his black US counterpart. I once had the opportunity to talk with some African Americans from Detroit, and they criticized the black people down here for never having heard of Martin Luther King, Jr."

"In Mexico, blacks have a problem with two parts," he continued. "One, you have the Afro-Mexican wiping himself off the map, not being able to hold on to anything that would strengthen his identity—that would even give him the chance to call himself black with pride. And two, you have the whole apparatus of the state. Politically, socially, culturally, it has made him invisible. The racism is disguised. On the national level, it's almost religious to state that Mexico is a country where there is no racism. Up front, people won't admit that there is racism. But behind closed doors, they have strong negative impressions of blacks."

Listening to Father Glyn, I was deeply moved. This was a man of God—I felt God in his presence—but also a great thinker. He understood the experience of blackness not as a curse or a blessing but as a fact. In his sympathetic eyes, I could see that he understood the struggle for pride in identity. He felt for every Mexican with black ancestors in his or her genome, with black blood in the veins, as the saying goes.

We began to talk about these issues, and the conversation, interestingly enough, soon turned to an unlikely subject: a comic-book character named Memín Pinguín, whose presence in Mexico dates back to the 1940s. He has come to be well known in North America. In 2005, the Mexican government issued a commemorative stamp featuring Memín Pinguín. Afro-Mexicans didn't seem to mind. In fact, everyone in Mexico seemed to love it, and the stamp quickly became a collector's item. African Americans, however, and especially Jesse Jackson, were furious. They looked at images of Memín Pinguín on the news and saw just another offensive black character with monkey-like features. They cried out that Memín Pinguín demeaned blackness. Rev. Jackson flew to Mexico to try and convince President Vicente Fox to recall the stamps and issue an apology. But Fox didn't budge. He said Mexicans loved Memín Pinguín, and the country never apologized for anything. He told Jackson that he was projecting a US context onto a Mexican text and, well, that he should just get over it. Memín Pinguín was here to stay. I don't think a US politician could have withstood such an onslaught; President Fox knew his constituency. Memín Pinguín is everywhere; just visit a newsstand.

I pulled some pictures of Memín Pinguín out of my bag, and Father Glyn and I looked them over together. I always have the same reaction. I think this character would be cute if he were a monkey, like Curious George. But this is supposed to be a black child! He's got big ears, exaggerated lips, and bowed legs. He even has fur on his face. The other characters in the comic book, who are all white, make fun of Memín Pinguín for the way he looks and speaks. He works as a shoe-shine boy and doesn't do well in school. Now, admittedly, I am an American, but to me, he is just another racist stereotype from the Western museum of racist caricatures, a refugee from a minstrel show. Perhaps it is a Mexican thing that this black man just can't understand? I am afraid that Rev. Jackson got this one right, at least from our point of view. So I asked Father Glyn what he thought, as a reality check.

"Mexicans, who are very intelligent people, their reaction was that you cannot judge him by the racist standards of the end of the century," he told me, shaking his head. "It was based on the 1940s. They're all stereotypes. Speedy Gonzalez? Memín Pinguín just represents a mischievous urban kid. His color doesn't matter. Mexican society accepts him. There's no way to say he represents North American racist history. People in the US can't use him to evaluate the racial interactions we have here."

I took a moment to think about distinctly American racism. Our circumstances gave birth to a civil rights movement—a movement that was desperately needed. And we were blessed with leaders who made an enormous difference. Those leaders, I remembered again with pride, ultimately made it possible for us to elect our first black president.

"Do you think, based on your experience, that black Mexicans will have a Barack Obama in this generation," I asked Father Glyn, "like they did at the beginning of the republic, back in 1829, at a time when such a thing was unthinkable in the States?"

"There's so much that has to be done," he said, sadly, "so much. Black Mexicans must have access to education, political participation, social acceptance. These things must be in place before you begin to produce leaders. But I would say I've seen some changes. Younger people are saying, with some assertion, 'Soy negro.'" I was encouraged to hear that. *Soy negro* means "I'm black."

"Why?" I asked.

"Because of the kind of visibility we've been able to generate and all the things that have spun off from that," he said with pride.

I wanted to learn more about these positive changes. I wanted to meet with someone from this new generation of proud, aware Afro-Mexicans who proclaim, "Soy negro!" So I said goodbye to the wise and caring Father Glyn. And I got in touch with journalist Eduardo Zapata.

Zapata was born and raised in the Costa Chica. Today, he celebrates his black identity and encourages other Afro-Mexicans to join him. In this spirit, he asked me to meet him at another church in Cuajui, where a festival was about to begin. I arrived to find throngs of laughing, happy black people gathered in a churchyard. They were loud and boisterous, and Zapata and I had to push our way through the crowds to reach each other. We met and introduced ourselves in the middle of the mayhem. I found myself shouting over the noise, trying to figure out what was going on.

"One of them was ordained a priest," Zapata beamed, waving at the crowd. "He makes many of the people here feel proud."

Music started, and the crowd began to push back, opening up a wide circle for dancing. Soon, a black male dancer came out wearing what looked like an enormous papier-mâché bull costume decorated with long, colorful streamers. The bull began spinning and bobbing about, and Zapata explained that the dance was called the "Toro de Petate." It's traditional in Latin America, but it takes on particular significance when danced by blacks. The bull's captivity serves as a metaphor for African slavery. When blacks dance it with joy, he said, they reclaim their own power, the power of a bull.

The crowd cheered and hollered, throwing their hands in the air and shouting out to the bull. It was an old-fashioned street party.

"Eduardo, this place looks like Harlem to me," I shouted. "This looks like the Africa of Mexico. It's great!"

"But we speak Spanish!" Eduardo joked in return. "And we believe in the resurrected Christ."

Memín Pinguín is a popular character in a comic book that was created by Alberto Cabrera in 1943 in Mexico and is still published today. A series of five stamps featuring him was released for general use on Wednesday, June 29, 2005. The release came just weeks after Mexican president Vicente Fox riled many people by saying that Mexican migrants take jobs in the United States that not even blacks want. (AP Photo/Dario Lopez-Mills)

He was right. The celebration was black, but the people were Afro-Mexican. I was still learning what this meant. "The Spanish culture, the European culture, we also have that in us," he explained, leading me away from the noise. "Because of that, it's difficult to say we're only blacks. What are we? A mix, a mix."

"Are you described as a black person, a *negro*, here in Mexico?" I wanted to know.

"Of course," he answered. "When you're little, no one questions it. When you leave here to study or go to Acapulco or go to the US, then you realize you're different—that you're Mexican, but you have something that's not the same as all Mexicans. You discover that you're black."

We were safely away from the crowd, and I was grateful to go back to speaking normally. I still didn't quite understand—Zapata said he was mixed but also black. I was starting to recognize that in Mexico, this duality was so common, it felt normal.

"Do black people suffer discrimination here in Mexico?" I asked next.

"We're a racist society," Zapata answered, nodding. "If you are in the cities, they stop you and ask you for your ID card. They make you sing the national anthem, and they accuse you of coming from Cuba to destabilize things. Nobody talks about it, but in every Mexican family, there is a little black person. And you know what the city folks say? 'He was born black, but we'll love him anyway.' "

"Tell me about Memín Pinguín," I said, curious to get Zapata's opinion. "Do you think the cartoon is racist or not?"

"No," Zapata said, shaking his head at me. "You go out into the street and ask people, and they're not worried. It's just a character. They don't identify with it. He's still just in stories. It's kind of like laughing at yourself, if you take it with humor, with sarcasm." Sort of like Eddie Murphy doing a postmodern version of Buckwheat, it suddenly occurred to me, or Paul Mooney on the *Dave Chappelle Show* doing Negrodamus, a black parody of Nostradamus. Or Jack White's Amos 'n' Andy/Buckwheat parodies on TheRoot.com.

"Why did Jesse Jackson come here to see Vicente Fox?" I pressed. It was so hard for me to believe that visit wasn't warranted. Just look at Memín Pinguín!

Zapata stopped short and turned to me. I recognized him then as the passionate activist he truly is. "Jesse Jackson should have worried about all the blacks that go to work in Mexico and aren't treated like people," he said with conviction. "They're treated like third-class citizens. He's not interested in the living black people on the coast. He's interested in Memín Pinguín. It's politics." I had to agree that it is much easier to engage in symbolic politics and to censor a stereotype than it is to affect the unemployment level. But, back home, Jesse Jackson and other black activists don't get called on this very much, in part because the history of racist representations of blackness is so long and deep and pernicious.

I was taken aback by the edge in Zapata's voice. Now we were getting somewhere. "Help me understand," I said, imploring. "I'm trying to figure this out. The difference between being black in America and being black in Mexico—it seems huge. And I don't want to be a typical gringo, or a typical gringo *negro*, or whatever it's called. I don't want to impose my values on you. I want you to teach me."

Zapata was silent for a moment. I watched him carefully forming his reply. "Spain conquered us," he said, quietly. "A religious culture conquered us. But the culture that conquered us was already familiar with blacks. Black slaves already existed in Europe, in Spain, in the courts—even before the conquest. So it's a different culture. The Africans that came here, who had talent and intelligence, had the capacity to get through the legal barriers that the Spanish put up. For example, if someone was a great artisan, the culture had to accept them and give them privileges. That explains much of the assimilation, the mixing. We're part of it all. We're not foreigners. We're Mexicans too. We also helped to build this country."

I thought about this. Black pride in Mexico was also national pride —at least in Zapata's view. He wasn't going to let talk of a cosmic race break his Afro-Mexican spirit.

(As a point of information, more Africans came to Mexico from Christian Africa—Angola, as we have seen in the chapter on Brazil— than from any other country, by percentage. The whole wave that populated Mexico from 1580 to 1640 was from Angola. So it is a misnomer to say that the Spanish imposed Catholicism on Afro-Mexicans; what they did impose was their version of Catholicism.)

Zapata wished me well as we parted. And he told me that if I wanted to know more about Costa Chica's black-pride movement, I should track down Israel Reyes, a teacher on the other side of Cuajui. I got right on it.

When Reyes heard about my project, he invited me over to his home to chat. The place was modest, but he proudly showed me a recording studio in a back room and told me, clasping his hands together with enthusiasm, that he has devoted his life to inspiring Afro-Mexicans to feel pride in their black roots. Every week, he records a radio program called *Cimarrón: The Voice of the Afro-Mestizos*, celebrating the African influence in Mexican culture. He wants his listeners to honor their African ancestry. And he wants Mexico to recognize the rights of its black population.

"The first step is being included in the census, to make it known that there are black people in Mexico," he said as we sat down together. "They aren't just in history books about the time of slavery. Blacks are here now, right now, today. And they are demanding that their rights be recognized."

I asked what he was doing to achieve this—and he shook his head in anger. "We started a process, we had talks with government authorities," he replied, urgently, "but at the last minute, they informed us that it was not possible to include a question on the census. But we're pushing forward with a pilot census for the black population in Mexico."

"Ah, that's good!" I exclaimed—this man's passion was energizing. "How do you think it will benefit the black community to be included?"

"Public policies for these populations," he answered readily. "Better

living conditions, education, health, housing, access to federal pro-
grams. But we have to start by finding out how many blacks there are in
Mexico." Black activists are making the same compelling arguments in
France, arguments largely falling on deaf ears.

I began to tell him that I couldn't agree more—and then, at the
front door, there was a sudden commotion. Reyes bounded up from
his chair and grinned. He led some children through the house to me
and explained they were there to record a rap song for his radio program. I couldn't believe my luck. And even though I could tell that my
presence made the kids just a little nervous, they were happy to have an
audience.

Reyes set up his recording equipment as I looked on, and the kids
rehearsed among themselves, snapping their fingers to create their own
beats. Soon enough, they were recording.

> If they despise me for being black, I don't deny my color
> Because among pearls and diamonds, black is better
> In the night, the shadow of my color protects me
> I don't care what these men, without taste, yell at me

Reyes asked me if I'd like to be part of the radio show, and I readily agreed. "We are being visited today by a very well-known professor,
Professor Gates," he spoke into his microphone. "Professor, what do
you hope the results of your work in Costa Chica will be?"

"I hope it makes Americans more aware of Mexico's complex racial
past," I answered. If I had come to understand anything, I realized, it
was that blackness in Mexico is complicated. One could make analogies
with the black experience in the States, but it would be foolish to try to
impose our interpretive frame onto theirs. All race, all racism, just like
politics, is local.

I left Reyes with his budding radio stars. And from his front porch,
I looked out at Costa Chica—black Mexico. Everywhere I saw brown
and black faces. It felt one-hundred-percent right to me that the nation's
black-pride movement should start here. But it must *start*.

Walking back to my car, it struck me that, in a sense, Mexico is a
victim of its own pioneering successes in race relations. It was quite a
noble act to abolish slavery in 1829, five years before Britain abolished
that pernicious institution throughout its empire, thirty-six years before

the United States. But despite these noble beginnings, over time race relations fell prey to a romantic idea—that by getting rid of racial categories officially, this could eradicate racism throughout Mexican society, by ridding society of privileges that stemmed from social and economic differences that were tied to apparent distinctions in race. That didn't happen. As in every Latin American society I visited, one group of people did not melt, to use the metaphor with which we in the United States are so very familiar; one portion of the Afro-descended group didn't blend, and they are, today, the still visibly black Mexican people with dark black skin, kinky hair, and thick lips who live on the Costa Chica and in Veracruz and are scattered throughout Mexico. And they are disproportionately poor.

When José Vasconcelos in 1925 declared Mexicans to be a new, cosmic race, the race of the future, you might say that Mexico—following a period of programmatic attempts to whiten itself—began to embrace and celebrate its brownness, answering Vasconcelos's call with enthusiasm. But brown pride only served to marginalize black culture qua black culture and to marginalize black people economically and socially who had not mixed with whites or with indigenous peoples even further. The Afro-Mexicans of today—as I was informed again and again by the descendants of slaves and free blacks—have paid a very high price for these experiments in race and what we might think of as "categorical racelessness," the living social death resulting from the invisibility of their black cultural and genetic heritage. If your ethnic group can't be counted, then your social presence and your rights as a citizen and as a wage earner, affected in some way by your phenotype, don't count either. And it is for this reason that restoring racial categories to the federal census is such an urgent matter to so many black activists in Mexico.

"Death and invisibility," I murmured to myself, recalling Cruz-Carretero's words, spoken as we looked at the walls of the port of Veracruz. They were chilling words. Was she right? It isn't the mark of a great nation to hide or deny its history, I thought, climbing into my car. But Mexico's blackness isn't gone. It lingers in places like Veracruz and the Costa Chica, where descendants of African slaves never became part of the nation's melting pot. And it lies hidden just beneath the surface of Mexico's national identity, an identity defined, perhaps, by sixteen lovely shades of brownness.

Vicente Guerrero (1783–1831), second president of the Mexican Republic, from April 1 to December 17, 1829. Portrait by Anacleto Escutia (1850). (Museo Nacional de Historia, Castillo de Chapultepec, Mexico/ Michel Zabe/AZA/INBA/Bridgeman Art Library)

Like Father Glyn, I saw sparks of hope in Mexico. But it's going to take a lot of dedicated political missionary work to create a movement of Afro-Mexicans to reclaim their history—and to be able to declare with unbridled pride, "*Soy negro*," in a society in which being *negro* seems only to be acceptable in the diminutive form of a well-known shoe-shine boy named Memín, or Lucky number 26 in La Lotería.

As I took my leave, I wished Father Glyn and Zapata and Reyes the strength to carry on, against enormous odds.

3

Peru

"The Blood of the Incas, the Blood of the Mandingas"

> In Peru, those who do not have the blood of the Incas have the
> blood of the Mandingas.
>
> —traditional

I HAVE TO confess that I was probably more excited to visit Peru than
I was to visit any other country in the series. I felt as if I were investi-
gating a great mystery. Peru's population includes somewhere between
six hundred thousand and three million Afro-Peruvians, depending on
who's doing the counting and how, even if not all of them self-identify
today as Afro-Peruvians or "blacks." Nobody knows for sure because,
like Mexico, the census does not include a place to identify race or ethnicity (a matter of bitter debate, as I learned, among black Peruvian activists). But estimates range from 2 percent to 5 percent to 10 percent of
Peru's total population of thirty million people—and Peru's very large
mestizo population (37 percent, according to "The CIA Factbook for
Peru") certainly includes many people who would be defined as "black"
in the United States. Whatever the final figure, it is far higher than most
Americans would ever guess because, after all, when you think of Peru,
what comes to mind? The majestic Andes mountain range? The myste-
rious ancient city of Machu Picchu, the great civilizations of the Incas?
Five thousand varieties of potato? How many of us know that one of
Peru's most famous saints is a black man, St. Martin de Porres, born in
Lima in 1579?

For most of my life, I certainly did not associate Peru with a strong,
historic African legacy. But that all changed a few years ago when I let
myself get way too far behind in my Christmas shopping. I was desperately scanning a rack of "World Music" CDs for gift ideas at HMV in

Harvard Square when a title caught my eye: *The Soul of Black Peru*. It was a collection of Afro-Peruvian classics recorded by various artists, including vocalist Susana Baca. I'd never heard of Baca, but what surprised me more was that I'd never heard of "Black Peru." I bought it for myself. When I took the CD home and played it, I was deeply intrigued. I recognized African influences in the music—and an unmistakable quality in the singer's earthy, lyrical performance. The record label was right: Peru, I found out, did have soul.

I started to do a little research. And I learned, as we have seen in Mexico, that more slaves had journeyed to Peru and Mexico combined than had traveled to the United States in the entire history of the slave trade. It turns out that the vast majority of Mexico's slaves arrived during the period of the Portuguese Asiento, between 1595 and 1640. They were heavily from Angola, as many as 80 percent. New scholarship by the historian David Wheat has shown that the Cartagena leg of the slave trade (leading to Colombia and Peru) had more African nations involved. While the largest single group still originated in Angola, their total number was about half; Senegambia and Sierra Leone come second, followed in a distant third by the Slave Coast, which is the modern Republic of Benin. John Thornton explained to me that "in the post-1640 period, when the formal Asiento stopped, Peru got slaves from Buenos Aires, shipped up the Rio de la Plata water system and overland to upland Peru and beyond. We think the Peruvian slave trade, like the Mexican, was concentrated in the early to mid-seventeenth century."

The more I learned, the more it puzzled me. My impression of Peru —with all its colorful images of people in traditional indigenous costumes—had never included black faces. I wondered why they weren't more visible. Had blackness in Peru disappeared, or was it buried somewhere deep in the culture, hidden or veiled? How had the black presence shaped Peru's history and culture, and how did Afro-Peruvians feel about their ancestry? I went to Lima to track down the answers to these questions.

I couldn't think of a better place to start than by talking to Susana Baca—the Afro-Peruvian whose music started me on this search. I met Baca in her recording studio in her lovely home. Warm and thoughtful, she was eager to help me in my quest to learn about black Peruvian history. I asked her if she had suffered from racism as a child. She told me she'd grown up in a seaside town, thoroughly integrated. As a child, she had no perception of her blackness or that blackness somehow made her different. It was only when she went to high school, outside her community, that she was forced to notice a difference between herself and other girls—and that is when she recalls experiencing racism for the first time.

"Something happened that was very ugly and very sad for me," she told me, ever more tearful as she related the story. "They told us in school that a teacher was going to come choose the girls who danced very well, and I thought, 'Well, I'm going to be chosen because I dance.' But she only chose the white girls. The Indian girls and the black girls did not belong to the dance group."

Virtually every African American autobiographer discovers that he or she is "black" in some painful way, and apparently the Afro-Peruvian experience conformed to this pattern. It was easy to picture Baca as a trusting child stumbling innocently into this experience, and I felt for her. I asked what had given her the strength to overcome such painful moments. She didn't hesitate in answering: "Our family gathered on Sundays," she said. "I would go to where they were playing music, to the uncles playing guitar, to the aunties singing. And there I was, in the middle. That was my salvation."

Baca told me she empowered herself through music, and she used that power to search for her ancestry, her family's cultural legacy. She said, in essence, that her love of music and her pride in her Afro-Peruvian heritage blossomed side by side. "I'm not a researcher; my specialty is not investigation," she explained. "But I started to search. I began with my mother. I asked her to tell me things about her life. After that, I interviewed my aunties, and after that I traveled through Peru, especially along the coastline where the Afro-Peruvians had settled. I almost reached the border with Ecuador, searching for music, poetry, verses. . . . I discovered what the Afro-Peruvians had contributed to Peruvian culture, and it filled me with pride and happiness."

"And then, happily, when I won the Grammy in 2002, a woman said to me, 'Because of you, the world knows about us,'" Baca said to me, beaming, referring to the presence of black Peruvians. "It was so beautiful for me to hear."

It was impossible not to smile with Baca. The young, shy, but de-monstrably talented teenager, unfairly overlooked in a dance competi-tion, had grown into a noble woman who knew her own value—and, in the process, had become a national treasure. "Today, I do not feel hate against those that discriminated against me," she confided. "But I feel, rather, that I am part of an important culture. I would love to see young Afro-Peruvians feel the pride and happiness of discovering themselves as part of a nation—a people—that they can feel, celebrate, and enjoy."

I was struck that this pattern of discovering one's blackness through deprivation or lack, a pattern that I had mistakenly presumed to be peculiarly American, constituted a defining moment in the life of a black Peruvian as well. The difference between Baca's experience, though, and that of most African Americans is how late in her life it occurred; most black writers—from Frederick Douglass, Zora Neale Hurston, and Richard Wright to Toni Morrison—had this painful experience early in childhood. So I wanted to understand how she could possibly have grown up as a minority person in her seaside town, unaware of her racial difference. She'd said she wasn't aware that she was black until she went to high school. How could Baca's story be true? I asked Carlos Aguirre, a professor of Latin American history at the University of Oregon. He told me that the answers lay in Peru's unique history. He agreed to meet me in Lima and to guide me through it.

We shook hands on a bright street corner in Malambo, now called the District of Rímac. It was a bustling, vibrant black neighborhood —the Harlem of Lima, I thought. A former resident of this great city, Aguirre strode confidently through the streets. I lagged behind, too curious not to look at everything around me.

Aguirre told me that the very first slaves to arrive in Peru came with the Spanish conquistador Francisco Pizarro in 1527. Pizarro's army included enslaved Africans to conquer the indigenous population, the "Indians" as they were then called. These indigenous peoples were baffled to meet Africans. As legend has it, when they first saw black people, they tried to rub their skin to "clean" the color off.

The African population of Peru grew rapidly as the indigenous population declined in numbers (though they remain quite numerous today, identified often by the term *Incan*, which is not historically correct, as the Inca were only one indigenous group among many). Many indigenous people died quickly under Spanish rule in the sixteenth century —killed in battle or by illness (the population had no immunity to the diseases, viruses, and bacteria that Europeans brought with them). The war and subsequent civil wars that made up the conquest of Peru took forty years (1532–1571), but we do not have reliable figures of the number of indigenous people who died in battle. Regardless, as the native population diminished, so did the local labor supply. So the Spanish imported over one hundred thousand Africans to help them mine Peru's gold, silver, and emeralds. In the sixteenth and seventeenth centuries, Peru became one of the richest colonies in the New World and one of the major recipients of victims of the trans-Atlantic slave trade.

"Malambo was the place where the slaves were first brought from the Port of Callao to be sold in a kind of marketplace," Aguirre told me, gesturing across an open square. "From here, slaves were taken to haciendas and plantations around the city, and even beyond." Over the course of the colonial period, he told me, about 25 percent of all slaves stayed in Lima, working as skilled craftsmen and artisans, as well as domestic servants, bakers, street vendors, and water carriers. The population in Malambo became 90 percent black, and Lima itself became between 30 and 40 percent black. Europeans considered Lima a black city, because Africans were everywhere. Almost every aspect of city life bore their stamp.

One slave's stamp is still recognized prominently in Peru today—though no one ever recorded his name. (Juan Martin de Porres, later canonized, was born illegitimately to a female former slave and a Spanish nobleman.) Aguirre led me to a lovely Catholic sanctuary seemingly built around a mural that had originally been painted on a wall—an extraordinary portrait of Christ on the cross. The painting was completed in the seventeenth century, when the wall was part of a slave quarters. One of the slaves living there, a man from Angola, painted it. I stood before the painting, frankly, in awe. It is rich, layered, sophisticated. I found I was holding my breath.

"There was a powerful earthquake, later," Aguirre whispered to me quietly, "and the whole area, including the slave quarters, was destroyed —except the wall. In fact, it survived not one but several earthquakes. And so a cult developed, initially among slaves, called *El Señor de los Milagros*, 'The Lord of the Miracles.'"

"I think the miracle is that the brother, an untrained slave, painted it in the first place," I whispered back.

"The cult spread throughout the rest of Peruvian society," he went on. "In the eighteenth century, the pope authorized, for the first time, a procession in the city. In the early twentieth century, the Peruvian state jumped in and started supporting these processions, and this became an almost official religious image. Today, in the month of October, people carry a copy of the painting through the streets, followed by hundreds of thousands of people. Congress even wants to name *El Señor de los Milagros* the Patron of Peru."

To this day, the annual procession for *El Señor de los Milagros* is one of the largest religious processions in all of Latin America, and I was deeply moved to learn that all of this had been set in motion by the vision of an Angolan slave. As we headed toward the doorway, I turned back for one last look. To think of an empty field full of rubble, with nothing but this wall standing . . . a crucifix, painted by an African slave, then embraced by a nation—I found myself wondering if Americans would ever have embraced a religious symbol created by an African American slave, or deified a black saint, as the Peruvians did with San Martín de Porres, who lived in the late sixteenth and early seventeenth centuries and whose cult has spread throughout Latin America.

Back in the sun, Aguirre began to tell me more about the history of Peru's black slaves, explaining that the living conditions in the city and the countryside differed markedly, and that the Afro-Peruvian population was shaped in dialogue with this difference, much as African American culture emerged from the blending of distinct rural and urban, southern and northern populations. Aguirre explained that in the city, a slave could become a *jornalero*, a type of free agent. *Jornaleros* moved about at will, looking for work and giving their masters some of what they earned. Over time, he explained, they could often save enough money to buy their own freedom.

"By entering into this arrangement, the master washed his hands of maintenance—feeding, shelter, housing, even discipline," Aguirre noted. "*Jornaleros* had to find employers on their own and work without supervision. But they had a degree of autonomy that others didn't have."

I found the idea of a class of semi-autonomous entrepreneurial slaves, and that upward mobility had been a possibility for some Africans in Peru, quite a contrast to the history of slavery in the United States. African American history records individual slaves with this degree of autonomy, but not a class on this order. Aguirre nodded when I mentioned the distinction but noted that the slave's experience on plantations was quite different.

"In general, slaves in the cities had a much better life in terms of

The Lord of the Miracles (*El Señor de los Milagros de Nazarenas*) is a mural of Jesus Christ that is venerated in Lima, where it hangs in the sanctuary at Las Nazarenas. It was painted by a black slave from Angola in the seventeenth century. The painting is also known as "Black Christ" or "Christ of Pachacamilla." (Miguel Chong/Wikipedia Commons)

treatment, chances to interact with other groups, and especially in terms of the possibility of acquiring freedom," he explained. "Slaves in plantation areas worked long hours, sometimes lived in miserable conditions, and were subjected to very harsh punishment. Urban slavery was generally more fluid—there was the possibility of freedom. Plantation slavery was more permanent—a static condition."

To learn more about the life of Afro-Peruvians during slavery, I visited the Palacio Municipal, where I met Peruvian historian Maribel Arrelucea Barrantes from the San Ignacio de Loyola University.

Arrelucea greeted me very warmly. She was excited to show me some works of art by a famous Afro-Peruvian artist—Francisco "Pancho" Fierro Palas, a mulatto who painted in the first half of the nineteenth century—and to see and hold the originals for the first time herself. I knew Fierro's work focused on urban life, so I was excited to see how he represented the experiences of both free and enslaved black people living in Peru in the nineteenth century. Besides, I love archives and archival research, being able to touch and smell original historical documents and works of art. And I found Arrelucea's energy infectious.

Fierro created vivid, almost documentary portraits of Afro-Peruvian life during his era. And he was prolific. Born in 1810, he died in 1879 having painted more than twelve hundred watercolors depicting almost every activity imaginable. Arrelucea told me that his paintings are considered so central to understanding daily life in this period that every schoolchild in Peru has seen them. A free man with a mixed racial heritage, Fierro seems to have been especially keen to represent the experience of slaves as fundamental to the shaping of Lima society. But he also possessed the artist's gift to observe and record life from a distance, often with irony, mischief, and sensuality. And best of all, for my purposes, he included many black subjects in his paintings, and many of his paintings depict small scenes, with three or four figures, almost cutaways of slavery.

Wearing white gloves to handle the originals, we carefully examined a group of the watercolors, laid out on a table for our view. I was immediately struck by his vivid colors, the generous round curves of the bodies, and the lighthearted spirit of Fierro's approach to his subjects. Most strikingly, Fierro's black subjects look integral to the construction of the scenes they are in; none is extraneous in any way to the action depicted. Many of them look quite contented, even those pictured at work.

Arrelucea handed me a pair of protective gloves, with her eyes shining. We had permission to handle the paintings, a rare privilege.

"It's exciting, yeah?" I said, holding up one of the pieces—gently.

"It's very emotional," Arrelucea replied. "This is the first time, as a historian, I have had the opportunity to see, and hold in my hands, an original painting by Pancho Fierro. He has left us the most important images. He shows us a society that we could not see from documents."

I picked up a painting of a funeral. I noted that all the pallbearers are black men.

"It is still a custom in Peru," Arrelucea replied. "It is highly criticized nowadays, but it continues to be 'the right thing to do.'" Tall, lean black men as the agents of Death—I sort of like that idea.

"Oh, my, this is like a picnic," I said, picking up a work featuring two women, in a leisurely setting, surrounded by food.

"It is very beautiful, isn't it?" Arrelucea sighed. "This is a typical pudding, and it is in the hands of Afro women, the slaves."

Next we looked at a portrait of three quite buxom women, quite

Pancho Fierro paintings: *above left, La Placera–Tres Razas; above right, Tapada y Sirvienta Negra; left, Vendedora con Zapallos.* (Maribel Arrelucea Barrantes)

suggestively exposed, surrounded by melons. I think I blushed. (If I didn't, I should have.) "I think Pancho Fierro was trying to leave us a joke," Arrelucea said, laughing. "Three races: Indian, black, white. So this scene is fantastic. It shows us three women, but the one who takes center stage is the Afro woman."

"He was something of an anthropologist," I ventured, but with a wicked sense of humor. The pun on melons was unmistakable.

"Yes," Arrelucea agreed. "He was in the street all the time. He painted as he looked at what was going on around him."

We lingered over the portraits, enjoying their exuberant air and our exuberance at being able to examine the originals so closely.

"When we think about slaves, we always think about plantation slaves, chained at the feet, constantly beaten up," she observed. "But Pancho Fierro gives us a lot to regain the past. Slavery in Lima was more relaxed, more flexible. I think Pancho Fierro wanted to show us the happiness that the Afro population could have."

Arrelucea walked me through a series of the paintings, each picturing small pleasures of everyday life and, everywhere in his work, sensuality. One especially suggested the abandonment of Pinkster, or Mardi Gras in the States, a time during the year when the slaves could step outside of their positions and assume new social roles, if only for a brief time. "This one depicts 'Amancaes,'" she said. "It was a festivity outside of Lima, in a field. People could openly have fun, without any rules. There was only pleasure—the pleasure of eating, the pleasure of drinking, the pleasure of the body, of sex, of dance, everything. There were no rules! It lasted almost a week."

As we carefully put the paintings away, I asked Arrelucea how she felt about Fierro's vision of slave-era Peru. It seemed so positive, so happily multicultural. Was it historically accurate?

"Yes," she told me confidently. "Pancho Fierro shows us people interacting, living together, having fun, whether they are men or women, rich or poor, black or white. He shows us a society which is more integrated, with fewer conflicts. This is a point of view. Peru has many different aspects. But in the end, we all try to connect."

For myself, I found that despite the paintings' great beauty and craftsmanship, Fierro's works were also somewhat disturbing, raising as many questions as they resolved. His vision of Peru reminded me of Gilberto Freyre's theory (or myth, depending on who you talk to) of

Pancho Fierro painting, *Baile Zamacueca*. (Maribel Arrelucea Barrantes)

racial democracy. I couldn't deny the exuberance of Fierro's work. But who could deny the simple hardship of being a slave? Was Fierro's name held up in glory—unlike the unknown slave from Angola—because he made slaves look so happy with their lot? Was Peru celebrating its black past, or trying to erase it?

I reconnected with Professor Aguirre. He listened while I explained what Arrelucea had told me, and he agreed that slavery was more "relaxed" in Peru than in the United States. But as I suspected, he said there was far more to the story than the scenes that Fierro chose to preserve.

Aguirre and I traveled together to Peru's historic Hacienda San José, two hours south of Lima. It was one of many plantations in the area that thrived from the sixteenth to the twentieth centuries, harvesting first sugar and then cotton. As I stepped out of the car, I could see immediately we were in a very different place. The hacienda—a sprawling compound with many buildings, including a chapel—felt a world away from the busy streets of Lima. The property had been badly damaged by Peru's recent earthquake in 2007, Aguirre explained. But it still offered a haunting view into the cruel treatment experienced by plantation slaves.

Aguirre told me that the master of this hacienda probably kept eight hundred slaves, making him quite rich. (I've seen less ornate chapels in small cities.) And the slaves who lived there, unlike those in the city, had little hope of ever leaving.

El Negro Mama cartoon of the Mexican Canal 2 TV character (supplied to the author by Monica Carrillo). Translation: "I found nice clothes, and I learned to speak better to be able to return to the television, my friend." "And what did your critics tell you?" "Even though he's dressed in silk, a monkey is still a monkey."

"For those working in the fields, they suffered," Aguirre told me. "It was hard to preserve a family, leave the hacienda, feed their own children. Their best shot at being free was to run away."

Hacienda communities could be quite complex. Some workers were slaves owned by the master, others were on rent from nearby haciendas, and some were even freed blacks for hire. Even among the master's wholly owned population, different slaves had different roles to play.

"Some of the slaves would live inside the house as domestic servants, but most of them would live in their own barracks," he explained. "House slaves tended to be female and also lighter—like mulattoes—as opposed to field workers, who were generally African and blacker."

Just like in the United States, I thought. There were house slaves and field slaves, and those who looked a little whiter, well, got treated a little whiter.

"Around any hacienda like this, you would have communities of runaway slaves called *palenques*," he went on. "They preferred to live in small groups of ten to twenty or so, generally speaking. The fewer people there were in one place, the greater the chances that they could survive."

Punishments for trying to escape were severe. Sometimes slaves tried to run to other haciendas where they thought they might receive better treatment. But it was easy enough for someone to spot them. And while some masters allowed for a little movement here and there, Aguirre explained, others brought down the whip—literally.

"Every hacienda had a place to punish slaves," he told me. "They were branded, and they were whipped. They were sometimes left there without any food. Punishment was a mechanism to enforce order and social control. Just imagine a riot or a rebellion of these slaves."

Imagine indeed, I thought.

I knew a little bit about the 1821 Peruvian War of Independence, so I wondered aloud whether plantation slaves had been part of it. After all, they didn't have the option to become *jornaleros*, as city slaves did. Did they see the revolution as their chance to gain freedom? Aguirre said they did. He told me that Peru's war for independence had two great

Left: "Female Domestic of Lima of the Class of Quarterons"; from Joseph Skinner, *The Present State of Peru . . . Drawn from Original and Authentic Documents* (London, 1805), plate 13, following p. 252 (courtesy of the John Carter Brown Library at Brown Library). *Right*: "Peru, Spanish colonization, Mestize are tortured—to carrying charges," engraving to *Nueva coronica y buen gobierno*, by Felipe Guaman Poma de Ayala, circa 1613 (Mary Evans Picture Library).

heroes: Simón Bolívar, a Venezuelan aristocrat, and José de San Martín, a general from Argentina. Bolívar was practically a professional revolutionary—he liberated six Latin American countries from the Spanish, and these revolutions set in motion other independence movements across the continent. Some people call him the George Washington of South America. The joke about Bolívar is that he has more statues than anyone else in the Western Hemisphere, which seemed to be true from my travels for the series.

Between 1821 and 1824, Bolívar and San Martín, who by the way don't seem to have been fans of each other, worked together to free Peru. San Martín's armies attacked Spanish forces from the south, while Bolívar's forces attacked from the north. Both were eager to add fresh soldiers to their ranks. And the haciendas were full of slaves just looking for the chance to fight for their freedom.

"When the troops led by San Martín arrived on Peruvian soil, they sent emissaries to neighboring haciendas to let the slaves know they would be freed if they joined the rebel army," Aguirre explained. "Hundreds of them left their haciendas, joined the forces of liberation, and fought in the War of Independence."

"Were San Martín and Bolívar personally antislavery?" I wanted to know.

"Not necessarily," Aguirre said, cocking his head. "It's a very complicated issue. I would say this: San Martín set up a process for gradual abolition, while Bolívar was much more ambiguous. In theory, he was against slavery, but he didn't enact legislation against it."

It turned out the leaders of this war for independence weren't so very concerned about the independence of slaves. First, slaves were told that everyone born after 1821 would be free. Then they were told that freedom would be granted to every slave when he or she reached the age of eighteen. Then it was changed to twenty-one. Finally, the slaves were told they would be free at age fifty! San Martín, Bolívar, and those who succeeded them as rulers of these nations just didn't keep their promises to the Afro-descendants in the countries they liberated.

"These leaders were liberal; they wanted independence from Spain," Aguirre explained, "but they were not ready for social revolution. They wanted to preserve social order and property and to protect landowners. If you take a pessimistic view, the war really just represented a change of masters—the country changed elites." In that sense, as far as the slaves were concerned, perhaps, this was a rebellion, not a revolution. In fact, Bolívar was famous for his racial thinking, which was retrograde by anyone's standards. He worried frequently about "*pardocracia*," or the idea that people of color would take over, and he was not at all sure about liberating slaves. He staged a show trial and executed one of his most able generals because he feared that he was plotting for *pardocracia*. San Martín and the Argentineans were much better on this issue, by a very long margin.

"Slaves had to fight against their masters and take them to court to gain the freedom they had been promised," Aguirre went on ruefully. "Some freed slaves were later reenslaved because they couldn't prove they were free. There were all kinds of complications."

That sounds familiar, I thought. Many freed slaves in the United States faced the same fate.

Slavery was finally abolished in Peru thirty-three years later, in 1854, under President Ramón Castilla. This was twenty-five years after Mexico's second president, Vicente Guerrero, a mulatto, liberated the slaves there and twenty-one years after slavery was abolished throughout the British Empire. But Aguirre told me that many former slaves in Peru continued to work on haciendas, just as former slaves in the United States continued to do, as sharecroppers on the land that they had worked formerly, before they were freed.

Just like their African American counterparts, many of these slaves simply had nowhere else to go, Aguirre explained . . . and some of their ancestors still don't. Today, over 150 years after abolition, there are still Afro-Peruvians working the same fields as their slave ancestors.

I wanted to meet some of these people, still bound to the land. So I left Professor Aguirre at the Hacienda San José to rest and recover from my endless questions. My driver took me through the vast surrounding cotton fields, looking for laborers. And I realized, with a start, that I had never been in a cotton field before, not even in the US South. Sitting silently in the back of the car, looking at acres and acres of cotton bolls, I was surprised to begin to feel the weight of my own collective ancestral past.

We pulled over near a group of laborers, and I stepped out onto a dry dirt road. I saw two women industriously picking cotton nearby. Their hands were quick, darting about. They seemed to be talking casually, but they never stopped working for a second.

I made my way toward them and introduced myself. I learned their names: Ana Peña Palma and Juana Portilla Palma. They seemed pleased, even excited, to explain how they did the arduous work they performed to provide for their families. I learned that both women lived in the nearby town of El Carmen. The town is largely inhabited, all these years later, by descendants of black slaves who worked at the Hacienda San José.

"I've never been this close to cotton before," I admitted. "Can you show me how to pick it?"

Ana and Juana patiently showed me how to pull each fluffy piece out of its prickly sharp cradle, called the boll. The trick is to pull the cotton away without bringing along any of the plant's dried brown leaves and stalks—and not to slice up your hands.

It wasn't as easy as it looked, as my bleeding fingers attested.

"Without straw, without the little leaves," Ana counseled, watching over my shoulder, as I pulled away a tangled mess of cotton and dried boll bits.

I tried again, with some determination. And then—ouch!

"I'm terrible at this," I said to them, admitting the obvious and wondering if I needed first aid for the cuts on my hands.

"It has to come off clean," Ana said sympathetically.

I asked my new teachers how long they picked cotton each day. They told me they worked from 4:00 a.m. to 6:00 p.m., Monday to Saturday: fourteen hours a day, six days a week. I asked if they get a lunch break. They do. It's fifteen minutes.

"Could I ask you how much you're paid?" I asked.

"Fourteen soles a day," Ana told me. That's about five dollars.

I asked Ana and Juana how old they were when they started picking cotton.

"I was seven," Ana answered first. "Yes, I was seven too, when I started to go out," said Juana.

They told me all of this cheerfully. I'm always impressed by hardworking people, but these two were blowing me away with their wide smiles and sunny outlook. I realized my associations with cotton picking—US slavery, the Ku Klux Klan, the painful years of Reconstruction after the Civil War—were not shared by these women. I asked how they stayed so positive while they worked so hard.

Women picking cotton near El Carmen, Peru. (Jemila Twinch)

"We always work with joy," Ana told me. "We have to work, and we're used to it, and we always go out and talk. It's our routine, the daily routine of work in the country."

I paused then to look around at the country she was talking about. It was hard to forget the women's grueling schedule. But the field was beautiful, the sky a brilliant blue bowl overhead. Breezes sent the cotton plants undulating in stiff little waves. I noticed other workers in the distance, bent over, their quick hands moving impossibly fast—and then I noticed that very few of them were children.

I asked Ana and Juana if they thought their own children would pick cotton one day.

"No, it's hard work," Juana told me. "We try not to have our children accompany us," Ana said firmly, "because they need to study. We're already gathering cotton because we're older, but them—no. The ones that are just growing up now, we don't want that for them."

I took a moment to marvel at these proud, happy women doing right by the next generation. And just then, incredibly, I began to hear a song in the distance. Far across the field, some workers struck up a call and response. It sent a shiver of recognition through me under the bright sun. Plantation slaves in the United States used to sing the same way.

I changed the subject, trying to forget how hard these women worked for such small wages.

"Most Americans don't even know there are black people in Peru," I informed them.

"Ah! No?" Ana exclaimed. "Yes, there are!"

"There are lots here, yes!" Juana piped in, laughing.

"You're our uncle!" Ana cried out warmly. "Nice to meet you, uncle!"

As I said my goodbyes, Ana and Juana handed me a ball of cotton to take with me as a souvenir and to remember them by.

I then decided to visit nearby El Carmen. I knew there was a famous Afro-Peruvian musical group based there, the Ballumbrosios. They're a family band—sort of like the Jackson Five, except with fifteen members! The late Amador Ballumbrosio brought the family's music to fame in the late 1960s, sparking a revival of Afro-Peruvian music. Today, the family and their hometown of El Carmen are known the world over for keeping Afro-Peruvian pride—and culture—alive.

As we drove over, I realized that Peruvian blackness seems to live most vibrantly in the arts—in the works of the anonymous slave from Angola, Pancho Fierro, Susana Baca, the poet and writer Nicomedes Santa Cruz, and the Ballumbrosios. Peru's blackness might be invisible in its politics and global persona. But as in Brazil, blackness in Peru couldn't be hidden or quieted. Here, blacks found their full-throated voice in arts and music, and they were calling out to be witnessed by the world.

I heard that voice—loud, proud, and joyous—as I walked toward the home of the Ballumbrosio family. Inside, people were calling to one another and laughing. And I could hear music: racing drumbeats and sharp bells. The energy behind this music was incredible.

Chebo Ballumbrosio, third in line to become the next patriarch, met me with a bright smile and a warm embrace, clasping my outstretched hand in both of his own. We settled in a couple of stuffed chairs in the family living room, and I asked him why he was so committed to keeping Afro-Peruvian music alive.

"We have an ancestral heritage of African music that goes back 350

years," he said with pride, "and we are a family with roots. We still preserve the black presence. The day that we play another type of music,
that we're featured on giant posters and we look really good, that will be
the day that we're making black culture disappear in this place."

Making black culture disappear. His choice of words struck me. But
it occurred to me later that the music that will replace his will probably
be hip-hop. I asked if making music was a way to fight for black political
power.

"Racism is everywhere," Chebo told me flatly. "The blacks are la-
beled as those who work in the doorways of hotels or in restaurants.
People think, 'This black guy dances really well; that's all he's good for
—he's not very intelligent.' I think the music gives you the strength
to fight."

Pride through art, awareness through celebration, power through
performance—I liked that. But I wondered if young Peruvian children
would understand and embrace what the Ballumbrosios were trying
to do. I told Chebo that back in the United States, most of the young
people I know don't want to listen to jazz or blues, let alone traditional
African music. All they want to know about is hip-hop. I asked if black
children in Peru know enough about traditional Afro-Peruvian music
to claim it as their own.

"In a way, yes," he replied. "It's about maintaining what's ours, our
traditions. In our universe, our African universe, there have been different groups in different parts of the world. I've listened to a lot of Brazilian music, Cuban music; there are lots of manifestations. We have to
listen to everything, but without forgetting the past."

"Many people don't even know there is an Afro-Peruvian community in Peru," I told him. "Do you think, through your music, you will
change that?"

"It's always a struggle to make the Afro-Peruvian presence known,"
Chebo answered. "But I have faith in that, yes. Things can only change
when people stop seeing this country as only Andean, which is how
they always see it. Peru equals Incas, or Peru equals Machu Picchu. No!
Peru is a lot of things together; it's a mix of races, neighborhoods, ethnicities, revolutions that all manifest together."

More talk of mixing, I thought. But the mix in Peru was nothing like
that in Brazil. The similarity ended with the burying of black roots. It
was difficult to see what had happened beyond that. There was certainly

very little mixing that I observed. Black destiny in Peru seemed more like an effort to resist invisibility than anything else.

I spent the next hour meeting many generations of this musical family, handling and even trying to play a few Afro-Peruvian instruments. As I left, Chebo graciously invited me to his daughter's upcoming *quinceañera* party—a traditional coming-of-age celebration for fifteen-year-old girls. I accepted, looking forward to seeing more of this beautiful family. But I wasn't ready to party just yet. Instead, I caught up with Professor Aguirre again, at the Hacienda San José, and we traveled together back to Lima. On the way, I told him about my visit to the cotton fields and my conversation with Chebo Ballumbrosio. I told him I had learned a lot about Afro-Peruvian history, but I wanted to know more. The black presence in Peru, even during my short visit, felt so rich. But from the outside world, you'd never know it was there. And Peru didn't seem to know its own history of blackness.

"I think the contributions made by Afro-Peruvians have been central to the shaping of the society," said Aguirre, thoughtfully. "But this hasn't always been recognized. We still live with a legacy of invisibility, with the usual exceptions: artists, singers, soccer players, boxers. The economic, social, political, cultural life of blacks in our society has not been recognized."

Why did he think that was the case?

"When colonialism ended, Peru became a society ruled by the heirs of the conquerors, who inherited ideas about the inferiority of blacks," he said. "And so the nineteenth century, which was supposed to create the conditions for everybody to participate in political life, ended up instead being a century in which discrimination, racism, and other forms of exclusion were only strengthened."

That puzzled me. Lima had once been considered a black city. I asked Aguirre how that could have changed.

"After independence, the country received an influx of new immigrants," he explained. "Chinese, Italians, Germans, Spaniards. Today, what we have are pockets of black population. In these places, the percentages of blacks are very high, but in the country as a whole, the percentage is small."

Some scholars estimate that Peru imported as many as 150,000 slaves, I thought. Where did they go? And what about miscegenation—

didn't the races get together and produce mixed-race children? I asked Aguirre for his thoughts.

"There was miscegenation, but not to the same extent as in Brazil," he explained. "And reproductive rates among the slaves were always very low and in some cases negative." Health had been so poor among African slaves, apparently, that a great portion simply died out.

I sat back in my seat soberly as Aguirre went on. Today, he told me, most Afro-Peruvians live in desperate poverty. Only 27 percent finish high school, and only 2 percent get a college education. He painted a grim picture. But as we neared the city, he began to speak with greater optimism about Afro-Peruvians' future.

Aguirre told me that Peru's pockets of impoverished blacks are raising their voices. Urban neighborhoods and rural districts which always had large black populations are becoming centers of black activism and culture. Peru's blacks are keeping traditional customs, playing the music, singing the songs—celebrating Afro-Peruvian life, not just enduring. And they're using their pride to fight the racism that still persists throughout Peruvian society.

I was ready to hear more about pride, activism, and celebration. So I thanked Professor Aguirre for all he'd taught me and climbed out of the car again at my hotel. I needed to rest and prepare for my next meeting, at LUNDU: Centro de Estudios y Promoción Afroperuanos (Center for Afro-Peruvian Studies and Empowerment).

The evening passed in a blur. I remember washing my face and tending to the several cuts on my hand, nearly forgotten. And then I remember spending hours in my hotel desk chair, thinking, turning over my notes. Last year, I recalled, the Peruvian government did something that no other country in Latin America has done—it apologized to its black citizens. I knew I had the apology written down, and I rummaged through a book bag full of notebooks to find it. When I did, I was impressed with the power of its forthright simplicity: "We extend a historical apology to Afro-Peruvian people for the abuse, exclusion, and discrimination perpetrated against them since the colonial era until the present." No mention of slavery, I noticed. But still, you had to give credit to the government for acknowledging these wrongs. I collapsed on my pillow and fell asleep wondering if the apology had satisfied any of Peru's black activists.

In the morning, I headed straight to LUNDU. I met the invigorating Mónica Carrillo, a leading Afro-Peruvian activist. And I found out, pretty quickly, that she is a natural fighter who isn't easily satisfied by symbolic gestures. As we were settling down to talk, I asked her about the government's apology to Afro-Peruvians. She fired off her response before my behind hit the chair.

"It's not enough, to say sorry, no," she said. "We need it to translate into public policies for Afro-Peruvian people. I believe that Peru is— could be—the most racist country in Latin America."

Carrillo explained that many Afro-Peruvians experience racism on a daily basis. The examples she gave me were alarming. "If you are an Afro-descendant, somebody might call out, 'You nigger!'" she told me. "If you're a woman, they might make both sexual and racist comments. If you're a kid, the teacher might say you're like a monkey."

"The teacher?" I asked. Carrillo nodded with a sympathetic smile.

"My history teacher, who was teaching Peruvian history, asked my sister and I if we could 'see the monkeys' in our class," she said. "At another school, they sat the black children at the back of the classroom and whites at the front."

These stories were, of course, evocative of the stories that Baca had told me my first day in Peru. I asked Carrillo what she was trying to do to fight this kind racism. She said that her mission is daily struggle and that it takes on many forms. That morning, she was working on her campaign against a TV character called "El Negro Mama." Carrillo's goal? To get the character taken off the air—for good.

"Here he is," she said, pulling out a photograph from between files on her desk. "In Peruvian, *mama* means 'stupid,' not 'mother.' So *El Negro Mama*? The name of this character is actually 'the stupid Negro.'"

Seeing El Negro Mama sent a shock through my bank of anti-black stereotypes. It made Memín Pinguín seem almost tame by comparison. The photo showed a man in blackface, with oversized lips and an ill-fitting and cheap black Afro wig, wearing black gloves to mask his white skin. His eyes were wide and vacant, his mouth hanging slack, his lips outlined in red. Carrillo gave me a moment to digest this terrible image. What century was this? I wondered.

"He walks like a monkey, too," she added, when I finally looked up. "He's always stealing or trying to rape women. In the last episode, he was trying to steal money so he could have an operation to become white."

A stupid, dishonest black caricature whose greatest wish is to be-come white—this is a modern-day Sambo. I'd seen some racist things on TV as a child: Buckwheat and Stymie from *Our Gang* and, of course, Amos and Andy. But I'd never seen anything as racist as El Negro Mama.

"I can't believe it," I sputtered. "It's disgusting."

"It is disgusting," she agreed, heaving a sigh. "LUNDU organized a protest against El Negro Mama, and it was removed from the air for two months. But as of a week ago, he's back."

"Why did it come back?" I blurted. This story was unbelievable.

"They said we were attacking free speech," she replied. "So now, we're trying to organize an international campaign against El Negro Mama, including institutions from the US too, of course." I told her she could sign me right up.

"It's positive because this is the first time in Peruvian history that we've had such a big racial discussion," she pointed out. "But at the same time, people have spat in my face. Someone else tried to run me over."

"*Run you over?*" I asked, genuinely shocked.

"These are the kinds of situations we live through in Peru," she said plainly. "My experience is particularly extreme, but we are all living with a dramatic problem."

I was amazed at Carrillo's composure. And I thanked her humbly as I left—not only for meeting with me but for the personal risks she takes every day to bring a better life to Afro-Peruvian people.

I tossed my briefcase into the back of my car, and I asked my driver to take me to visit someone who could offer a different view, that of the political establishment: Congresswoman Marta Moyano. Moyano understands the potential perils of activism in Peru, such as those faced by Mónica Carrillo: her sister, María Elena Moyano, a community or-ganizer and activist, was assassinated by members of the Maoist Shin-ing Path movement on February 15, 1992. Congresswoman Moyano was instrumental in getting the Peruvian government to apologize to its black citizens—the first time, I believe, a Latin American government has done such a thing—and I wanted to hear what she had to say about the effectiveness of that apology. Was it merely symbolic, as important as that symbolism might be? If El Negro Mama was still on the air, to take just one example, had Afro-Peruvians really made genuine prog-ress up the social ladder in contemporary Peru?

Moyano is a thoughtful, ordered, and passionate politician with a large agenda for Afro-Peruvian rights. She made me understand, with admirable efficiency, how hard it had been to get that simple apology accepted in the first place.

"In Peru, there are many organizations for people of African descent that have been working for twenty or thirty years," she explained. "In the year 2004, we celebrated 150 years since the abolition of slavery in Peru. So we decided to hold a national Afro-Peruvian conference. We gathered Afro-Peruvian representatives from around the country. And we invited the World Bank, US aid organizations, and all the Peruvian government institutions, so they'd listen to us."

Moyano's struggle, and the struggle of others like her, has been to get the Peruvian government simply to acknowledge that Afro-Peruvians exist. Listening to her, I started to perceive the depth of the problem. There was no public dialogue, no formal exchange of ideas. At some time in the distant past, Peru had simply eliminated blacks from its national portrait. And as in Mexico, the federal census has no category for Afro-descendants. While that might not sound like an important political decision, it reflects a peculiar logic about race: if black people don't exist legally, then how can anti-black racism exist? A similar argument has been put forth by the Mexican and French governments.

According to Moyano, Afro-Peruvians weren't recognized in the country's constitution as a people, as a distinct ethnic identity. They had no representative presence in government. There were no holidays celebrating any aspect of Afro-Peruvian culture. Peruvian census forms didn't include any questions about ethnicity, so the number of Afro-Peruvians has never even been counted.

"We want people of African descent to be conscious that they're of African descent," she said simply. "But after so many years of discrimination, many of them don't want to be of African descent."

Her words landed on me like a blow. How could any black-power movement take root when poverty, racism, and helplessness had convinced so many to disown their own heritage? I mean, you can't exactly have a mass movement of black people if they are too ashamed to admit that they are black. I asked Moyano what kinds of changes could begin to make a difference.

"Concrete ones," she answered confidently. "Changes that affect quality of life. In many places, there isn't any water, they have no sewage, they don't have legal health coverage, their work in the fields isn't

recognized. And then there's the whole education question. Afro-Peruvians need universal rights."

Moyano's obligations were pressing. So I shook her hand and
thanked her for the time she'd given me. Outside, I walked slowly along
the sidewalk. My visits with Carrillo and Moyano had left me somewhat drained. I was starting to understand why my images of Peru had
never included Afro-Peruvians, and their uphill battle toward visibility
seemed awfully steep.

I was ready to spend some time talking about all this with a scholar
whom I had admired from a distance. So I asked my driver to take me
to Lima's San Marcos University, where I could find Professor José
"Cheche" Campos Dávila.

I can't say enough about the bond I share with Cheche. We are both
academics, we've been inspired by the same great Pan-African leaders, and we've traveled parallel paths in our activism. In the late 1960s,
when I was entering Yale as part of its first affirmative-action generation, Cheche was part of a small cohort of talented black students in-
tegrating Peru's elite universities. Back then, Peruvian universities en-
rolled only seven or eight black students at a time. Cheche was one of
those, pursuing his degrees with spirit and determination. Today, he's
the dean of social sciences and humanities at Universidad Nacional
de Educación Enrique Guzmán y Valle, La Cantuta, one of the most
well-known black academics in the entire country, and a champion of
an affirmative-action policy in Peru. I was honored to meet a man with
whom I shared so much in common; we have similar statures, and we
both even use a cane!

We spent several minutes discussing our education, our mentors,
the writers we admire, our favorite books. We soon learned that we
share a deep admiration for the Nigerian Nobel Prize laureate Wole
Soyinka. I told Cheche about my travels through Peru. I told him I'd
never seen blackness buried so deeply. I wanted to know how the country had changed since he'd been a student.

"I think it has changed significantly," he answered, thoughtfully.
"Because before we were totally invisible."

Cheche told me that when he was a young man getting ready to
enter college, the United States contacted Peru offering scholarships for
black students. The Peruvian education ministry, incredibly, responded
by saying that there were no black people in Peru—and that therefore

no scholarships were needed. Cheche was one of many young Afro-Peruvians to respond to this outrage with action. He helped organize the Peruvian Youth Cultural Association. This group, and others like it, then worked for decades—and have begun to change the complexion of Peru's middle class, not through a black nationalist embrace of "Africa" but by stressing the history and integrity of Peru's black traditions as part of the larger national cultural mix, an ingredient of equal portion and flavor in a savory cultural stew. For Cheche, black, white, and indigenous are mutually constitutive in Peru, and that relationship should be preserved, officially.

"Now, we are visible," he said, his words coming with a certain satisfaction. "And I, after many years, believe it is not an issue of finding Africa. It is an issue about finding Peru. At its depth, it is about finding integration."

"So the future of blacks in Peru is to be found in multiculturalism?" I said, leaning forward. My new friend had genuinely surprised me.

"That's right," Cheche responded. "I believe that the black organizers have to worry more about other aspects, rather than waste energy on the fight against discrimination and racism. The fight for development and culture is a bigger fight that, in the long run, brings better results."

I found that an interesting point. You can't just fight against the negative without having something positive to fight for. Otherwise, there's no meaningful progress—no agenda for change.

"Barack Obama would not have been able to take on the presidency of the US if he hadn't presented himself as being above the issue of color," he argued. "Because if you are involved in the issue of color, you are only the president of the black people."

But what about El Negro Mama? Surely fighting to remove this racist caricature from Peruvian consciousness would be good for Afro-Peruvians. I asked Cheche if he agreed with Mónica Carrillo and thought it was important to get the character off the air.

"I think we have to be concerned about free speech and that in a free country, the fight is not in whether or not you are against it," he said, with a patient smile. "Because if they get it off the air, they are going to give it more value. But if people don't pay attention to it, don't give it value, then gradually, it's going to start disappearing."

I respect Cheche's political strategy. But resting my head against the back of my chair, I wondered if racism goes away by ignoring it, especially in a country in which black culture is struggling to gain legitimacy. After all, the Peruvian government didn't just wake up one day and decide to issue its historic apology to its black citizens; it responded to pressure, to a campaign that had been organized by Congresswoman Moyano. Without some official acknowledgment of and respect for black culture in Peru, can there be an effective way to fight against acts of anti-black racism or to dismiss them, as Cheche was arguing to me, as isolated or insignificant? And without the courage to acknowledge Peru's multiple cultural roots, it can't become the great multicultural society that Cheche envisions for it to be. Many countries, including the United States, are obviously far richer for their multiethnic heritage. But it has taken a very long time to effect this change in the US public cultural identity, and it has not been an easy process. The culture wars of the early nineties rage on today, but in new forms. Just listen even casually to speeches of members of the Tea Party or consider recent regulations in Arizona banning certain forms of ethnic studies. Cheche and Carrillo and Congresswoman Moyano, in their own ways, argue that if Peru wants to reap a similar benefit as the United States has, it must reconsider the way it narrates its entire history, from school curricula and national holidays to the funding of cultural organizations and diversifying its print, electronic, and digital media beyond throwbacks like El Negro Mama. That means including Afro-Peruvians—as slaves and as descendants of slaves—in Peru's official story, as builders of Peruvian history and culture, as preservers of black traditions almost half a millennium old, and perhaps most important, as members of Peru's vibrant middle class, a process that necessarily starts with access to education.

I bade farewell warmly to Cheche, a long-lost soul mate or doppelganger, explaining that I had a *quinceañera* to attend. We parted with the best of wishes and promised to exchange books, which we have done. I headed back to my hotel to put on my white linen suit. And that evening, I watched a ritual that culminated when Chebo Ballumbrosio's daughter, a beautiful young woman aged fifteen, danced with her father, far into the night, in high-heeled shoes for the very first time.

The *quinceañera* is a broadly celebrated Latin American tradition, not by any means a specifically black one. I wanted to see how this pan-Latin coming-of-age ritual might be embraced, or even transformed, by an Afro-Peruvian family. It was then that I saw the wisdom in Cheche's words. Chebo's daughter was breathtaking: she was wearing a white dress with blue butterflies on it, and they had been painted onto the dress by her aunts and her mother. She was also wearing wings, as did the little girls who escorted her. Her face was painted with a blue butterfly mask. It was magical, like seeing a fairy princess emerge before your very eyes. That night, the Ballumbrosios claimed Peru and this Latin American ritual as their own, effortlessly celebrating and manifesting and infusing their Afro-heritage into the forms of this received ritual. They played Afro-Peruvian rhythms but also "Speak Softly, Love," the theme from part one of *The Godfather*, traditional Mexican music, salsa, Cunan son, soul music, and hip-hop. They didn't welcome multiculturalism; they embodied it, seamlessly. They celebrated the promise of their daughter's future, dancing joyfully in the various rhythms of their inextricably mixed cultural identity.

I tapped my own foot at the edge of the dance floor. And I thought of all that was possible for this nation. Just a short time ago, I'd been one of the many people who didn't even know there was a black Peru. And there's a reason for that: black Peru has been muzzled. It's hard to hear if you live in Cambridge, Massachusetts—or indeed, almost anywhere on the international stage. But black Peru is not silent, and, in fact, the voices of Afro-Peruvians are only growing in strength. They're fighting for the cultural visibility they deserve. They're fighting to claim the truth of their past and to seize the potential of their future. The outcome of this fight is, I think, by no means certain. But what is important is that they have begun the fight. And with their first victory an unprecedented apology for the crimes of racism from their federal government, I think their chances of longer-term success are remarkably good.

At the end of the evening, I left the banquet hall and walked back into the darkened streets. I reflected on all I'd learned. I especially thought of Ana and Juana—the two women I'd met in the cotton fields. They'd be waking soon, going off to work, struggling even today to see their children leave the inherited hardships of slave ancestry behind. I don't know why, but in the half-light, this suddenly inspired me and filled me with hope. It seemed clear to me that Peru could in fact embrace its rich African legacy, study it in the classroom, and celebrate it. I realized I had seen it with my own eyes, heard it with my own ears, felt it in my heart. And perhaps, I thought, one day soon, all of Peru —a most unlikely center of black culture to most Americans—will do the same.

4

The Dominican Republic

"Black behind the Ears"

We are in the presence of a mulatto population that calls itself Indian, which gives us much food for thought.

—Frank Moya Pons

HOW DO RACE and racism play themselves out in the Caribbean? To
see for myself, I boarded a flight to the Dominican Republic, on the
island of Hispaniola—which it shares, somewhat uneasily, with Haiti.
The people here, on opposite sides of this island, have faced each other
across this body of land for 360 years. And their two cultures are studies in contrast. Haiti was colonized by the French; the Dominicans
were colonized by the Spanish. In Haiti, people speak Creole; in the
Dominican Republic, they speak Spanish. In Haiti, the national sport
is soccer; here, the national sport is baseball. In Haiti, the national religion is Vodou and Roman Catholicism; in the Dominican Republic,
it is Roman Catholicism. On the Haitian side of the Massacre River,
which divides the two countries, when it is 7:00 a.m., it is 8:00 a.m. on
the Dominican side.

Hispaniola is an island divided by two peoples who, to some extent, have shaped their identities in opposition to each other. In fact,
the Dominican Republic is the only country in the New World that celebrates its independence from another American country, because for
Dominicans, the separation from Haiti in 1844 is their Independence
Day. (Between 1822 and 1844, Haiti occupied the Dominican end of
the island.)

From afar, I thought, the Dominican Republic seems like heaven
on earth. I thought of its seemingly endless beaches, its long tradition
of merengue, and its dominance in baseball. And I love its cuisine,

especially the dishes such as *chofán* and *locrio*, characterized by its flavor-filled burnt rice, called *concón*. I knew that the nation was filled with black faces—over 90 percent of Dominicans possess some degree of African descent—and that the very first rebellion of black slaves occurred here in 1522. But I also knew the Dominican Republic has a complex past; few people here self-identify as black or *negro*; rather, a wide majority of Dominicans—82 percent most recently in a federal census—designate their race as "Indio," while only 4.13 percent designate themselves as "black." And I wanted to understand why. After Christopher Columbus stopped in the Bahamas, the northern end of Hispaniola was his first stop—his ships landed here in 1492—and, racially at least, it has been a troubled melting pot of Europeans, Africans, and native people almost ever since, its people and its government deeply ambivalent about the country's relation to its black past.

Santo Domingo, the capital city, was founded in 1496 by Columbus's older brother Bartholomew. It was the first permanent European settlement anywhere in the New World. (Columbus had created a small fort at La Isabela on his first voyage, but when he returned, all its inhabitants were dead.) It was also the first city in the Americas to import slaves from Africa. The first boatload arrived just ten years after Columbus, in 1502. Surely none of those slaves or the newly arrived colonists (or even their royal patrons in Europe) could ever have imagined that over eleven million Africans would follow that first boat's path to slavery in the New World. Traders called Santo Domingo the "Gateway to the Caribbean." It might as well have been called the Gateway of the Slaves.

Santo Domingo has an unmistakably Spanish flair, its architecture in the Zona Colonial recalling Spain, but Spain with a tropical ease and flavor. My hotel was near the center of town, in a grand square with a majestic, Spanish-style cathedral at one end and an enormous statue at the other. Though I was tired, dusty, and thirsty when I landed, I asked the driver to pull over and let me take a look. He told me that this was Columbus Square and that the church, the Catedral de Santa María de la Encarnación, was the first cathedral in the Americas.

I stepped out to get a closer look at Columbus's imposing statue. There he was, looking regal and well fed, pointing a finger toward new horizons. No surprise here. But as I thought about it, I found it a bit odd that the central square of the capital of a Caribbean country was dedicated to the European who first colonized it. (Curiously enough, in 1986, at the time of the overthrow of "Baby Doc" Duvalier, a Haitian crowd actually knocked over a statue of Columbus in Port-au-Prince and threw it into the sea.) Perhaps I was overreacting; still . . . I wondered if there were any monuments to the Dominican Republic's black heroes. I looked around hopefully, but I saw nothing suggesting a connection to blackness in this quasi-Spanish square. (Of course, in the United States, we celebrate all those early European ancestors because we believe that the Native Americans don't count as much, having been driven off their land or killed, and because we believe that we are all descended from those early Europeans in an almost cosmic sense. I think that even African Americans share a version of this, though of course they interpret the story of colonial America through a filter of slavery, and—unlike the way Mexicans and Peruvians might see their relationship to the conquistadors—most African Americans don't see themselves as having been colonized.)

I asked my driver, Adolfo Guerrero, if he could take me to such a monument. He turned his head one way and then the other, looked back at me, and shrugged. The quizzical expression on his face spoke volumes.

I did find a statue eventually, honoring Lemba, a great leader of the maroon slaves in the sixteenth century, positioned not in the central square but at the entrance of the Museo del Hombre Dominicano, in Santo Domingo. But that discovery was still in the future. Climbing back into the car, I realized that my first interview was already under way. I love meeting with scholars and historians, politicians and activists. But there's so much you can learn about a place by just chatting with everyday people, whose understanding of where they live is, of necessity, profound.

I told my driver about my project, learning about the black experience in Latin America, and I asked him about blackness in the Dominican Republic. He told me amiably that Dominicans don't think of themselves as black. They call themselves "Indio" instead, in a reference to the color of their skin, echoing a myth of the extent of their genetic descent from the island's indigenous inhabitants.

I knew those tribes were long gone from the island. So I asked him to define *Indio* for me more clearly. I wanted to understand why the term is used to describe a people who, back home in the States, would be described as black. But he struggled to find an explanation that would satisfy me. It seems that anyone who isn't white—whether the person is lightly tan, medium brown, or dark black—self-identifies as Indio. It is more about being Dominican, he explained, than being African or indigenous. Who is black? Who is *negro*? Why, the Haitians! And the fact is that if we applied the United States' "one-drop rule" to Dominicans and made Indian ancestry that one drop, most Dominicans would, in fact, be descended from Taíno roots, as DNA evidence reveals quite clearly.

I sat back, thinking about that, as we neared the hotel. The Dominican Republic was born a Spanish colony named Santo Domingo, and as a maturing nation, its Eurocentric ruling elites identified it as Caribbean but proudly declared that its heritage was primarily "Spanish, Catholic, and white"—and this in a country where mitochondrial-DNA evidence reveals, as the anthropologist Juan Rodríguez pointed out to me, that "85 percent of the residents of the Dominican Republic have African ancestry, 9.4 percent Indian, and less than 0.08 percent European! And on the father's side, through y-DNA, we now know that only 1 percent of us descend from an Indian male and 36 percent from an African male. Yet the average person here describes their race as 'Indio.'" In other words, this country acknowledges its indigenous past but not its African heritage. But where had its blackness gone, outside of its music and baseball? Where was the cultural mark—and the cultural recognition—of the hundreds of thousands of slaves whose labors built this country? I was determined to find out.

The next day, I drove out to visit a colonial plantation, the kind of place the first black slave in the New World would have worked. Called the Nigua Plantation, it was one of the very first sugar plantations anywhere in the Americas, and I knew it had once housed hundreds of African slaves. I was excited to see Nigua. But I was especially looking forward to meeting my guide, Professor Frank Moya Pons. He's one of the Dominican Republic's most respected academics, and he is widely considered to be the leading expert on the history of the Dominican Republic.

As our film crew pulled up to the plantation's ruins, I saw Moya Pons walking toward us, waving. I was struck by the gentleness in his face. We grasped hands, warmly, and he talked me through the birth of slavery in his country. Moya Pons told me that plantations like Nigua were the center of sugar production in Santo Domingo. They launched

Cutting sugar cane. (Jemila Twinch)

the sugar boom that spread across Latin America, the boom that de-manded the mass importation of African slaves, first in the Dominican Republic, then in Brazil, then in Haiti, and then in Cuba. Indigenous people were the colonists' first pool of slave labor, he explained, until smallpox, carried across the sea from Europe, decimated the popula-tion. Incredibly, within less than twenty years, he told me, the indig-enous population collapsed, from an estimated four hundred thousand when Columbus arrived to less than five hundred by 1550. It is difficult to think of any other way to describe this decimation of a people than as genocide. Faced with the growing demand for sugar back in Europe, and with a rapidly disappearing labor supply, the colonists imported Africans to fill the gap, and the country's sugar empire was born.

But the sugar economy didn't last long. First Brazil and then Barba-dos and Martinique, then Jamaica, and then Saint-Domingue (today's Haiti) began to outproduce the Dominican Republic by a significant margin, and so the country gradually transitioned to cattle ranching. This change transformed race relations, Moya Pons told me, planting the seeds of the very complex contemporary Dominican ethnic identity.

"Slavery in plantation societies works differently than slavery in cattle-ranching societies," he explained. "As cattle ranching became the dominant occupation, slaves had to be used as ranchers, too. And with ranching, there is little difference between master and slave. They were both riding horses, they were both using machetes, so master-slave relationships here became quite different from the rest of the Caribbean."

Moya Pons then told me that there was less tension between masters and slaves in this cattle economy—that the treatment of the slaves was fundamentally different. Moreover, he said, the new economy brought about a tremendous population shift that was felt along racial lines. Blacks, he said, gained more status in Santo Domingo as cattle ranching became the only game in town. Many white men—those born in Spain and their descendants born in Santo Domingo—were less interested in ranching than in gold and silver production, and so they left the area for Mexico and Peru in large numbers. Increasingly, Santo Domingo needed people of African descent and their children (many of mixed race) to work on the plantations and cattle ranches. Eventually, and increasingly, some managed to enter the colonial bureaucracy, to serve in the church, and to enlist in the military. And these colored people stepped eagerly into these roles, Moya Pons said, embracing the Spanish Crown as sovereign. They came to be known as "whites of the land."

"The population did not look Spanish at all," Moya Pons told me. "But if you look into the official documents, most people signed their letters, 'From the most Spanish and loyal city of Santo Domingo.' This created, I would say, an ideological superstructure of 'Spanicity,' or 'Hispanicity,' no matter how dark your skin was." In other words, they thought of *Spanish* as a nationality, perhaps, and not a race.

Plantation life on the other side of Hispaniola, in what was to become the French colony of Saint-Domingue and then, in 1804, the country of Haiti, was quite different, he noted. Haiti was under French rule, not Spanish—and plantation conditions were cruel for the slaves there. However, there was a surprising measure of upward mobility for some. Saint-Domingue actually had as many free people of African descent as there were whites by 1789, and many of these were quite wealthy. For instance, Toussaint Louverture had gone from slave to plantation manager and even slave owner in his lifetime, so there definitely was social mobility in the society for black people, though

"The Veins of Gold Ore Having Been Exhausted, the Blacks Had to Work in Sugar," by Theodor de Bry, sixteenth century. (Photo by Lebrecht Music & Arts; Corbis UK)

Haitian slaves had an unambiguous relation to their colonial master: they, rightly, hated France, though many free blacks and mulattoes developed quite an attachment to France and French intellectual life. (The new black and brown elite in Haiti even after independence—and well after independence—had a quite complex relationship to France.) But upward mobility here was driven by a different process: in Saint-Domingue, social mobility took place in a massive economic boom that actually opened up possibilities for free people of African descent. But Afro-descendants in the Spanish colony of Santo Domingo felt more of a fellowship of identity with their colonial masters and their culture because of a kind of marginality within the Spanish Empire for everyone in Santo Domingo, a situation that opened up social possibilities. Black people in Santo Domingo were being treated—by comparison to the slaves in Saint-Domingue—quite well, integrated into the lifeblood of the society in ways unthinkable, save for a small mulatto elite, at the island's western end, in Saint-Domingue. And so, metaphorically, a society slowly grew that was oriented, quite dramatically, far more toward its white, European, colonial past than either to its African heritage or to the black nation that was born of violent confrontation to its west.

It is a truism that every relation between a colonizer and the colonized is a complex love-hate relation. But the cultural relation and the relation of identity between the Dominican Republic and Spain, at least symbolically, seemed, at times, to have been almost incestuous. I wondered if the slaves in Santo Domingo had resented Spain for taking them out of Africa and making them slaves. Had these slaves ever banded together and rebelled, as the Haitians did? Moya Pons's answer was intriguing.

"The first blacks were brought from Seville," he explained. "There was a fairly large black population in Seville at that time, and they spoke Spanish, so they could communicate with each other. And in 1522, they rebelled—unsuccessfully, but they rebelled." (Actually, the sixteenth-century historian Gonzalo Fernández de Oviedo y Valdés claims this revolt was led by Wolofs from Africa.) "As a result, after 1522, the colony decided to only import slaves directly from Africa—blacks who spoke different languages and dialects, so they couldn't communicate." That was the goal, at least. "But they still had a preponderance of Senegambians united by Mandinka and Wolof, and a long tradition of maroonage and rebellion, stretching into the 1560s. And soon thereafter, the collapse of the sugar industry and the rise of cattle created a different relation between slave and master, black and white, than that which unfolded in more traditional plantation economies." (Other scholars, such as Silvio Torres-Saillant, point out that this history of rebellion of Afro-Dominicans extended well into the eighteenth century.) Thus, what we might think of as a Dominican difference came to be born.

I had an appointment back in the center of the city, and Moya Pons had a meeting at the Dominican Academy of History in just a few hours. So I left him walking pensively toward his car, as I walked pensively toward my own. Maybe the peculiar history of US race relations had not prepared me to understand the complexities of racial identity in a society as complex as the Dominican Republic; perhaps, as I questioned this "Indio" ethnic identity so firmly embraced here, it was incumbent on me to try, at least, to understand how a genuinely multicultural identity could be forged, even in a land as black, culturally and genetically, as the eastern end of Hispaniola. Was what is meant by *race* just too subtle for me, as an American, to understand? Wasn't "Indio" just another socially constructed identity? Perhaps the Dominicans weren't passing at all, in the American sense of that term, and perhaps I needed to be critical of my own assumptions as an outsider visiting a land where ideas about race were quite strange to me.

When you want to find out about the heart of an Afro-descended culture, I believe that it often helps if you can check out the music that people listen to—and the dances they dance. It was time for a little merengue. I'd managed to get in touch with celebrated musician Francis Santana, a man who has been singing merengue in the Dominican Republic for over sixty-five years. His partner, Frank Cruz, joined us as we sat on the steps of the ruins of the San Francisco monastery where this weekly ritual unfolds, as the crowd gathered and as his band set up. (Las ruinas del monasterio de San Francisco are the ruins of the oldest monastery in the New World.) It was a Sunday night, and each week, he told me, Dominicans come together in the center of Santo Domingo to dance merengue. Who doesn't love good music and dancing? I couldn't decide what I wanted to do more: to talk to Santana, to hear his band play, to watch a bunch of Dominicans get down, or to hit the dance floor myself.

I had arrived just before sundown at the open square in the shadow of the ruins of the monastery to find a sprawling public dance party. Everyone else seemed like a regular. It was fun to look around and see entire families there—old couples moving gracefully together, young couples sharing young or new love, teens goofing off with their friends, and mischievous children darting around, chasing each other through the crowds, sometimes dancing with their elders, all the time learning the rhythms and movements of merengue almost by osmosis.

And then, of course, there was the music, the hauntingly rhythmic music, music made for dancing. Like Mexico's fandango, merengue has clear African and Spanish influences. But the rhythm is different, the vocals are different, and the flourishes are different from fandango. Merengue has an unmistakable Caribbean flavor, the black sound of the islands. Fandango, it seemed to me, is more of a spectator sport; we sat in chairs and watched performances of couples and groups who had trained specifically in its techniques. Fandango, for all its vibrancy

Francis Santana's merengue band at Las ruinas del monasterio de San Francisco. (Jemila Twinch)

and immediacy, is, in this sense, something of a museum piece, a cultural artifact self-consciously preserved almost through school training, a bit like the Irish dance form called stepdancing—something to be watched, rather than performed. Merengue, on the other hand, is a dance form still very much practiced throughout the culture; it is a form most alive on the dance floor, a form kept alive spontaneously, with mastery of its techniques broadly based throughout the culture, regardless of class, something performed primarily for pleasure, for joy.

I found Santana again, glistening with sweat from his performance, at the edge of the square, on the steps of the cathedral. Anyone could tell just by looking at him that he loves what he does. But he is no spring chicken, and he was happy to sit down with me and rest for a moment! He shook his head, trying to catch his breath. Before I knew it, he had me doubled over with laughter, as he described to me how merengue had changed since his youth.

"Merengue has changed: now they play it too fast," he said, pulling a handkerchief from his pocket and wiping his brow. "Now it is so fast that any old person drops dead from a heart attack. Before, you could put your arm around a girl if you were in love. You could embrace her and dance closely together. Now, one is over here, the other is over there, and they're dancing bottom to bottom!"

When we were done laughing, Santana told me proudly that merengue is the great symbol of the Dominican Republic. People the world over know about the small island nation, he said, because they love its music.

"Merengue is a mixture of the music of the African slaves, the Spanish—with the guitar—and the *güira*, which is a native Dominican instrument," he told me. "They mixed up their instruments to make merengue."

Dominicans themselves love merengue fiercely. They all come together—white, brown, tan, black—united by the music. Mixed-race people created merengue, Santana said, fusing their influences, their histories, their future. And today, they dance together freely, no matter what color they are, to its unique rhythm. I had wondered if this curious insistence on an "Indio" identity might manifest itself in the selection of partners on the dance floor; it did not. Through this music, he said, Dominicans found a way to celebrate being exactly who they are—a genuine blend of cultures. The musicians and the dancers don't think about where their ancestors came from. They think about what those ancestors created together. Merengue, Santana said, was the birthright and legacy of every Dominican, though it was made the country's national music by none other than Rafael Trujillo, the man who ruled the country for thirty years. (Some Haitian cultural historians, however, describe the merengue similarly as a kind of Haitian national music— the two cultures are deeply intertwined in this way, naturally enough.)

I wondered if merengue could be thought of as the musical manifestation of an Indio culture.

"We feel it as ours," Santana said passionately, clasping his hands together in a universal embrace. "This is our life. Without merengue, we can't live."

I looked out again at the dancing crowd. It was hard to argue with him. These were ordinary people on an ordinary Sunday night. This wasn't a special celebration. This was just a culture in action, loving its music and embracing itself, a culture moving its feet.

I left Santana in the buzzing square, catching one last glimpse of him as he pulled himself back onstage for another set. I thought about Santana's definition of the social significance of merengue as a great cultural contribution to the world, and I understood that Dominicans want to see themselves as a proud mixed-race people. But I was here to find out how Dominicans feel about their African heritage, and the legacies of slavery—and no one seemed to want to talk about being black. All I was hearing, once again, was about a blended or a brown pride. And brown pride would be wonderful—if everyone were treated the same. But as I've seen, over and over again on this journey, brown pride often masks a distinct disdain for people who are darker than brown.

I paused for a moment to look around me, just watching the crowds on the sidewalk. Everywhere, there were people of various shades of skin, including dark brown but also, yes, black. Yet these people would only call themselves Indio, I thought, not black. And they want to be Caribbean—not Afro-Dominican. What was going on?

I needed help understanding this cultural roadblock. So back at my hotel, I got on the phone and scheduled a meeting with Juan Rodríguez, an anthropologist who serves as director of cultural diversity at the Ministry of Culture. I wanted to talk to him to make sure the Dominicans' pride in their mixed identity wasn't just cultural denial of an indisputably black past.

I met up with Rodríguez bright and early just near Columbus Square. He is quite dignified and keenly intelligent—and it was plain to see that he has African ancestry. I remember looking at him sideways as we walked through the square. As an American, I'm used to the ways Americans judge color. I couldn't believe he wouldn't be considered black. And I had to believe there were Dominican categories of blackness just beneath the Indio label.

Rodríguez looked at me, a bit puzzled, as I studied him. He knew all about my project and was very supportive. But I'm not sure he was ready for the barrage of questions I had for him as we walked through the center of this lovely city. I started out by asking him how he'd describe his race, given his dark coloring. "Well, here I am Indio," he said knowingly, cocking his head and smiling.

I asked him what the word means. He replied carefully, choosing his words. "I am supposed to be Indio. *Indio* means somebody—a black person that is kind of in the middle: not too dark, not too light, right in the middle."

"Help me understand, as an American," I said. "Where does this word come from?"

"Well, they have been using this for a long time," he replied. "But it has been really a product of the nineteenth-century word *indigenismo*, with the difference that by the nineteenth century, we didn't have any more indigenous people like South America did, so it didn't really apply to us. But to use the word *Indio* was a way to negate our African ancestry and start being something else. Because when you look at Dominicans, we cannot say honestly that we are Anglo-Saxons. Look at me. I'm black."

"You're black!" I blurted back—it was such a relief to say and to hear him acknowledge. "By American standards, you're certainly black."

"Yes," he replied, still smiling, "and the way I feel, I'm African American, I'm Afro-Dominican."

I asked Rodríguez if he'd always known he was black. I'd already spoken to several people in Latin America who discovered their African roots in adolescence or even later. So I wasn't surprised when he admitted he'd had to learn about his own blackness.

"I had to discover that I was black. And I discovered that I was black in America, when I first went to New York. Most Dominicans don't discover that they are black until they go to New York," he laughed. "And all of a sudden, I felt that my roots were in Africa, not in Spain—although, even today, everybody here says that the motherland is in Spain."

"So who is black in Dominican society?" I asked. "In America, all these people would be black. But here, who's black? Who is *negro*?"

Rodríguez smiled, knowingly. "Nobody's *negro* here," he said. "If we are told we're black, we say, 'Oh, no, I am not black! I am something else.' Dominicans are in complete denial about who they are."

Denial. That's the word I was afraid of.

As Rodríguez and I walked through the center of town, we happened on a window of curios, ceramic figures representing different scenes from the island. To my horror, one set of figures was Sambo images, vulgar caricatures of dark-skinned people of African descent, figures crafted with jet-black skin, huge behinds, monstrously large breasts, and absurdly thick, red lips. I found them sadly familiar, images commonly distributed in the United States more recently than we would like to admit. But these images were meant to be those of contemporary Haitians. I was stunned at the violence inherent in these abhorrent images and even more stunned when Frank Moya Pons later told me that he believes that some of these images have been produced "by Haitian artisans who have moved to Santo Domingo and have brought with them their art and their popular representations of the Haitian people and the blacks in Haiti." I found this difficult to believe.

"Look at this," Rodriguez said. "For the Dominicans, this represents African heritage: Sambos. This is the way they portray Africans. This explains why a kid will not say, 'I am African.' Because this is what they give you, this is what they show you being African means."

I thought of young black Dominicans seeing these images, and my heart sank. Then I thought of young white Dominicans, or light-skinned blacks, seeing them—and I wondered what kind of racist behavior these stereotypes might inspire.

"Have you ever experienced discrimination because of your color?" I asked, fearing I already knew the answer.

"Yes, I have indeed," he answered steadily. "I went to a very fancy nightclub with my nieces. I was told I couldn't enter. 'Members only,' they said. But then I noticed lighter-skinned Dominicans going in, no questions asked. I went back to the guy at the door, and he said, 'Look, I'm as dark as you are, but I have to keep my job. I have orders from above not to let *negros* like you in.' So the next week, I took a hidden camera to six different places like that—and in all six places, I was not let in. I made a big scandal in the press." This reminded me of the brown-paper-bag tests among African Americans in the past, when a person darker than that bag could not gain admission to the party.

I hadn't heard about this before our interview, and I now felt a huge amount of respect for Rodríguez's courage as well as his acute grasp of contemporary race relations in his country. He wasn't going to go down without a fight—and he wasn't going to let Dominicans flatter themselves that they were beyond racism. Again, I thought to myself, that dream shared by all the countries in Latin America that have embraced the logic of *mestizaje*—that a country could be so mixed that darkness of color didn't matter—had not become a reality here. I turned back to Rodríguez.

"So you said the rich people at the club, the ones that could go in, were lighter skinned," I said. "Does that mean that most of the poor people in the Dominican Republic have darker complexions?"

"Yes," Rodríguez said. "If you really see our social stratum, you will see that the most powerful people, the most influential people, are lighter and almost European-like. And of course, the darker people are poorer. The most depressed neighborhoods are completely dark. It's the same thing in the prisons."

I asked Rodríguez about the origins of the desire to be Indio—to claim Indian blood rather than African blood. Where did that come from? His answer surprised me.

"Nobody here is black because that word is reserved for Haitians. I think it is really the desire to negate anything that would be Haitian."

Haiti—that close neighbor, just on the other side of the great island of Hispaniola. Blackness in this country doesn't mean African; it means Haitian. I was fascinated. I thought I'd come to some conclusions about racial identity in the Dominican Republic, but I realized then that my journey was only beginning.

When I left Rodríguez, my joyous chat with Francis Santana about merengue felt like a distant memory. According to Rodríguez, the Indio label was just a myth, a function of a sort of race hatred. I wondered if others would agree. So I decided to talk to more black people who don't necessarily embrace the Indio label and who don't embrace Spanish identity over an Afro-descended one.

I'd heard of a brotherhood, the Holy Spirit of the Congo Drums of Villa Mella, that celebrates its African legacy—right on the outskirts of Santo Domingo. It's a Roman Catholic brotherhood, but like those who created Brazil's Candomblé, its founders combined African religions with Catholic teachings. They believe that the Holy Spirit performed miracles, giving their African forebears musical instruments so they could worship their ancestral gods. Of course, we now know that many of the Congos in question were already Christian before Columbus ever set foot on Hispaniola. Today, the group keeps African roots alive on this island, along with the Guloyas in the eastern part of the country and the Gagá believers throughout the Bateyes—in the long shadow of Christopher Columbus.

I located the brotherhood on a quiet street at the edge of the city, under a canopy of tropical trees. Román Minier, the group's leader, greeted me with enthusiasm. I love the many traditions of African ancestral gods and their attendant stories, and I deeply respect how Africans in the New World looked to their various faiths to endure slavery. Minier recognized me quickly as a kindred spirit, and he carefully explained to me the nature of the ritual they were performing for a family that had engaged their services for the day—a commemoration of the seventh year since the passing of a maternal ancestor.

"The brotherhood has been handed down from generation to generation," he told me. "Maximiliana Minier, the great-grandmother of my grandfather, was twelve when she was named the queen of the brotherhood. From that day on, we've had this tradition, which is over five hundred years old."

One of the brotherhood's primary duties is to honor dead ancestors. Over the course of the day, Minier told me, he and his group of musicians would perform a ritual to mark this seventh anniversary of the loved one's passing, her photograph installed at the center of a makeshift altar, around which his group of players was stationed. As a man of God, he would perform these rituals for anyone who asked, white or black. But he confirmed that the people who come to the brotherhood are mostly dark skinned. This is one of the ways that Afro-Dominicans who embrace African tradition find community and comfort.

I asked Minier if there are many other groups like his in the Dominican Republic—groups that keep African traditions alive. He shook his head. Those that do exist, he said, are in jeopardy because so many Dominicans reject their African roots. The United Nations Educational, Scientific and Cultural Organization (UNESCO) has even designated the brotherhood's activities as an endangered cultural practice.

The brotherhood confirmed that Afro-Dominican cultural practices do still exist in the Dominican Republic today and that at some point African customs had been part of Dominican life, despite its extraordinary degree of hybridity. But today, those customs are in danger of being forgotten or discarded. I climbed back into my car, delighted to have witnessed this centuries-old cultural form but also worried about its survival.

If Afro-Dominicans aren't embracing their ancestral customs, what is important to them? I knew they had embraced sports—especially baseball. In fact, it is hard for me to think of a major-league team that doesn't have a Dominican player. So I tracked down Dominican pitcher José Rijo. I knew he'd returned to his home country to start a baseball camp for young boys, and I was eager to see a successful Afro-Dominican in his element—a dark-skinned Dominican at that.

I traveled to Rijo's camp, which he named "Lomas del Cielo"—"The

Hill of Dreams"—after the great American film *Field of Dreams*. And I found a professional, orderly, and efficient operation at work. Baseball is big business in the Dominican Republic. Rijo was in the field with one of his young protégés, correcting his arm angle as he threw to the plate. He saw me walking up and strode over with a wide smile, gesturing to the open space around him with both hands.

"If you build it, they will come," he said, joyfully quoting the movie.

Rijo told me he was inspired to build this camp by Roberto Clemente, the stupendously talented right fielder for the Pittsburgh Pirates. Clemente, a tireless humanitarian, was killed in an airplane crash on the way to assist victims of an earthquake in Nicaragua in 1972. "Somebody that give his life trying to help another people?" Rijo said, gazing across a sea of young baseball players. "People he don't even know? I think if you don't find a motivation in that lifestyle, you have a problem."

Rijo uses his camp to help the talented become even better, to teach them academic skills, and to start them on a path to professional baseball. Athletes come here to prepare for a career in the majors; for scouts from the major-league teams, Rijo's camp is a must-see. The sport isn't just a pastime for Rijo and these boys, I realized. It is a way of life. In baseball, he had found success—and also a way to give back.

I asked him what baseball means to a young boy in the Dominican Republic.

"Everything," he answered simply. For young Dominicans, baseball is opportunity, he explained. "They can pursue a dream, one that they've seen come true for many others like them. They can embrace a passion that might one day make their lives better and make it possible for their families to live comfortably. Every single boy at the camp came from poverty. This is their way out."

"So baseball's a meal ticket?" I asked.

"Absolutely, yes," Rijo replied. "They say the only way to get off the island is by swinging or throwing. Baseball players usually have no education. But the sport gives them a chance. They just want the opportunity to become somebody."

Dark-skinned Dominicans are the poorest people in the country, he told me, echoing what Rodríguez had said. For these Dominicans especially, sports often provide the only possible avenue for success. Rijo does his part to—pardon the saying—level the playing field by running his camp. The business community might discriminate against blacks based on the color of their skin. But in this country, no one denies a great baseball player, whatever his complexion.

We chatted for a while about Roberto Clemente, about major-league baseball, and about the young boys who'd come to train with him. This one has a good arm, he said. That one over there? He can hit anything near the plate. Rijo is clearly proud of the work he is doing. But even more important, he is consumed with the desire to help these young men escape poverty.

Rijo and I said goodbye with a hearty handshake — and a few predictions about the upcoming seasons in our respective countries. I headed back to my car to continue my journey. I needed to delve deeper into Dominican history to understand how we got here.

My next appointment was with Silvio Torres-Saillant, a Dominican scholar from Syracuse University. We planned to discuss the Dominican Republic's fight for independence. And I knew this had to have some impact on the country's feelings about its blackness. Having seen so many of those feelings in action, I wanted to know more about their historical roots.

I met up with Torres-Saillant in Santo Domingo's Independence Park. Here, on February 27, 1844, Dominicans raised a flag over a free Dominican Republic for the first time. I thanked the professor for making time to share his wisdom with me. And I asked him to paint me a picture of that day.

"This was an open space, a meadow with a gate called the Puerta del Conde — the 'Gate of the Count,'" he explained, gesturing across the park. "There was an old building, which had political significance, and all the people congregated there. They declared the birth of the Dominican Republic."

He explained to me that the Dominican Republic's independence movement was different from any other in Latin America. Every country I'd visited had broken free from its colonial master in Europe. But the Dominican Republic freed itself from Haiti, its next-door neighbor, after an occupation lasting from 1822 to 1844.

This aspect of the country's history is riveting. Blacks in Haiti, who detested their French rulers, won independence in 1804 after a bloody revolution — and became the first black republic in the New World. In 1822, Haiti — convinced that the only way to ensure its safety from foreign invaders was to secure its eastern flank (which unfortunately happened effectively to be another country!)—moved into the former Spanish colony that had just proclaimed its independence, as "Spanish Haiti," from imperial Spain in December 1821. The Dominicans found themselves independent from Spain—that was the good news; but they were soon occupied by the Haitians, and that was, for them, the bad news.

Haitian leaders said they had to do this to stop French or Spanish forces from attacking them from the east. Some Dominicans welcomed the Haitians and greeted them like liberators. But most Dominicans, understandably, didn't care about Haiti's military needs. Some had been quite content under Spanish rule; and even if others chafed under Spanish rule, many also resented being dragged into a union with a country whose traditions already were so different from theirs. Ultimately, most simply wanted to create and run their own country themselves. After all, why substitute one master for another?

There were periods of collaboration with Haiti, Torres-Saillant noted, and even camaraderie between the two countries. But over the course of twenty-two years, hardship and resentment accumulated. Haiti needed money, so it taxed Dominicans and their institutions—making many Dominicans feel they were nothing but a piggy bank. To make matters worse, Torres-Saillant said, Haitians didn't show much respect for Dominican culture.

"The Haitian government imposed French as the language of instruction, when it had been Spanish for centuries," he explained. "They taxed and even appropriated land from the Catholic Church, and the people here were very Catholic. This angered everyone."

Relations between Haiti and the Dominican Republic continued to sour. And the occupation left an indelible mark on Dominican identity. "This era solidified the idea that these were two separate peoples," Torres-Saillant said. "Dominicans started recognizing themselves as their own. This was a period when that could be seen emerging distinctly."

"So Dominicans started to say, 'We're not like Haitians, we're different'?" I asked.

"That's right," he answered, nodding emphatically.

Juan Pablo Duarte, the architect of Dominican nationhood, wrote admiringly of the Haitian people. And the original Dominican constitution embraced some of the more progressive features of Haitian law.

Over time, however, distaste for Haitians became part of the Dominican cultural psyche, as it were. Being Dominican increasingly meant being "not Haitian." And when the Dominican Republic finally broke free in 1844, its people rejected just about everything about their island neighbor. They cast off Haitian culture, its language, its ideas—and to a certain degree, its color. Haiti was black, so, suddenly, black was no good.

Torres-Saillant asked me to follow him into the main hall of the site, to examine the permanent exhibit of sculptures of the Dominican Republic's founding fathers, the heroes who had led the fight for independence: Rosario Sánchez, Juan Pablo Duarte, and Ramón Matías Mella. They were great men, equivalent to George Washington, John Adams, and Alexander Hamilton, he said. Yet when we arrived at the exhibit and looked at their monuments, you'd never know that one—Sánchez—had African ancestry. His features had been changed to look like those of Europeans.

"This reflects the tendency of the Dominican ruling elites to whiten their heroes," Torres-Saillant told me. "If their heroes are too black, they changed the features."

But he pointed out that the Dominican relation to Spain, and to whiteness, was not as simple as one might think. "Here, we need to consider the War of Restoration, between 1863 and 1865, fought successfully to expel a Spanish invasion that had come to recolonize the country. You should know that Dominicans use such terms as *los blancos* and *blanquitos* often pejoratively. This chapter in our history may be said to have accentuated the Dominican sense of non-whiteness." Later, Torres-Saillant said, another occupation intensified Dominicans' dislike of Haitians—and blackness. Shortly after the Spanish-American War and a short-lived US occupation in Cuba, President Woodrow Wilson took a keen interest in the island of Hispaniola. Ostensibly, Wilson wanted to exert more influence over the United States' closest neighbors in the Caribbean—and to look out for his country's best economic interests there. In 1915, the United States occupied Haiti. And in May 1916, the occupation expanded to include the Dominican Republic.

When World War I cut off the United States' European sugar supply, leading to terrible shortages, the United States rebuilt and expanded Dominican sugar plantations to meet its domestic demand. The United States had only one problem: a shortage of labor. Dominicans

The Altar de la Patria (The Nation's Altar), in Santo Domingo, honors the three found-ing fathers of the Dominican Republic: Francisco del Rosario Sánchez, Juan Pablo Du-arte, and Ramón Matías Mella. (Jemila Twinch)

would not accept the extremely low wages offered for this kind of work, Torres-Saillant told me. But instead of raising wages, American land-owners brought thousands of Haitians into the Dominican Republic to do the work. By 1920, the national census recorded 28,256 Haitians living there, with thousands more, perhaps, living in the country ille-gally and unrecorded. This began the flow of devalued immigrant labor from Haiti to the Dominican Republic, a flow that remains unabated to this day. And these workers are defined, legally, in a recent case of the Dominican Republic's Supreme Court of Justice, as "in transit," a "re-serve army of labor," as the historian Franklin Franco Pichardo put it to me. Haitians were so desperately poor, Torres-Saillant explained, that they would work for next to nothing. They had never organized labor unions as Dominicans had, and they would accept much harsher work-ing conditions.

They also didn't have much of a choice. The United States appro-priated land in Haiti, and many rural Haitians were forced from their homes and farms. They had to survive somehow—so many of them traveled to the Dominican Republic to do it. But Dominicans were out-raged. They looked on Haitians as usurpers, with less respect than ever. In the popular press, Haitians were demonized.

"The plantation dehumanized Haitian workers," Torres-Saillant told me. "They were reduced to a condition of total destitution. It is then that Dominicans learned to see themselves as superior to Haitians."

"In other words," I clarified, "the Haitians became the migrant work-ers—doing jobs that no self-respecting Dominican would do."

"That's correct," Torres-Saillant replied. "They became a new class. And because they were so homogeneous in terms of their hue, their blackness was considered different than the blackness of ordinary Do-minicans."

"During the occupation, class became color coded?" I asked.

"That is correct," he said, nodding his head. "That is exactly what happened."

For some Dominicans, *black* meant poor, desperate, dirty, unedu-cated, stupid, degenerate. Everything these Dominicans thought about Haitians became what Dominicans thought about blackness. Today, some Dominicans stereotype Haitian people the same way whites have historically stereotyped blacks. Conservative Dominican newspapers are constantly portraying Haitians as Sambos.

"Caricatures like those are always offensive," Torres-Saillant said. "But they're especially important for understanding Dominican race relations. Negative Haitian sentiments and racist sentiments blend to-gether, and they reinforce one another."

Torres-Saillant then told me that until the 1960s, racist anti-Hai-tian attitudes were taught in Dominican schools. The state generated propaganda that was staunchly anti-Haitian—and by extension, anti-black. One politician, Torres-Saillant said, did particular harm to the Dominican Republic's relationship with Haiti—and its relationship to its own black roots. His name was Rafael Leónidas Trujillo: "Remark-ably, he was the grandson of a Haitian woman named Ercina Chevalier, whose name graced schools and other institutions during his dictator-ship." Trujillo was a Dominican general. He rose to power by means of a coup and ruled the country from 1930 until he was assassinated in 1961, following years of brutality. As a leader, he craftily used anti-Haitian sentiment to solidify his power and perversely to unite the na-tion around a supposedly common enemy. Trujillo argued that the Dominican Republic was actually a white nation—in spite of its obvious heritage of slavery and even in spite of his own Haitian ancestry! Over time, he proved a vicious dictator and is considered to be responsible for the deaths of thousands of Dominicans at the hands of the army and his secret police force.

"Trujillo was a child of the US occupation," Torres-Saillant told me, shaking his head. "He received his political education in the National Guard, which was created by the US. So when Trujillo requested assistance after taking over, assistance came."

Torres-Saillant offered to put me in touch with a person who had studied Trujillo, Sabrina María Rivas, to learn more about him. I was soon able to arrange a meeting with her at the Santo Domingo National Museum of History and Geography, where she works—and where visitors can look at President Trujillo's personal effects and learn about his time in power. (The exhibit even includes a car, perched next to a mannequin outfitted with his formal uniform used at functions of state, the very car that gunmen used to assassinate Trujillo.)

To my delight, I found Rivas informed, frank, and enthusiastic. She wanted to know all about my time in the Dominican Republic so far. She also couldn't wait to show me, piece by piece, all the relics of Rafael Trujillo. She has an impressive eye for detail.

"This was his formal uniform," she said, striding up to one of the cases, which housed what appeared to be a linen suit, covered in gold braids, epaulettes, and buttons. "It was made in France," Rivas told me. "It has a very French style."

She then showed me an important ledger called the "Gold Album of Trujillo." The dictator published it in 1956, she said, to share his image of the Dominican Republic with the world. It was a strikingly white vision of the country—featuring a strikingly pale portrait of its leader.

"All white," I said, looking at a photo of finalists in a beauty contest. "Not even a mulatto."

I noticed a twinkle in Rivas's eye. She turned to me and smiled, mischievously.

"In all his photos, he is wearing makeup," she said.

"He'd powder his face?" I asked, sticking my nose closer to the image. For a man with a brutal reputation, Trujillo suddenly looked downright silly. Maybe Sammy Sosa had been inspired to lighten his skin by Trujillo's example, rather than by Michael Jackson's.

"Powder, yes," Rivas laughed, "white powder. And look at the rose cheeks." Then, she pulled out a wooden container still full of Trujillo's white powder, all these years later, along with the brush he used to apply it.

"I'll be damned, look at that," I marveled. "So he was trying to represent the Dominican Republic as European, Spanish, and quite literally, white?"

"Yes, that was the image he wanted to give," Rivas explained. "Others even saw it as a symbol of stability. If he showed an elegant, rich, white population, that was the proof. And so that's the image he projected."

Trujillo's anti-Haitian views were well-known and perhaps even formed the basis of his power. But in 1937, he took his antagonism up a notch. He ordered an attack on the Haitians who were living along the Massacre River, the Dominican Republic's border with Haiti. As Rivas explained it, the border between the two countries had always been quite porous. Many Haitian migrant workers lived on the Dominican side of the river, alongside Dominicans of Haitian descent and some mixed families. These Haitians worked as farmers, and some even owned land. They spoke Spanish just like Dominicans. And for a long time, Dominicans tolerated their presence, even if they didn't enjoy it. "It was precisely the coming together of Dominicans and Haitians seamlessly," Torres-Saillant told me, "that terrified ultranationalists. It was the sense that the contours of the nation were being eroded by the transnational rapport at this site of confraternity."

Trujillo decided that these Haitians were a threat. So in October 1937, he launched a military attack. His goal? To kill all Haitians living in the Dominican territory. It was a tragic event, and I listened to Rivas tell me the story in silence. Trujillo's troops arrived and immediately closed the border, trapping Haitians on the Dominican side, at the border town of Dajabón. The Haitians were, rightly, terrified. They knew that many of them were about to die. So they tried to flee across the river. But on the shores and even in the water, Trujillo's forces caught and massacred them. No one really knows how many Haitians died, she told me. But the estimates generally put the number at about fifteen thousand.

Despite this brutal massacre, Rivas told me that Trujillo never did succeed in eradicating Haitians from the Dominican Republic. In fact, the Haitian workers on his own plantations were left undisturbed. And

Haitians crossing the Massacre River at Dajabón on market day. (Jemila Twinch)

the importation of Haitian immigrant labor continued soon after the horrors. Today, there are more than a million Haitians living and working in the Dominican Republic. They aren't always welcome, as we have seen—but they do quite a lot to make the Dominican economy function, especially its sugar industry. And they're striving to make a better life for themselves and their children, even though those born in the Dominican Republic do not become citizens automatically, as they would in the United States. Neither citizens of Haiti nor of the Dominican Republic, they are stateless and work for substandard wages and struggle to build lives for their families in substandard living conditions.

I realized I needed to see Dajabón and the Massacre River for myself. So the next morning, very early, we drove in darkness for the few hours it takes to go from Santo Domingo to Dajabón, to arrive just after dawn, in anticipation of the opening of the border for Market Day. We arrived just before 8:00 a.m., the hour when the border opens and Haitians flood across—to set up stalls and sell their wares to Dominicans or to purchase goods and return them to waiting trucks that will take them for resale throughout Haiti. This series of commodity exchanges every Friday on the border is a big, organized, thriving business. I noticed that many of the Haitians were already there, arranging their products, their vegetables, fruits, dry goods, and crafts, having waded across the river, miraculously escaping the watchful eye of the massive numbers of officials in the border patrol, who were seemingly desperate to preserve the sanctity of the official starting time, forcing dozens to wade back to the Haitian side of the river until they said it was time. Perhaps these Haitians already on this side had moved into Dajabón the way I did, in darkness. They seemed willing to do just about anything, I realized, to gain the slightest advantage and to make a tiny bit of extra profit for the day.

I looked across the river at Haiti. It was so close that a strong arm could toss a coin or a stone from this shore to that one. And yet there was almost no measuring the cultural and economic gulf between the two countries. Haiti stood with its French colonial past—its Creole, Vodou, and love of soccer; the Dominicans, by contrast, had their Spanish roots, Roman Catholicism, and baseball. There was no gulf, however, greater than that between their ideas about race—their own and each other's.

As I drove back to Santo Domingo, to catch a flight to Port-au-Prince, I thought about what I had seen in the Dominican Republic. It seemed to me that what I'd found there was a people deeply in denial about their roots, confused about the relation among color, class, and inferiority—people whose historical anger at their Haitian counterparts, with whom they have shared the island of Hispaniola for almost half a millennium, had warped their view both of the Haitians and of themselves. On the one hand, the Indio identity in the Dominican Republic spoke to a long history of intermarriage and cultural and genetic hybridity, rendering received categories such as *black* and *white* inadequate to account for their complexity. As Torres-Saillant put it, "What about Edward Glissant's notion of identity as rhizomatic, meaning not a vertical root reaching down to a singular origin but a horizontal dispersion of roots connecting with multiple other roots and origins?" And there is something to be considered here. On the other hand, there can be no denying that a great amount of schizophrenia, denial, and racial tension lie just beneath the surface of this nation's skin, buried in many of the various connotations of this curious ethnic designation, Indio.

Colonialism, an occupation by Haiti in the nineteenth century, Spain's annexation between 1861 and 1865, and still another occupation by the United States in the twentieth century (leading to the adoption of baseball as the national pastime here, yet stubbornly resisted during the simultaneous US occupation of Haiti), and manipulative, opportunistic, demagogic leaders had done their share to bring the Dominican Republic to this place. It is only Dominicans themselves who can reshape their national character and nurse black pride back into being. It will happen when they look in the mirror and come to love the blackness in their own faces as much as they admire the traces of their European colonial masters, and when scholars of the black diaspora recognize and give credit to Afro-Dominicans for their glorious past. But perhaps things are changing: I took much comfort and encouragement from the fact that the first country to cross the border and offer aid to the Haitian people after the earthquake was their fraternal neighbor, the Dominican Republic. And perhaps this will lay the groundwork for the beginning of a new era in their foreign and domestic relations and, by extension, a new era in the estimation of the role of the African past in the hybrid, resistant Indio present that is Santo Domingo. For me, it was time to cross the border.

5

Haiti

"From My Ashes I Rise; God Is My Cause and My Sword"
(*Motto on King Henri Christophe's Haitian Flag, 1811–1820*)

[The rebelling Haitian slaves are] the cannibals of the terrible republic.

—Thomas Jefferson, February 11, 1791

Their slaves have been called into action, and are a terrible engine, absolutely ungovernable.

—Thomas Jefferson, March 24, 1791

We receive with regret daily information of the progress of insurrection and devastation in St. Domingo. Nothing indicates as yet that the evil is at its height.

—Thomas Jefferson, January 5, 1792

Never was so deep a tragedy presented to the feelings of man.

—Thomas Jefferson, July 14, 1793

EVEN BEFORE I landed at Port-au-Prince, my mind and my heart were engulfed by Haiti—by the country's incredibly complex, still unfolding saga of glory and shame, honor and suffering. From the air, all I could see were checkered fields of blue and white. I discovered, as all visitors to Haiti do since the earthquake, that these were tents—tents housing an estimated 1.2 million Haitians, tents that will have to serve as homes for the dislocated citizens, some estimates say, for the next twenty years.

Haiti is the poorest nation in the Western Hemisphere. Today, its very name conjures up images of suffering: of the massive earthquake that devastated Port-au-Prince, of brutal dictators and the Tonton Macoutes, of military coups, riots, food shortages, crowds of people lining up for international aid, images of terrible poverty and unending political unrest. And, of course, "voodoo," the stereotypical denigration of the religion Vodou. But when I think of Haiti, I think first of its unique place in world history, as the birthplace of one of the most inspiring revolutions in the eighteenth century, the Haitian Revolution and its victory over Napoleon Bonaparte's France, the most powerful army in the world. When Haiti won its independence from France in 1804, its slaves did something that had never happened before: they overthrew their European masters and established their own nation, a republic, at least initially. It was, and should be recalled as, one of the most thrilling moments in human history. When Haiti was born, it was the first (and only) black republic in the New World or in Africa (Abyssinia, now Ethiopia, was a monarchy, which Haiti soon also became, but it was not initially); and theirs was the only truly successful slave revolt in the whole of the New World.

Moreover, as part of its historical origins and cultural legacy, Haiti remains, to this day, an indisputably black culture, even if color tensions between mulattoes and its darker citizens have been quite problematic over the entire history of the colony and the republic. In fact, in an attempt to speak to this issue of color as class, Haiti's very first constitution—Dessalines's constitution of 1805—declared, "Because all distinctions of color among children of the same family must necessarily stop, Haitians will henceforth only be known as blacks." Haiti was keenly aware of its role as a putative center of what we later came to think of as Pan-Africanism, as a transnational "black" political consciousness: indeed, Alexander Pétion in his constitution of 1816, in article 44, actually declared, "Any African, Indian or those who carry their blood, born in the colonies or in foreign countries, who come to live in the Republic will be recognized as Haitian." This act of welcoming all black people around the world to become Haitian citizens—which Frederick Douglass actually announced that he was considering accepting on the eve of the Civil War—can be thought of as one of the earliest, and perhaps the earliest, signal acts in the history of Pan-Africanism, the first time certainly that a government thought of all persons of African descent positively as "citizens" or members of a unified or related group—the flip side of considering all Africans as members of a single group of people who are potentially enslavable, even though

Alexandre Pétion, president of Haiti, 1806–1818. (New York Public Library)

we know that not all African ethnic groups were enslaved in the trans-Atlantic slave trade and even though we know that some African ethnic elites made it their business to sell other African ethnic groups to Europeans for transport to the New World. This is a remarkable development in the history of black peoples in the Western Hemisphere: one can rightly say that the slave trade ironically created a pan-ethnic "black" identity, as manifested in many ways but especially profoundly in this declaration in the Haitian constitution.

(Douglass, by the way, served as the United States minister and general consul to Haiti between 1889 and 1891 and delivered several speeches about Haiti and Toussaint Louverture, including his widely reported address at the dedication of the Haitian Pavilion at the World's Columbian Exposition in Jackson Park in Chicago on January 2, 1893.

Douglass also was the assistant secretary to the commission to the Dominican Republic under President Ulysses S. Grant, from January 24 to March 26, 1871, and actively endorsed the attempt in 1871 to annex Santo Domingo as a new state in the United States. Despite many severe objections, including from his friend Senator Charles Sumner, Douglass did so, he explained, to create the first black state in the Union, "a black sister of Massachusetts," one whose "racial ambiguity" was proof that racial categories were not fixed by nature as the historian Sarah Luria has clearly shown in "Santo Domingo, or the Ambiguities: Frederick Douglass, Black Imperialism, and the 'Ku Klux War.'" Douglass also thought that this annexation would begin a process of annexing much if not all of the rest of the Caribbean to become part of

Frederick Douglass sitting at his desk in Haiti. (National Park Service)

a "Great Western Republic," forever transforming the racial balance of the citizenry of the United States and thereby increasing the number of black votes and increasing the potential opposition to the growth of the Ku Klux Klan.)

Nevertheless, in Haiti, as in the Dominican Republic but with its own patterns of development, color as class has been an important and deeply problematic aspect of the nation's history from its inception, as captured in this popular proverb commonly used in Haiti today: "The rich black person is a mulatto; the poor mulatto is black." Actually, as the historian Laurent Dubois informed me, this version of the proverb is a revision of the nineteenth-century form: "The rich black who can read and write is a mulatto; the poor mulatto who can't read or write is black." This version ties the discourse of race in Haiti to that of such Enlightenment philosophers as Hume, Kant, Jefferson, and Hegel, each of whom pointed to the absence and presence of reason or literacy as justification for ranking persons of African descent lower than Europeans in the great chain of being. At times, rivalries and confrontations between mulatto and black Haitians have been almost as vicious and as pernicious as those between Haitians and the French, starting at the very beginnings of the fight for independence from France and persisting to this day in less severe but still pronounced forms. I wanted to see how race manifests itself at the western end of the island of Hispaniola, in comparison to what I had seen in Haiti's mirror image, the Dominican Republic.

The Trans-Atlantic Slave Trade Database estimates that 770,000 slaves were brought to Haiti over the course of the slave trade. (Some historians place the figure higher, closer to one million, estimating the numbers that came illegally.) Gazing idly out my car window in Port-au-Prince, I shook my head in amazement as I recalled that number. This small nation—a country that takes up about one-third of the island of Hispaniola, about the size of Maryland—absorbed perhaps 350,000 more slaves than the total number that came to the United States.

What happened to those slaves? What inspired them first to fight, so improbably, for their freedom and then to found their own nation, a black nation in a sea of Spanish, Portuguese, Dutch, English, and French colonies? And more important, how do Haitians today feel about their past? How does their blackness reverberate through their lives? How does it feed their spirits? And how had the earthquake affected their sense of themselves, their sense of regaining a foothold onto a democratic, upwardly mobile future? I had seen so much of Anderson Cooper's coverage of the devastation of the earthquake on CNN; now I was ready to meet the people of Haiti, to talk to them, to witness their struggles, and to try to find some answers.

The first stop on my trip was Port-au-Prince—the devastated city that has become Haiti's global face. On January 12, 2010, the worst earthquake to hit Haiti in over two hundred years struck here with terrifying power. It registered a 7.0 out of 10.0 on the Richter scale and leveled nearly the entire city to the ground. Over 220,000 Haitians lost their lives, and today, a million and a half are still homeless. The world has pledged ten billion dollars to help, but much of it hasn't arrived— only 38 percent by January 2011—and much of the remainder won't arrive for a long time. Haitian officials have said rebuilding their shattered capital could take twenty-five years.

I had tried to prepare myself to see tragic suffering. And I expected to be ready for it. I've seen poverty-stricken inner cities all over the United States and traveled to twenty African countries—as well as to much of the Caribbean. I've seen a lot of hardship. I didn't think any poverty or destruction could shock me, no matter how bad it was. And I had attentively watched the coverage of the devastation of New Orleans and the Gulf Coast following Katrina, in addition to watching the 24/7 coverage of Haiti on CNN.

But when I stepped out onto the streets of Port-au-Prince for the first time, I realized that I was wrong—that nothing, truly, can prepare a human being to see something like this. I was surrounded by utter devastation. Office buildings, hotels, homes of all shapes and sizes had been reduced to piles of broken wood, plaster, and crumbled concrete, virtually everywhere. There was almost nothing else. Buildings had just collapsed, caving under, it seemed, rather than being blown around. Rubble was pushed to the sides of the streets so cars could pass, but there weren't many untouched buildings standing anywhere in sight.

I saw tens of thousands of large families living in veritable tent cities, without electricity or running water, relying on fraying tarps for shelter, open taps for water, and porta-potties for toilet facilities. I knew there were hundreds of thousands more, living in possibly even worse conditions, scattered throughout the city and in enormous aid camps, constructed in any available open space, including every major park in the city. These were the worst living conditions I'd ever seen. The enormity of the disaster, and the stench, took my breath away.

I walked down one road after another. Anyone who had tried to talk to me would have found me speechless. But as I continued along, I began to sense a survivalist spirit in the streets. There was hope in the air. I might have been staggering around with my mouth hanging open—but Haitians weren't. All around me, they were carrying on. I saw people greeting one another, talking, making plans, working, and helping one another. I even heard people making music. Life was impossibly hard, but these people were living. I don't know how other victims of earthquakes have responded, but it was clear that these Haitians were amazingly resilient.

Then, suddenly, in the middle of one of these tent cities, I stumbled on something quite wonderful. There amid the rubble stood a monument to Haiti's founding fathers—and they were black men: Toussaint Louverture, Jean-Jacques Dessalines, and Henri Christophe. I stood in front of it in awe. I'd seen many things in my travels, but nothing like this, not even in Africa: a bold, public recognition of a nation's black founding fathers. Slaves and their descendants fought in many wars for independence in Latin America. They even led some of those wars, as Morelos and Guerrero did in Mexico and as Antonio Maceo did in Cuba. But their nations did not embrace them like this. Most Mexicans had long forgotten about Guerrero's and Morelos's black roots, and even Maceo's features had been whitened over time. This country, Haiti, was the only one I'd seen on my journey that did not whiten its heroes. They were proud of their blackness.

It didn't take long for me to witness that pride in action. That afternoon, I visited Port-au-Prince's National School for the Arts. The building had suffered major damage, but in a room that had escaped damage, a teacher was holding class. The students surrounding him held drums —African drums. They were learning polyrhythms from their teacher, a man named Louis Lesley Marcelin, known simply to his students as Zhao. As I walked up, I saw him leaning over a book, showing one of the young people how to read drum notations in a musical score.

"Now, as you can see here, it shows you a zero for bar one," he instructed, pointing emphatically with one finger. "Now it is only your foot that is tapping."

As his students pored over their books, he came over to greet me.

I introduced myself eagerly, and I learned that Zhao is the head of the school's percussion department. Everything that he teaches has African roots, he explained. But all the musical traditions taught at the school are distinctly Haitian. The country's music was born out of a rich cultural mix—an African mix.

"Haiti is a country of imitation," said Zhao. "So many different ethnicities have come from Africa. And we Haitians have imitated them all. And that is why we have so many musical styles. For example, there is Dahomey, which comes from Benin. Or you take Nago, which we inherited from the north, from Gonaives, that comes from Nigeria. Because we are descended from so many places in Africa, everything Africa had to offer, we inherited."

Those who don't know Africa tend to lump all Africans together. But Africa is itself, of course, a multicultural continent, the most genetically diverse continent in the world. Fifteen hundred languages are spoken in Africa. It was a rare thrill to talk about cultural mixing with someone who both acknowledged that plainly and had the sophisticated training to explicate the parts that had been combined in Haiti to make new cultural forms.

Of course, European influences left their mark on Haiti too. Today, Zhao told me, nearly the entire population speaks Creole—a beautiful language that first appeared when early Haitians combined the tongues of several West African nations with elements of eighteenth-century French, Spanish, and, some scholars speculate, Arabic. Creole is a totally unique creation, Zhao said, a national language forged by Haitians, just for Haiti. (It should be noted that every Caribbean country has a creole language, and they were all built pretty much like Haitian Creole was. In Aruba, for example, with almost no African past, the people speak not Dutch but a creole based on Spanish with a lot of African loan words, which came in through Curaçao. This language, Papiamento, is every bit as unique as Haitian Creole.) Remarkably, it was only in 1987, during the presidency of Jean-Bertrand Aristide, that Haitian authorities consented to give Creole the status of the country's official language, alongside French, which most of the poorer people do not speak fluently.

Zhao then turned to his class, a sparkle in his eye. He asked them if they'd like to serenade me with a song about Creole. I was tickled by the prospect, and they seemed to enjoy having me as an audience.

A normal day at school had become something special for all of us. The next thing I knew, they were shouting out proudly, their voices ringing off the broken walls around them:

Creole, oh
Creole is spoken, Creole is understood
Creole, oh
Creole is spoken, Creole is understood
The language of my mother
Creole, oh, that is home
The language of my father
Creole, oh, that is home

The song was echoing in my head the next day, as I made my way around Port-au-Prince, preparing to go north to the country's second-largest city and one of its most historic. The French first landed in this area in 1625. Petit-Goave, founded in 1654, is usually considered the first formal settlement (by that time, Spain had already settled on the eastern side of the island and built Santo Domingo). The first French settlers were buccaneers, and their first settlement in the region was on Tortuga. They were outlaws, not representatives of France. They also made illegal settlements across the water on Hispaniola in the 1640s, but the formal French presence began with the appointment of Bertrand d'Ogeron in 1665, a situation not recognized by Spain at the time.

Spanish forces were too small and weak to hold the entire island. Yet neither France nor Spain was prepared to go to war over this territory, so in 1697, the two great powers formally divided the island in two, and Cap Haïtien (originally called Cap-Français, nicknamed "Le Cap") became the centerpiece of the French side. The formal division was made in 1697, by the Treaty of Ryswick. (The Treaty of Aranjuez in 1777 formally divided the island into two distinct colonial sites.) It was a fortuitous agreement for the French. Indeed, Le Cap soon became France's most important trading post in the New World and a primary entry point for African slaves—at least three-quarters of a million of them—as Haiti became the richest colony in the Western Hemisphere. It was the jewel in France's crown—the French even called it the "Pearl of the Antilles."

The reason? That magical five-letter word: *sugar*. European invest-

Sugar-cane lithograph, "Planting the Sugar-Cane." (New York Public Library)

ment, combined with Haiti's ideal climate and all that slave labor, turned the colony into a giant sugar producer. By the middle of the eighteenth century, Haiti was producing nearly half the world's sugar. And it accounted for two-fifths of France's overseas trade.

There was a reason that Haiti's sugar plantations made so much money. The conditions were horrific. Slaves were frequently worked to death—treated more like cheap farm equipment than human beings. Running plantations this way was highly profitable for France, but it created a very different kind of slave society from the one on the Dominican side of Hispaniola. Later, as we have seen, these contrasts between the two cultures led to hostility between them, as well as to the visible differences in their citizens' phenotypes. While Haiti, from the beginning of its revolution in 1791, had a clearly defined free mulatto elite, the masses of its people—and its three founding fathers—were unmistakably black.

Before leaving Port-au-Prince, I called on sociologist Guy Alexandre. Alexandre is an expert on the history of relations between Haiti and the Dominican Republic, and he also once served as Haiti's ambassador to the Dominican Republic. As we walked through the city, he quickly began to explain how slave conditions had set the stage for the modern-day animosity between Haiti and the Dominican Republic.

"In Haiti," he said, "there was a plantation economy linked to the exploitation of a large number of African slaves, whereas in the Dominican Republic, the number of slaves was infinitely lower—and the economy was based on livestock. This meant there were major differences in the way these populations were formed, at the outset. And there was a much higher rate of racial mixing in the east than we had here in Haiti."

I asked him if these different historical circumstances had led to the two countries' having such different feelings about Africa and the relation of their histories and cultures to their African slave forebears. When it came to embracing black roots, I noted, these two countries were like night and day.

"Basically," he replied, without hesitation, "in the traditional view held by Dominican society, the black, the African, bears connotations of savagery, of primitivism with regards to the religions—such as Vodou in Haiti's case—which are associated with the black world. And there are also connotations, for Haiti, of belonging to a world which is not a civilized world because Haitians speak a language which is not a civilized language: Creole. So Haiti and Haitians represent, in Dominican society's mainstream ideology, what Africa is, what Africans are: a human race outside of civilization, savage, etc."

"Now specific parts of Dominican society," Alexandre continued, "have lately been very slowly discovering that Dominican society is a mixed society and are gradually beginning to accept the non-European element—the African element—in their culture. But this is a recent phenomenon. For the most part, the Dominican elite simply rejected, almost completely, the African component of their culture. While Haitians, and specifically the Haitian elite, accepted their African origins to the point where our African origins are part of the national culture."

But in fact, the Haitian elite—even the leaders of the Revolution—rejected Vodou and Creole and maintained a very long and passionate love affair with most things French. Jean Price-Mars wrote his famous book *So Spoke the Uncle* (published in 1928 in French as *Ainsi parla l'oncle*) to dignify the African roots of Haitian culture against the vilification of the ruling elites. Price-Mars's book was part of a larger discourse of transculturation, also exemplified by the work of Vasconcelos and Freyre, as we have seen, and of Fernando Ortiz in Cuba.

I was deeply familiar, however, with the long and terrible history of intraracial color prejudice within Haiti, the discrimination of the mulatto elite against darker-skinned Haitians, going back to the time of the Haitian revolution against slavery, which started in 1791. As early as 1797, Moreau de Saint-Méry, a French lawyer and historian, published a book about the island of Saint-Domingue (as Haiti was called before it became independent in 1804), in which he described the community's racial admixture, using twelve categories including white. He then proceeded to show what happens when a white person mixes with one of these categories of racial admixture, leading to 128 possible combinations of mixture from these twelve categories! Shades of Brazil! But I was delighted to think—to hope—that Haitians, remarkably, respected and celebrated Africa's legacy in the New World and that this long history of color as class had abated in recent years. I wanted to examine Haiti's appreciation of its African legacy, as Alexandre suggested thrives here today, to determine if this is a romanticization or if it is true. Would a Creole-only speaker, for instance, be able to get ahead professionally in this society? Bidding a warm goodbye to Alexandre, I traveled to the outskirts of Port-au-Prince to learn about Vodou.

We've all seen the Hollywood-movie version of the religion commonly referred to as "voodoo": zombies, dolls stuck with pins, black people with bones in their noses wreaking havoc in scary trances, rituals culminating with the slaughter of a squealing black pig. It's been called devil worship, most recently by the Reverend Pat Robertson, who attributed Haiti's past and present suffering to a supposed pact with the devil that the revolting slaves supposedly made (after all, Robertson reasoned, how else could black slaves have defeated the French?). And it's been called black magic. Time after time, those who don't really know the first thing about this New World African religion have reduced it to a racist caricature of itself. But in fact, Vodou is a complex, fascinating religion. It's as sophisticated and as sacred as any other faith on earth.

Like Brazil's Candomblé and Santería in Cuba, Vodou is a mix of African and European religions. The slaves who came to Haiti brought their own ancestral gods with them, of course, and those from Angola brought their own tradition of Catholicism. Most masters, curiously enough, were really not interested in having slaves practice Catholicism, and indeed the Jesuit order was expelled in 1763 in part because their active work among the slaves made the planters suspicious. These

Africans held on to the old but also embraced the new. They fused new forms of belief from both religions. And out of these sources emerged Vodou—an unquestionably African religion with deep Catholic influences that can be traced to Africa, as John Thornton has shown in great detail, because the most common ethnicity in Haiti among the slaves was Congo, and they were Catholic already, as we have seen, before they were enslaved. French priests wanted nothing to do with catechizing the slaves; they spent all their time with the whites, so the proselytization of the African arrivers was in the hands of the Congos, as surprising as this seems.

Even many of Haiti's black leaders initially condemned Vodou's practice, of course, but they could never eradicate it. Today, much of the country is officially Catholic, but a majority of the populace are Vodou worshipers. And most Haitians actually practice both faiths at the same time, seeing no real conflict between them.

I wanted to learn more about this intriguing religion. So I got in touch with Vodou's highest priest—a priest is a *houngan*—who practices in the small village of Trou-du-Nord, outside of Port-au-Prince about an hour's drive. His name is Max Beauvoir, and he leads Haiti's most important Vodou shrine. I wanted to see Beauvoir and his devotees before attending a more spontaneous expression of Vodou ritual in the town of Trou-du-Nord. Every year, the town of Trou-du-Nord throws a big party following a church service at St. Jean Baptiste Church in honor of its patron saint, Saint James. Saint James (Major), as Linda Heywood and John Thornton have shown, was the patron saint of the Kingdom of Kongo, because he intervened miraculously in the battle between Afonso I and his brother, Mpanzu a Kitima, in 1509. Throughout the precolonial period, Saint James's day, July 25, was celebrated in Kongo as a national holiday. This day is recognized in Haiti as having Kongo roots (though it is celebrated on June 24, not July 25 as it is in Africa and most everywhere else). So I thought it would be interesting to compare the rituals at Beauvoir's temple with those three days later that the people practiced on the street, after a night of worship, drinking, and celebration.

I caught up with Beauvoir at his temple (called a *hounfour*) in Mariani, on the outskirts of Port-au-Prince. And I was fascinated to learn about his personal history. Beauvoir was a professional biochemist. He had trained at both City College in New York and the Sorbonne

Max Beauvoir and Vodou worshipers. (Minna Sedmakov)

in Paris! But he felt an undeniable calling to serve as a Vodou priest. Thirty years ago he became a *houngan* in Haiti. And he loves his life, he told me. He sees Vodou as all embracing—and he believes this openness is central to Haitian identity.

"Inclusiveness is the aim of Vodou," Beauvoir said, beaming, as we strolled across the grounds outside his *hounfour*. "When Vodou was constructed, the point was to include each African group. Senegal was part of it. Mali was part of it. Dahomey was part of it. Upper Nigeria was part of it. Southern Nigeria, with the Ibos, was part of it. The northern Congos, with Cameroon and Gabon, they were also part of it. So it was inclusive, not exclusive. And in fact, I think that was the basic strength of Vodou." Beauvoir was only part right about the origins of the slaves.

While it is true that slaves in some numbers came to Saint-Domingue from many parts of Africa, the majority came from just two regions. In the Dominican Republic, slaves arrived very early in the trade, mostly before 1600, and mostly from Senegambia, Upper Guinea (Sierra Leone), and, later, Angola. In other words, ethnic groups were often concentrated, varying by region. Indeed, this was true throughout Latin America: in Brazil, some 70 percent of the slaves came from

Angola. Mina, or the Fo-Aja-Yoruba region, was another major source of Brazilian slaves. Here in Haiti, just across the river from the Dominican Republic, slaves from different ethnicities and regions in Africa collaborated and fused their belief systems to create a new religion. But half the slaves in Saint-Domingue in the last thirty years of the trade, when Vodou was formed, shipped through the Kingdom of Kongo. Roughly another third were from Dahomey and its region. So actually the two nations accounted for 70 percent of its slaves. Slaves in the Dominican Republic made African cultural forms, too, including a religion called Gagá. But it didn't have the status or popularity of Vodou, just across the border. Everyone in Haiti whom I interviewed seemed to have a stake in embracing Vodou as particularly "Haitian," something key to their national identity. And I found that phenomenon quite intriguing, especially given the way that Vodou has often been demonized in the West but also traditionally in Haiti in previous generations, demonized as it was by the educated and ruling classes.

The slaves drew a lot of comfort from their common faith, Beauvoir told me. It also united them. In Vodou, they found common solace but also common cause—and together, they found the strength to fight their oppressors. Slowly, in fits and starts, they began to organize effectively against their French masters. They chose leaders and, eventually, they dreamed a common dream: to end slavery. And although not all black people joined their cause, and although there were tensions and fissures between the slaves and the free mulatto community, enough black people chose to fight for their freedom as a unified force. And they won.

I was full of questions for Beauvoir about the Haitian Revolution. I wanted to know how he thought his people had pulled it off. He laughed at me a bit, but I could also tell he is proud of his nation's history—and of this event in particular. He said the revolution had been planned in a place called Bois Caïman (in Creole, *Bwa Kayiman*)—the "Forest of the Alligators." He said a Vodou ceremony, led by a slave named Boukman, had launched the revolution there in the woods in 1791. And then he told me his daughter, Rachel, an anthropologist, was an expert about Bois Caïman and could tell me more about it. So I traveled to Cap Haïtien to meet her.

The journey required a brief flight and then a long drive. As I watched the fields and hills pass outside the car, I tried to imagine them through the eyes of eighteenth-century slaves, yearning for their freedom. I thought of how that first group of independence fighters must have felt, in their hearts, as they traveled to their rendezvous in Bois Caïman to plan their revolution, in the dead of night, against all odds.

I was beside myself by the time we arrived. I was just so excited to see the place. I hopped out of my car and started looking everywhere around Bois Caïman, like a crazy man. I don't know what I expected to see—monuments, flags, a giant museum? But all I saw was a humble village, spreading out around a large tree. And it was under that tree that the revolution was launched, through a Vodou ceremony, supposedly launched by Boukman's prayer (first set down by Haitian poet and politician Hérard Dumesle in 1824):

> The god who created the earth; who created the sun that gives us light. The god who holds up the ocean; who makes the thunder roar. Our God who has ears to hear. You who are hidden in the clouds; who watch us from where you are. You see all that the whites had made us suffer. The white man's god asks him to commit crimes. But the god within us wants to do good. Our god, who is so good, so just, He orders us to revenge our wrongs. It's He who will direct our arms and bring us the victory. It's He who will assist us. We all should throw away the image of the white men's god who is so pitiless. Listen to the voice for liberty that speaks in all our hearts.

As I recalled Boukman's words, I realized there wasn't so much as a tiny plaque on or near the tree marking the spot where the Haitian Revolution began. But people knew the power of this place: many evangelical Christians had attempted, even recently, to have the tree cut down, as a symbol of devil worship. They even constructed a church nearby, as a protest and as a way to ward off evil, and have tried to poison the tree!

Rachel Beauvoir met me in the center of Bois Caïman. She is a warm, friendly scholar with a beautiful smile who reminded me of her father. She is an anthropologist, I learned, and she's spent her career researching the Haitian Revolution, secret societies in Haiti (in a book written in Creole and published in Cuba), and the history of the now destroyed Port-au-Prince cathedral. I was fascinated to hear about her process of researching the origins of the revolution. There were few written records kept about what happened in Bois Caïman. But the

Henri Christophe, a leader in the Haitian Revolution, winning in-
dependence from France for Haiti in 1804, was made president of
Haiti in 1807 and in March 1811 was proclaimed Henri I, King of
Haiti. (Illustrated London News Ltd./Mary Evans Picture Library)

Haitians have a rich oral tradition—and for generations, the people in
the area passed down the story of the revolution. Rachel has collected
those narratives, dissected them, cross-referenced them, and put the entire story together. She knows, she said, what happened in these woods,
two hundred years ago at midnight on August 14, 1791, the night the
revolution was born.

"August 14 is the day of the Mother of the Earth, and that's why
they chose this day," she began, gesturing to the forest. "And they got
together in a Vodou ceremony. And everyone, together, said, 'It's over.
Slavery is over.' They sacrificed an animal, a black pig, and during the
sacrifice, everyone touched the pig. This was the sacred 'Oomph!' From
then on, above everything else, liberty was most important."

The ceremony culminated with a call to revolution—and within two weeks, slaves had taken control of the entire Northern Province of Haiti, destroying thousands of plantations and killing slave owners by the hundreds. French forces soon captured and executed the priest Boukman, but the uprising he inspired could not be stopped.

I asked Rachel to tell me more about the role of Vodou in the revolution.

"Vodou represented the cement," she replied, urgently. "You had all those slaves coming from so many different areas on the African continent. Haiti was like a microcosm of Africa. And the glue was Vodou, making sense of it all and making everyone make sense to everyone else. And then they had Creole, which became the national language. So they had a religion and they had a language together. This gave the slaves the unity that was necessary to create the most powerful slave revolution in the New World."

She wasn't kidding. The Haitian Revolution was an extraordinary event, by any measure. In the eighteenth century, France was among the strongest nations on earth. The idea that a bunch of slaves on a small Caribbean island could overpower French forces and put an end to slavery, on their own terms, was unimaginable. But the revolutionaries were savvy. Their leaders took inspiration—and key lessons— from both the American Revolution and the French Revolution and, of course, from the Kongo speech of Boukman's at Bois Caïman:

Eh!, Eh!, Bomba, hen, hen
Canga ba fiote
Canga moun de le
Canga doki la
Canga le

John Thornton's translation follows:

Hey, hey, Mbomba [the name of the rainbow deity], hey, hey
Tie up/restrain/save the Blacks
Tie up/restrain/save the white man
Tie up/restrain/save [in the religious sense] that witch/sorcerer
Tie up/restrain him/save him

The progress of the war was complicated. It was led by men who did not always share the same allies or ambitions. The most remarkable of these leaders was Toussaint Louverture. He was born a slave on a Haitian plantation, gained his freedom at the age of thirty-three, and although completely lacking military experience, proved a genius on the battlefield, leading guerrilla troops against a host of European armies. Toussaint played a central role in the uprising of 1791, and by 1793, he was fighting on the side of the Spanish, who had entered the conflict, seeing an opportunity to weaken the French. Toussaint was quickly promoted to "Général d'Armée du Roi d'Espagne" and helped precipitate the abolition of slavery in Haiti. But a year later, following the ratification of this decision by the French and its expansion to the entire French Empire, Toussaint switched sides in the European war that was overwhelming his country, and in July 1795, he was appointed brigadier general of the French Republic by a decree of the National Convention. That was the same year that Spain ceded to France the ownership of the Spanish part of Hispaniola in the Treaty of Basle. In 1797, he was promoted again, to major general, serving effectively as a commander in chief against Spain's armies and establishing himself politically as the leader of the former slaves in the north.

In the "War of the Knives" (Guerre des Couteaux), fought between 1797 and 1799, Toussaint defeated his rival, André Rigaud, the leader of the free mulattoes in the south of Saint-Domingue. In May 1801, the Central Assembly of Saint-Domingue ratified a constitution for the colony, and Saint-Domingue became an autonomous political regime within the French Empire (in other words, it remained a French colony). Toussaint was appointed governor for life. That constitution reaffirmed the abolition of slavery, even if plantation wage labor persisted. Toussaint marched into Santo Domingo to annex it and to unify the two parts of the island, thereby enforcing the terms of the Treaty of Basle. He was acting, at that time, under the authority vested in him by the French state.

So, following the uprising in 1791, the abolition of slavery in 1793, the ratification of this decision by the French in 1794, its expansion to the entire French Empire, and then the establishment of Haiti as a semi-independent country, black slaves were free—in no small part due to Toussaint's singular skills as a military strategist. It was Napoleon's

Toussaint Louverture, by François Seraphim Delpech, 1838.
Louverture (1743–1803) was a Haitian revolutionary and
statesman. (Mansell/Time Life Pictures/Getty)

reversal of emancipation in 1802 that set off the war for independence
in Haiti.

But before we discuss that noble effort, it is important to consider Toussaint's own complex attitudes about slavery and labor. As
Carolyn E. Fick points out, Toussaint was not a radical reformer, to say
the least: "he maintained the large estates, invited the white owners to
return and take possession of their properties, leased out sequestered
plantations to his top generals and placed the workers under direct
military supervision. It would have to take outright coercion, to engage
the workers in plantation agriculture and to keep them from fleeing the

Haiti: A Drama of the Black Napoleon, by William Du Bois, with the New York cast, 1938. (Library of Congress)

large estates, most of these by now farmed out to high-ranking army officers or run by the former white masters." Indeed, Toussaint declared, "I never believed freedom to be license, or that men who have become free should be able to give themselves over to disorder and idleness: my formal intention is that workers remain bound to their respective plantations; that they receive one-quarter of the revenues; that they not be mistreated with impunity. But at the same time, I want them to work harder yet than they have ever worked before, and that they be subordinate and fulfill their duties correctly. I am resolved to punish severely he who strays." In a sense, one could say that Toussaint saw slavery as the enemy, and not France or the plantation economy: his wars certainly freed the slaves, but he also sought to cement the place of the black military officers in the country's elite, alongside the white planters. Above all, though, he sought to keep the former slaves in place as workers on the large plantations.

Toussaint, in other words, was determined to end the legal status of slavery, but he replaced it immediately with forced labor, including serfdom on the old estates, which he restored to their former owners. Realizing that Toussaint hated slavery but loved forced labor and the old-fashioned way of making sugar is a bit like first realizing that George Washington owned slaves. It wasn't easy for Toussaint to cut off foreign revenue that came from selling export crops, and he claimed that his re-institution of the essence of slavery while denying its name was to buy weapons, which is probably true and makes a lot of sense. But it does make him less mythical. As John Thornton has shown, the real rebels against him were Kongos, like Macaya, who understood his complexity from the start. And, accordingly, it is no surprise that Haitians even today see Kongos as ugly, primitive Africans, and the word is used as an insult, because the Kongo slaves didn't and wouldn't compromise the way the mulattoes (who created the idea that the Kongos were primitive and collaborationist) and the elite of the slaves (Toussaint, after all, was an elite slave, not a field hand) were willing to compromise.

Unfortunately, emancipation in Haiti lasted only about a decade before Napoleon Bonaparte attempted to reinstate slavery in 1802. Toussaint and his compatriots were incensed. But after a brutal military struggle with France, lasting a few months, he retired and agreed to meet with French leaders to negotiate matters. The meeting, however, turned out to be a trap. He was arrested at his home and immediately shipped back to France, where he died in prison. Haitian blacks were enraged by this turn of events. They rallied to arms once again, refusing to be put back in bondage and determined to get rid of the French, for good. And a new leader emerged to take Toussaint's place. His name was Jean-Jacques Dessalines.

Rachel told me that to Haitians, Dessalines is an enormously inspiring figure. Like Louverture, he was a former slave and a brilliant general. He fought ferociously—so much so that they called him the Tiger. And his army gave the French an old-fashioned thrashing at a place called Vertières, just outside Cap Haïtien. This was the decisive

Coronation of Jean-Jacques Dessalines as emperor of Haiti.
(New York Public Library)

battle in the struggle, and when it was over, Dessalines delivered a stirring, impassioned speech, on January 1, 1804. He declared Haiti an independent black nation.

Rachel had a copy of Dessalines's incredible speech with her. And
in the center of Bois Caïman, the place where it all began, we stood
closely together, reading: "Let them tremble when they approach our
coast, if not from the memory of those cruelties they perpetrated here,
then from the terrible resolution that we will have made to put to death
anyone born French whose profane foot soils the land of liberty." These
words were somewhere startling to me, even a bit scary. But as Rachel
explained, they were understandable. The French had agreed to abolish

slavery in Haiti—and then gone back on their word. They lied to the man they saw as most directly responsible for the abolition of slavery, they captured him, and then they threw him in prison back in France, to die a slow and agonizing death. There were many reasons to believe the French might try, once again, to take control of the island. So Dessalines was defiant.

Dessalines's fears unfortunately got the better of him. In a crude attempt to eliminate any lingering threats to his new republic, Dessalines ordered attacks on French planters—and a massacre ensued. Not all whites on the island were targeted, Rachel stressed. Some French colonists, along with Americans, were left alone. French whites who had sided with the blacks during the war, Polish deserters, and a few others were spared. But the bloodshed sent shockwaves across the world. Just two years later, Dessalines was assassinated. His killers were some of the same generals who had fought side by side with him to drive the French out of Haiti. Even some of his own supporters thought he had gone too far.

Dessalines's successor was a man named Henri Christophe. A former slave, he had served as Dessalines's right hand during the fight for independence. In 1811, after serving as president, he declared himself the king of Haiti. And of course, he did next what all kings do—he erected a palace in his own honor. In the countryside, outside of Cap Haïtien, Christophe built the incredible Sans Souci—French for "without worries"—modeled after the summer palace that Frederick the Great, the king of Prussia, built in Potsdam, near Berlin.

In "The Three Faces of San Souci," a fascinating chapter of Michel-Rolph Trouillot's *Silencing the Past*, Trouillot suggests that Christophe built Sans Souci just a few yards away from the spot where he killed a colonel in the revolutionary army, a man born in the Congo named Sans Souci, who fought against both Christophe and Dessalines. In this interpretation, Christophe, by now a king, named his palace after his enemy in order to absorb his spirit, imitating the myth of origins of the Fon people of Dahomey. Trouillot points out that not only did Christophe admire and praise Dahomeans as great warriors but many Dahomeans served in his elite cadet corps. Either way, Sans Souci is an astonishing structure to encounter in the north of Haiti. Rachel described it to me so vividly that I had to visit it. Though a devastating earthquake destroyed much of it in 1843, it remains a grand, imposing,

The author at Sans Souci, Henri Christophe's palace. (Minna Sedmakov)

gorgeous structure, something right out of a fairy tale—incongruously constructed in Haiti in the nineteenth century, for Haiti's first king.

But life for Christophe was hardly the stuff of fantasy. This man had immense responsibility on his shoulders. He needed to lead Haiti as it joined the community of nations, yet the rest of the world wasn't interested in welcoming Haiti. In fact, it seemed like Haiti's fight to exist as an independent state had just begun. Virtually the entire Western world banded together to choke the new republic in its crib. Even as France, England, and the United States squabbled among themselves, they stood united against Haiti. They refused to acknowledge it as a legitimate nation. The very idea of Haiti was too much of a threat, Rachel told me. They couldn't let Haiti's story inspire other blacks in the Caribbean, in Latin America, and especially in the southern United States, to fight for freedom from slavery. But of course, that's exactly what the example of the revolution did. Even though it was a sign of trouble with the revolution that Christophe decided to crown himself king and start building a palace, the fact remained that Haiti had overthrown its slavemasters.

Christophe knew it was only a matter of time before his enemies

sent armies to attack Haiti. So he embarked on a second ambitious un-
dertaking—just as he built his fantasy palace, more pragmatically, he
decided to build an enormous fortress that could withstand any assault.
It was to be called the Citadel. It sits on a three-thousand-foot mountain peak near Cap Haïtien, and it took twenty thousand men to build
it. To this day, it's still the largest fortress anywhere in the entire Western Hemisphere.

That night, I traveled back to Cap Haïtien, thoroughly exhausted
yet captivated by Haiti and its story. It was as remarkable as I'd imagined. At least among the people I had interviewed, there seemed to
be very little rejection of black roots for the sake of a hybrid "brown"
pride. Despite a long history of troubled relations between the mulatto
elite and the black masses, I hadn't seen any crazy charts or heard about
catalogues of words employed in everyday conversation categorizing
and ranking dozens of shades of blackness today, as I had encountered
elsewhere in my journey. And modern-day Haitians weren't trying to
whiten their past. I arrived at my hotel astonished at all the history I
had seen that day. And very soon, I fell asleep with images of a giant
fortress in my head, clearly visible to ships sailing toward Haiti. Silhou-
etted against the sky, it must have terrified Haiti's enemies, I thought
drowsily. This was a nation that knew how to fight and how to protect
itself—and it was ready to keep fighting to defend its principles.

In the morning, I revisited my notes on the Citadel. It had recently
undergone some renovation, and I knew there had to be a leading Haitian preservationist on the project. There was—and it was the Howard
University–educated architect Patrick Delatour, who happened to be
the minister of tourism. I was able to track him down, and we arranged
a time to meet at the Citadel. I wanted to learn all about the fort—both
structurally and historically. Delatour would make the perfect guide.

I traveled to the Citadel by car, and I'm not sure how to describe
seeing it for the first time. Knowing you're going to visit the biggest fortress in your hemisphere is one thing, but seeing it with your own eyes
is another. And recalling, always, that it was built by black men to defend a black nation is another still.

I first glimpsed it between trees, far off in the distance. It seemed
huge, even from afar, and as we drew closer, it just got larger and larger
and larger. In the end, it loomed over me, casting an enormous shadow.
I could scarcely believe this monumental edifice was built with simple

tools and human labor. The fact that it still stands is a testament to its engineering. But I sensed something greater when I looked at the Citadel. It was the size of Haiti's ambitions for itself. It was as outsized as the hopes of the Western Hemisphere's first black nation.

I met up with Delatour on the grounds. He is a tall, solid man. And at first, his demeanor came across as a bit academic. But I soon came to understand that this was just an expression of his seriousness. He treats the history of Haiti and its architecture with great respect. And I appreciated his sincerity and his diligence as he showed me around. As he realized that I appreciated his admiration for this edifice, our conversation became quite warm and relaxed.

We climbed to the very top of the Citadel. The view—Haiti's mountains all around, in the distance the ocean—was sublime. I learned that we were quite close to the very spot Columbus first landed on this part of the island. On that ground, Delatour explained, the Haitians built their defenses to stop other Europeans from landing on their shores.

"Take a look on top of the mountain, right there," he instructed, pointing along the ridge. "There is another fort and, next to it, another fort."

I couldn't believe the amount of strategic planning that had gone into thinking through how to counter a military invasion, in fear of which the early Haitian leaders lived for decades.

"They could sustain a guerrilla war against any invading force," he said.

I replied with all honesty, "I had no idea it would be this awe inspiring."

I asked who built the Citadel. Architecturally, it was a work of pure genius. Were its makers black? Some of them were, he said. Engineers and architects of both Haitian descent and French descent worked together. Color lines didn't matter among those who believed in an independent Haiti.

The Citadel was beyond impressive. But was all the time, effort, and money needed to build this colossus really necessary? I asked Delatour what Christophe was so afraid of.

"The return of the French," Delatour answered simply, "and going back into slavery. As soon as France made peace with England, and as soon as it made peace with the rest of the European powers, Christophe knew France could consider coming back to attack Haiti. And the pain of slavery was terrible for Haitians. Whenever you're making an analysis of Haiti or the Haitian people, you must always come back to it. Many Haitians wrote they would rather die than go back into slavery."

With the Citadel standing to defend them, Haitians were at a crucial juncture in their history. And they made a decision that still has ramifications today. They decided to reject every vestige of slavery. They refused to work on sugar plantations, even to maintain the properties for some future use. All they were trying to do was to leave a painful past behind, Delatour explained. But in the process, they destroyed their greatest economic asset. As Adam Rothman points out, in 1789, Haiti was the leading producer of sugar in the world, exporting almost fifty million pounds of white sugar and more than ninety million pounds of raw sugar (roughly 30 percent of the world's sugar exports). But by 1801, the country's exports had fallen to less than twenty thousand pounds of white sugar and less than twenty million pounds of raw sugar.

"Haiti was the most profitable colony in the history of colonization," I said. "If they had just maintained the plantation system, Haiti would have been rich — it would have become one of the world's richest economies."

Delatour nodded. It was a complicated fact but nonetheless a tragic one. "They systematically destroyed all the means of production," he said ruefully. "Anything that was associated with slavery was destroyed. Ultimately, they would destroy the whole village system, the road system, along with the investments for sugar-plantation machinery and even coffee. Basically, their lives became based solely on the notion of individual survival, family survival."

I'd come here to find Haiti's soul, I remembered. And it seemed that, at times, Haiti itself had lost track of it. I was coming to understand that Haiti's first years of true independence were marred by terrible mistakes. But in that moment, I took Delatour's advice, and I reminded myself of the pain of slavery. Only truly inhuman circumstances could have compelled Haitians to abandon their country's best chances for success, which would have been to maintain their level of sugar production, soon to be assumed by Cuba. In their passion for freedom, in their urge to leave the slave past behind, Delatour argued, they inadvertently brought economic destruction on themselves, by not developing alternative economic options.

Jean-Pierre Boyer, president of Haiti, 1822–1843. (New York Public Library)

"They helped do the work of their enemies," Delatour said. And he was right. No one ever had the nerve to attack the Citadel. But Europe and the United States found other ways to keep Haiti at the bottom of the global food chain. They continued to deny its sovereignty. They denigrated Haitian people. And they spoke out, actively, against the very idea of blacks governing themselves. Thomas Jefferson, then the US president, famously referred to Toussaint Louverture and his followers as "cannibals of the terrible republic." One might argue, I realized as Delatour spoke, that the Dominicans' anti-Haitianism was, in part, a result of this unfortunate pattern of Western vilification of Haiti, as Silvio Torres-Saillant insists.

Trade between Haiti and the world did continue, Delatour noted, including the United States. But the relationships were inherently unequal. The other nations exploited Haiti, refusing to treat it fairly—and desperate Haitians had no choice but to take whatever paltry deals they could get. France was particularly hard on its former colony. It threatened a blockade of Haiti's ports if the country did not pay reparations to its former plantation owners. The budding nation had no military allies—and therefore no choice. It paid France more than one billion dollars between 1825 and 1947 in exchange for formal recognition of its status as an independent state—and guarantees that it would not be invaded, at least immediately. The United States finally acknowledged Haiti's independence in 1862, during the Civil War, Delatour noted—but only because President Lincoln hoped to send some of the freed slaves there.

The country struggled to pay its debts, but it did succeed for a time, laudably, at providing the highest standard of living for blacks anywhere in the New World. Had it not been for the reparations France demanded, Haiti might have stabilized and found prosperity. But by 1914, 67 percent of its budget was devoted to the payment of foreign debt. One form of slavery, I thought to myself, had simply replaced another. And the situation soon worsened. On July 28, 1915, US military forces landed in Port-au-Prince and occupied the country. (A year later, they also occupied the Dominican Republic.) The Americans claimed that they needed to bring stability to Hispaniola. They wanted to make sure Haiti paid its remaining debts. But, as we saw in the Dominican Republic, the United States also wanted to use the island to produce sugar—filling the supply gap left by a war-torn Europe. Haiti's sovereignty just wasn't on their minds. It didn't make me happy to learn this, but I can't say I was surprised. US presidents used to call the Caribbean their "backyard." They felt entitled to do whatever they liked with it.

During the nineteen-year occupation, Delatour explained, the United States appropriated Haitian land. It exercised veto power over the government's decisions. It even rewrote the country's constitution, making it legal for whites from other countries to own land in Haiti. Thousands of Haitians had to flee to the Dominican Republic to find work, many of them accepting terribly low wages to work on plantations there, in exile. Haitians tried to mount a rebellion. But it was put down with brutal force by the occupying US military. The United States sent its most racist troops to Haiti, I learned—Marines from the South who thought of blacks as less than human. This reopened many of Haiti's colonial wounds. Politically, socially, economically, the country was set back again, by decades.

This nation had technically been independent since 1804. But foreign powers never even gave it a chance to flourish, free from their interference. In fact, all they did was punish, sabotage, and abuse Haiti. And corrupt leaders in Haiti, hungry for power, did as much as they could to help the foreigners by repressing their own people and stifling the growth of democratic institutions and free enterprise.

Delatour reached out to me sympathetically, patting me on the back with some formality, but also with warmth. Not all of Haiti's problems were caused by the outside world, he explained. During the Haitian Revolution, the country chose great leaders. But since, it has suffered under some terribly corrupt and brutal ones. None was worse, he told me, than François "Papa Doc" Duvalier.

Duvalier served as Haiti's president from 1957 until his death in 1971. He was a true despot. He had his own private militia, called the Tonton Macoutes, which terrorized ordinary Haitians. He stole millions of dollars in international aid. And oddly enough, he announced publicly that he felt dictators didn't deserve their poor reputation. Delatour shared a transcript with me from one of Duvalier's speeches, and this is what he said: "To have peace and stability, you should have a strong man in every country. Not a dictator, but a strong man. What you call democracy in your own country another country can call a dictatorship."

In spite of Duvalier's corruption and cruelty, the United States supported his presidency—just as it supported General Trujillo in the Dominican Republic. Why? Because Duvalier and Trujillo both opposed nearby Cuba's Communist regime. Any leader who stood with the United States against Communists, it seemed, could count on US backing, regardless of how brutally he treated his own people.

As we drove back toward my hotel in Cap Haïtien, I got on my cell phone. I had been given a contact in Haiti, a journalist named Bernard Diederich, who had covered a great deal of the Duvalier presidency. He recommended that we meet up at Fort Dimanche, outside Port-au-Prince. The fort was central to understanding Duvalier, he said, because the president had used the complex as a prison. The conditions there spoke volumes about his character.

Diederich and I arrived at the crumbling structure—as damaged by time and neglect as much as by the recent earthquake—surrounded by the worst slum in all of Port-au-Prince. And together, we looked at the walls and stones that made up Fort Dimanche. The day was extremely warm, the stench of open sewers nauseating. But I felt a cold chill pass through me. Diederich shot me a look—he felt it too. This was deeply troubled ground, the site of terrible evils.

"This was an old army headquarters," he told me. "It was the worst place to be during Duvalier's reign. He just put people in there, and they died. Tuberculosis was the first thing to strike them, and then dysentery. They gradually got worse and worse and died. Some of them basically wanted to be put on death row."

Only one prisoner, he told me, ever escaped. Inmates were tortured, brutalized. To be Duvalier's enemy was the stuff of nightmares. But this brutal dictator did more than torment his enemies and terrorize his people. His practices caused Haiti's best and brightest to flee their country—denying the country their talents. The nation pays the price for this exodus to this day.

"He allowed the country's best to leave the country," Diederich lamented. "And we never really survived this, because we lost all the best teachers, all the best writers. He had kicked them out."

We slowly walked away from Fort Dimanche together. Like Port-au-Prince, it's surrounded by poverty. A slum surrounds it in all directions. Some ten thousand people live in its shadow, I learned. But these Haitians steer clear of the fort. The history is too grim and the memories still too fresh.

Diederich left me then, standing at the side of the road. From hardship to hardship, I thought. From cruel slavery to cruel imprisonment. From one bondage to another, and always, for Haiti, a life of poverty. This country has come full circle, but its circle was made of suffering. These thoughts crowded my mind and saddened me, as I climbed into my car once more.

I ended my journey where I began—in the center of Port-au-Prince. I drove past the tent cities, past the crowds of poor black people. I realized with a start that as much as I'd come to Latin America to find its blackness, this was a sight my eyes grew weary of seeing. The Haiti I wanted to see was the Haiti of the future—the nation that recovered from this earthquake, from its legacy of slavery and its decades under corrupt rule.

The Haiti I'd seen was many things. It was small, it was poor. It was cast out by the Western world for being free and black—and it's still paying the price for that exclusion. But Haiti is also strong as iron. Its people are extraordinarily resilient. And they're proud of being black—

which sets them apart from many of the other people I'd visited in Latin America.

This is the tiny nation that defied the French Empire. These are the descendants of those who founded the first black nation in the Americas. But let's not paper over the historical significance of their own internal forms of intercolor tension and intraracial color prejudice—of the mulatto elite against darker Haitians, which seems to have abated among this generation of Haitians. It is a troubled part of their past. Today, however, if anyone can turn Haiti's tragic story into triumph, it is the Haitian people. They have faced greater odds in their history. They have the resilience and courage to rebuild their society and to construct more prosperous lives. And perhaps now, after all these years, the world will welcome this great black republic as a full and equal partner in the community of nations. If not now . . . when?

6

Cuba

The Next Cuban Revolution

AS AN AMERICAN, it's difficult to think of Cuba beyond Fidel Castro's revolution of 1959, Castro's embrace of Communism two years later, the Bay of Pigs, the row over Elian González, and a fifty-year-old dictatorship just ninety miles from Miami. But these recent events obscure the shared history between the United States and our closest Caribbean neighbor, dating back centuries. And nowhere is this connection deeper than in race relations.

Between 1651 and 1866, Cuba received about 779,000 slaves from Africa—329,000 more than the total number that arrived in the United States—and most of these arrived after 1801 and the Haitian Revolution, after Haiti's sugar economy collapsed. Cuba replaced Haiti as the world's leading producer of sugar. I wanted to know what happened to these Africans and what their descendants experienced. According to the last census, in 2002, 65 percent of Cubans are white, 25 percent are black, and 10 percent are mulattoes. But some scholars estimate that at least 65 percent of the Cuban people are "black" as defined in the United States. I knew that Afro-Cubans shaped the country's music, cuisine, and way of life, but does Cuba recognize their contributions today? Castro famously announced that his revolution put an end to racism. He promised opportunity for all. But did the revolution deliver? I couldn't wait to find out.

I began by calling Professor María del Carmen Barcia, who's made a career studying slavery in Cuba. She agreed to meet me at the ruins of a slave plantation called Angerona in the Artemisa province. On my drive out of Havana, which had lived up to its reputation as elegantly shabby and in post-revolutionary disrepair, I was struck again at the natural beauty of the Caribbean islands—how verdant and lush everything is, how inviting is the sea, how compelling are its beaches and seemingly endless sunshine and blue skies. For a place that has suffered so much political and economic turmoil, Cuba's natural beauty must have looked like paradise to its early settlers. It is easy to see why so many people have for so very long been willing to risk their lives to live here, on their own terms. There is something irresistibly charming and sensual about this island, even after half a century of a Communist regime.

I arrived to find Carmen Barcia waiting cheerfully, shielding her eyes from the sun with her hand. We began to stroll around the richly verdant property together, battling mosquitoes, discussing the history of the Angerona plantation. Though Columbus landed in 1492, Cuba's economy didn't take off until the Haitian Revolution destroyed Haiti's booming sugar trade. Seeing an opportunity, the Spanish and the white creole elite imported hundreds of thousands of slaves into Cuba to push sugar production into high gear. By the 1820s, Cuba was the biggest sugar exporter in the world and the largest slave economy in the Western Hemisphere. What's more, slavery didn't just help Cuba produce sugar; it defined Cuba itself—the country held on to its slave system until 1886, twenty-one years after the United States abolished its pernicious institution and just two years before Brazil finally abolished its.

Carmen Barcia told me that Angerona had once been one of Cuba's most important plantations. It housed over four hundred slaves, who first produced coffee and then sugar. Slave labor was so critical to the economy, she explained, that masters housed their slaves in mixed quarters—keeping men and women together—to encourage reproduction. By the middle of the nineteenth century, Afro-Cubans and mixed-race people outnumbered whites on the island. This ratio might have been no cause for concern, Carmen Barcia noted. But whites on the island were anxious after Haiti's 1791 slave revolt. When Haitian slaves threw off their chains and announced Haiti's independence in 1804, news reached Cuba quickly. And the white masters got very nervous.

"It fueled the fear of the blacks," Carmen Barcia told me, "the fear that another revolution like the one in Haiti could happen here. So two paths were taken. On the one hand, concessions were made to the slaves regarding their living conditions, while on the other hand, repression and controls increased. This fear was real."

She showed me the remains of a watchtower on the grounds of the plantation and explained that after the Haitian Revolution, many Cubans monitored their slaves around the clock, as if they were running

a prison. Some concern was justified, she said, because there were oc-
casional uprisings. But, as Carmen Barcia explained it, the white elites
in Cuba also worked to enflame this fear. They used it to convince
whites to band together—and to stay loyal to the Spanish Crown. For
a long time, this cynical tactic worked. By 1825, every Spanish colony
in Latin America had become independent except for two: Puerto Rico
and Cuba.

I asked Carmen Barcia about day-to-day life on plantations like
Angerona. Were slaves worked to death in Cuba, the way they were in
Brazil?

"It wasn't as extreme," she said, shaking her head. "Of course, some
owners were very cruel. But slaves were expensive. So generally, masters made an effort to keep them alive and fit for labor."

Hardly a desirable destiny, I thought, but better than dying of ex-
haustion and abuse. "So what happened to all those slaves?" I asked.
"What happened to their descendants? Far more Africans came here as
came to America? How come there aren't more black people here than
in the United States?"

"The descendants of the slaves in Cuba are here!" she announced,
opening her arms wide enough to embrace the entire island. "Slavery is
ever present, in both a positive and negative way. Great Cuban athletes,
famous painters and musicians—many of whom are black or mixed
race—bear the surnames of the slave owners that owned their great-
grandparents. But many black people still live in poverty."

"When slavery was abolished in 1886, the labor market was flooded
with over two hundred thousand men," she continued. "They were illiterate and had no profession. And so they were destined to perform the
most menial and poorly paid jobs. That had a long-term effect that can
still be felt today. Not all poor people are black, but more black people
are poor, and that is a consequence of slavery."

I wanted to learn more about Cuba's transition out of slavery. So I
thanked Carmen Barcia and began a long journey—traveling six hundred miles southeast from Havana toward Oriente province, the birthplace of several Cuban revolutions. Oriente has a major Haitian influence, historically, because of its location. There, on October 10, 1868,
a sugar-mill owner named Carlos Manuel de Céspedes called all his
slaves together for a mysterious meeting and announced that he intended to free Cuba from Spain by force. He told his slaves that they

were his army—and he freed them on the spot. The news must have been a shock, and many of the slaves did not initially trust Céspedes, but they fought with him, launching a conflict that grew and grew, eventually becoming what is now known as the Ten Years' War.

This was the first significant effort to overthrow Spanish rule in Cuba, and one of its chief aims was to abolish slavery. This wasn't as noble as it sounds. The leaders of the revolt were primarily white Cuban landowners and merchants, and their motivations were complex. To achieve independence, they needed soldiers, and they desperately wanted to weaken Spain's economic power. Their talk of abolition accomplished both these things by simultaneously depleting plantations and filling their armies. So their agenda was not purely humanitarian. Nonetheless, they made promises to free the slaves, and they set in motion a chain of events that accomplished that goal. Though their rebellion failed, it sowed the seeds of what eventually became Cuban independence, and it had, ultimately, a tremendous impact on relations between the country's African and Spanish populations.

When I arrived in Oriente province, I went to the town of Santiago de Cuba, and the first thing I saw was a bust of Céspedes in the town square. He is a fascinating man, but I wasn't here to investigate his story. I was interested in the life of one of his successors. Céspedes was deposed as president of the republic in 1873, and Spanish troops killed him in February 1874, in a mountain refuge, four years before the end of the war he launched and the defeat of his friends and allies. (The new government refused to allow him to go into exile.) Like so many others who fought for Cuba's independence and freedom, he died before he could see his country free from Spain. But a persistent band of Cuban rebels didn't give up. After a second attempt to throw off the colonial yoke of Spain, in the "Little War" between 1879 and 1880, they renewed the fight, starting another war in 1895—and a new hero, Antonio Maceo, emerged. Many of the soldiers fighting for independence were black, and so were a few of their leaders. Maceo was of mixed race, the child of Marcos Maceo, a free mulatto, and an Afro-Cuban woman, and he became a national treasure.

I was immediately fascinated by Maceo. I wanted to know how a black man was able to rise to such power. Just looking around Santiago, I felt I could see some clues. Santiago is the blackest part of the island. It struck me that this place could be analogous to Brazil's Bahia (though

José Antonio Maceo, 1845–1896. (Library of Congress)

J. Lorand Matory feels that the "Black Rome" of Afro-Cuban religion is found in Havana and Matanzas). I could feel Africa's presence here. I could smell African dishes and see the customs being practiced in the streets. A great Afro-Cuban walked from these streets into national prominence, and he is venerated here for his role in gaining Cuba its freedom.

I made a pilgrimage to Maceo's monument, located at the entrance to Santiago in Antonio Maceo Revolution Square. It's quite different from Céspedes's monument. For one, it's massive—the tallest statue anywhere in Cuba. The somewhat abstract sculpture presents Maceo on horseback, gesturing to rally the troops behind him. The horse is up on its hind legs, signifying that Maceo died in battle. It's a stirring work of art, even if it is squarely in the genre of monuments to war heroes.

But maybe I liked it so much because Maceo was a black man, and we have nothing even remotely approaching it in grandeur in the United States celebrating the achievements and courage of an individual African American military woman or man.

I then traveled back to Havana to meet with Ada Ferrer, a historian at New York University and an authority on Cuba's wars for independence. She was able to tell me much more about Maceo, launching enthusiastically into his story. "Antonio Maceo joined the Ten Years' War in 1868, as a common soldier," she said. "He was promoted within weeks, maybe even within days, and rose to the rank of general. But there was always anxiety about his rise to military power because he was a man of color. He was accused of wanting to create another Haiti. He defended himself very eloquently. He said, 'Yes, I am a man of color, and I don't think I am any less than anyone else.'"

Maceo, I learned, was promoted to the rank of major general in 1878, when he was thirty-two years old, and was so successful in battle that he came to be known as the "Bronze Titan." I told Ferrer that I was astonished to learn that Cuba had black generals as early as the 1870s. Nothing like that could have ever happened in the United States at the time. It was about seventy years later before we had our first black general, Brigadier General Benjamin O. Davis, who was promoted to that rank in October 1940. But Cuba had black generals in the nineteenth century.

"But it wasn't easy," Ferrer responded, nodding. "Everyone in Cuba wasn't anti-racism or antislavery. But Maceo emerged as part of the war itself, the greater struggle for independence. He ascended in that context. And he truly became a hero for all of Cuba. People knew him far and wide. In Havana, young men hung out at coffee shops eager to meet him and shake his hand."

"As a black man, I find that almost unbelievable," I stammered in response. I remembered Maceo's massive statue. I listened as Ferrer told me about the museum the Cuban government built in Maceo's house— a museum that celebrates his African ancestry. I learned that he married a mulatto woman in Cuba and fathered a son with a Jamaican woman —a son who would grow up to be educated at Ithaca College and Cornell. I couldn't stop myself from being amazed. Here was a mixed-raced man, just like Frederick Douglass, I thought. He died just a year after Frederick Douglass died. But this black man's accomplishments were treated with so much more respect than even those of Douglass are in the United States.

Ferrer told me that Spain, unsurprisingly, used Maceo's blackness to stir up more fear among Cuban whites. The Crown told colonists that if Maceo drove Spain out of Cuba, Afro-Cubans would take over and create a black-dominant society—the way the Haitians did. Many whites bought the story, spurred on in their fear by the fact that about 60 percent of the revolutionary army was black. But the father of the revolution rose to Maceo's defense: the poet and journalist José Julián Martí y Pérez. According to Ferrer, Martí became an active champion of Maceo, repeatedly insisting that Maceo wanted Cuba free for all Cubans. In fact, they even plotted strategy by meeting in New York, following the end of the Little War.

Together, Maceo and Martí argued that Cubans had a right to their own culture, one that they'd created and should share together—whether they were black, brown, or white. Spain was the enemy, they said, and racism was not the answer. As leaders, they were generations ahead of their time. And they eloquently called Spain's bluff.

"They reminded everyone that slaves fought together with white men," said Ferrer, "that they died together, their souls rose up to heaven together. They said, 'The only people talking about race wars are the Spanish, who are trying to divide us.' And so, out of the war, they created a vision of a nationality that transcended race. They made racism an infraction—not against an individual but against the nation. That they said it didn't make it real, but saying it—and casting it as an ethical pillar of the nation—was significant and powerful."

Here was another society announcing that it could be beyond racism, I thought. It was hard not to be moved by hearing this common cry again.

The stories of Maceo and Martí have a complex ending. By 1896, they were dead, both killed in battle. For almost two years, the outcome of the revolution was uncertain. Then, in January 1898, the United States government decided to step in and protect its own interests. This was the era of the emergence of expansionist imperialism in US foreign policy, so some forces advocated annexing Cuba, while others wanted an independent Cuba to eliminate European influence from the region. At about 10:00 a.m. on January 25, 1898, the battleship USS *Maine* arrived in Havana, claiming it was needed to guarantee the safety of US citizens living in Cuba. Historians widely believe that the government had other aims as well—and that the battleship was at least partially intended as a show of force to intimidate the Spanish into negotiating with the rebels. Regardless of its purpose, the incident ended tragically, when the warship mysteriously exploded and sank in Havana Harbor on February 12, killing 268 sailors. No one ever found out what destroyed the *Maine* (it remains a great mystery even today), but the United States blamed the Spanish, and in April 1898, US forces formed an alliance of convenience with Cuba's rebels, which effectively marginalized them and launched what is now called the Spanish-American War (in Cuba, it is properly called the Cuban-Spanish-American War). Within ten weeks, Cuba was free from Spanish rule. US intervention interrupted the victory of the Cuban troops over Spain, enabling it to claim the victory for itself. The United States played the role of spoiler. The Cubans would have defeated Spain on their own.

Cubans rejoiced as one: black, white, rich, and poor. But Cuban forces, many of them fighting for equality among Cubans, were in for a surprise. When the Americans swarmed into Cuba to "stabilize" the country, they were shocked to find blacks and whites fighting in mixed units. Back in the United States, it was the racist era of Jim Crow. So the Americans began reordering and resegregating Cuban society, vowing to leave only when the budding new nation was "capable of self-rule."

"In some sense," Ferrer said, "in that moment, the Cuban definition of civilization, of capacity for self-rule, came to be defined as white."

"Are you saying that the difference in the history of race relations in Cuba was determined by the American occupation?" I asked, irritated. "Did the four months of the Spanish-American War really reverse this potential for an interracial democracy, the first interracial democracy in the free world?"

"That's partly true," Ferrer explained, furrowing her brow as she tried to think of the best way to explain. "The tension over race was already there. You had Martí killed, you had Maceo killed—this weakened the antiracist position. And then at the same time, you had the US come in. It gave the advantage to forces that were already there, though it didn't bring them in. A lot of the black officers already saw their ascent blocked as the end of the war neared. And as the Americans came in, their ascendance was blocked even further. There were black leaders who protested, but the white Cubans always responded, 'Right now what we need is unity so the Americans will leave.' The project of anti-racism took a back seat to the simple project of independence."

It was a project, it seemed to me, that never got finished.

"So the American presence exacerbated a situation that was inherent?" I asked. "It could have gone one way, but history didn't allow that way to become reality?"

"Right," she said.

I struggled with a number of very strong emotions in reaction to what Professor Ferrer had told me. I'm not a romantic about anti-black racism, in any society. I know that there was racism in colonial Cuba, even as mixed infantries fought for independence and even as the incredible interracial duo of Maceo and Martí came to prominence. It's just not possible for a culture to see black people as slaves one day and to treat them as equals the next. But I was deeply troubled by how far US intervention reached into the history of Cuba's racial relations. The country's nascent black-equality movement was suppressed before it even had a chance to take root in a nation made independent to a considerable degree by the sacrifices and courage of black men.

I wanted to understand exactly what happened during the United States' occupation. So I was thrilled to secure a meeting with history professor Marial Iglesias Utset in Havana. She suggested we go to Havana Harbor to visit the remains of the *Maine*, the ship that served as such a catalyst in Cuba's struggle for independence. She said its sinking was an unparalleled event that split Cuban history in two.

"It put an end to Cuba's colonial history, to the four hundred years of Spanish colonization," Iglesias explained, as we looked out over the water. "The US intervened in the war between Cuba and Spain, and they expelled Spain from the country."

"Do you think the history of race relations in Cuba would have been different if the Americans had stayed out and just let the Cuban interracial army defeat the Spanish?" I asked. I wanted to get her take on all this, to make sure that I wasn't imposing US Jim Crow race relations on Cuban history.

"I think so," Iglesias answered. "The official policies of the North American government were incredibly racist. And they tried, during the occupational period, to impose segregationist policies. There was also a Cuban elite that was racist. They cooperated with the military and with the policies of the occupying government. But the Americans

The PIC rebels as apes (orangutans), *La Discusión*, June 19, 1912. (Marial Iglesias Utset)

led the way. When it came to formalizing the police force, which had been integrated by Cubans, US government officials made Cubans create separate divisions of blacks and whites. This unleashed a protest. Many veterans of the liberating army argued that during the wars for independence, black and white people fought side by side, and therefore these military bodies should be interracial. But the North Americans managed to impose their views."

Some white Cubans, Iglesias told me, did fight for Afro-Cuban rights, resisting US efforts to keep blacks from voting. But the white elite —wealthier and more influential—simply overpowered them. These elites welcomed the chance to whiten Cuba and even, in retrospect, to whiten the war for independence. They claimed Cuba as their own.

Professor Iglesias led me to Havana's large harbor-side exhibit of cannons and chains that were once part of the USS *Maine*. She explained that when the ship exploded, it didn't sink completely right away. In fact, Cubans could still see pieces of it above the waterline for fourteen years. To Afro-Cubans, it must have been a haunting symbol.

"The 'patriotic' story would be that Cubans had been fighting Spain for thirty years and finally won," Iglesias sighed. "But by their intervention with an occupying military government, the US prevented the birth of a truly independent republic."

As I listened soberly, she told me that Cuba simply traded one form of colonialism for another. The country elected its first president in 1902. But the United States continued to exert a strong influence in Cuba for many, many years.

We were wrapping up our tour when Iglesias asked if I had a little more time to spend with her. She explained that while conducting some research for her doctorate, she discovered a rare letter written by a man named Vicente Goytisolo, a black civilian and former slave. The letter was sent to a white military leader, and it is a significant find. Ninety percent of Cuba's slaves were illiterate, incapable of writing such a letter. And most incredibly, the letter offered a direct view into the heart of a black Cuban before independence. "It's a very, very interesting letter," Iglesias stressed, "because he shows his nationalistic sentiments. He calls Cuba 'our country.'"

After I saw the letter, I was as excited as Iglesias about her discovery, and I wanted to know more about the author. I asked her if the man still has descendants living in Cuba. She told me she believed he does. With a bit of effort, we eventually located the man's family, living in one of the poorest parts of Havana, and Iglesias and I traveled together to share the letter with them.

We arrived at the modest house of an Afro-Cuban named Penélope Gato Moré. She welcomed us graciously and introduced us to her two children. Among them was a sweet nine-year-old boy, a precocious young man who seemed especially fascinated by his great-great-grandfather's accomplishments. Professor Iglesias read their ancestor's letter to them:

I take up my pen to express how happy I am to know that all the country hears my joy. You've indeed endured many terrible moments for the sake of our homeland since 1878, without food, without drink, without sleep, all for the good of our home land, for the well-being of all. I prayed to Santa Bárbara, patron saint of warriors, to watch over my brothers, some of which are still alive. And also to watch over you, father. I promise not to sleep in a bed until the day I learn the Cubans have won.

Vicente Goytisolo. (Marial Iglesias Utset)

The family hadn't known about the letter, but they knew all about their ancestor and took pride in his story. Penélope led me over to a hand-painted photograph hanging over the mantlepiece in the house. The image was aged and weathered but unmistakable. This was a former Cuban slave.

"The kids asked, 'Mom, who is that person?'" she said, laughing and shaking her head. "And I said, 'This is your great-great-grandfather.' And they asked, 'Well, why is he dressed like that?' I said, 'Because he was from the time of the wars of independence! And that's how they dressed.'"

I wanted to know more and more about Vicente. What was he

like? What did he do? Mrs. Gato's answer surprised me. Vicente, she said, was a Santería priest. He presided over a *cabildo*, an African congregation, and spoke Lucumi, a dialect of the Yoruba language and the liturgical language of the Santería religion, Cuba's version of Candomblé and Vodou, religions that are cousins. He was devoted to the major Yoruba deity, Shango, also known in Spanish as Santa Bárbara in the Santería syncretic code, a central figure in Santería, Candomblé, Vodou, Lucumi, and the other Yoruba-based religions throughout Latin America, including in Puerto Rico and Venezuela.

Santería, like Brazil's Candomblé and Haiti's Vodou, as we have seen, was a religion born of the slave trade. Cuban slaves combined their Yoruba faith with Catholicism in a mix that's unique to the island, its population, and its culture. Once again, the Yoruba orixás and Catholic saints worked together to help slaves bear their bondage with faith and dignity. Santería is sometimes even called the "Way of the Saints."

Vicente's descendants spoke with me proudly about his life as a Santería priest, and I told Professor Iglesias that I would love to see a ceremony during my time in Cuba. She told me about an old slave plantation named Taoro, where Santería ceremonies are performed regularly. And thanking God, Olodumaré, Santa Bárbara, and whoever else might be responsible for cell phones, I started making my arrangements.

Driving to Taoro, I noticed something striking. I kept seeing a tree that reminded me of the iroko, a species that's common in West Africa. I asked my driver about it, and he told me that it is called a ceiba tree. I suddenly had a vision of African slaves arriving in Cuba, being shipped to the countryside, having no idea where they were—and then seeing ceiba trees. At that time Africans were deeply tied to nature, so this visual reminder of home must have had great impact. But not every tree was a ceiba tree, I reflected. And not every African custom could have survived an entirely new life as a slave. I thought about Santería as I sat back in my seat. It made sense that this new world created a new faith.

When I reached Taoro, my guides into Santería were two *babalawo*, or priests, Nelson Rivera Vicente and Juan Bencomo Pedroso. Nelson is white, and Bencomo is black. They told me that many Santería rituals are conducted only in secret and that I was not welcome to participate. But they did offer to let me watch one entire ceremony to witness their way of worship.

What I saw fascinated me, as something of a student of the Yoruba religion. The ceremony involved a sacrifice to a god the Cubans call Elegua, the same god the Yoruba faith calls Esu Elegbara, the messenger of the gods, like Hermes. He is called Exú, as we saw, in Brazil. Clearly, from these names alone, we can see his Nigerian roots. Drummers played, a woman started dancing, and soon the devotion was in full swing. I was struck by the similarities between this Santería ceremony and those of Candomblé and Vodou. Each begins its worship with a sacrifice to Esu. It was plain to see that these three religions all share historical antecedents with Nigerian Yoruba and Beninese Fon religions. They are clearly cognate traditions. Their common roots are strong and indisputable and were alive in front of me.

Afterward, I waited patiently for Bencomo and Nelson to complete their duties. I wasn't about to leave them just yet. I asked these men, equals in faith, how important Santería is for ordinary Cuban people today. Does it live in their hearts, in their souls?

"People have a great faith in Santería," Bencomo answered, with Nelson nodding beside him. "And through that route, they find a way to escape their social, economic, and family problems. They search for a way to be more free." Practitioners, he said, used to be persecuted. But modern-day Cuba embraces Santería as a uniquely Cuban creation. Whites are even joining the faith, in great numbers. The men told me that for every Afro-Cuban who is initiated today, there are four whites.

Bencomo led me to his humble home, where he makes sacred drums. Each one will be consecrated, he explained, in a ceremony whereby a spirit called Ana will enter the drums and live inside them. I asked if I could try one, and he let me handle several of the newer drums that hadn't yet been consecrated. But he wouldn't tell me a thing about the secret ceremony that would invite Ana inside. I knew I'd reached my limits. But I was especially intrigued by its Yoruba roots.

"African roots in Cuba are not only rooted in religion," Bencomo said in response—it seemed important to him that I understand this. "They can be seen not only in religious ceremonies but also in its festivities, dances, songs, in its way of thinking. Africa is present in Cuba's daily life. These desires of doing what we feel like doing were the same desires that the slaves had in the barrack huts. Because the black human being is a free human being. We show what we feel."

I found it especially gratifying to learn that Afro-Cubans embraced

Santería ceremony. (George Hughes)

cultural forms that had an explicit ancestral memory of their own sovereignty as human beings. Hundreds of years of slavery and fearful oppression had failed to obliterate their self-conscious connection to Africa here.

"You know what?" Bencomo asked me, leaning forward with a glimmer in his eye. "You know what Ochún, Santería god of love, says? Ochún says, '*Iquiriada.*' It means, 'Get your machete sharp again.' And that is something that all black Cuban people say, because we have a national conscience."

The next day, humming the song I'd heard Bencomo play, I headed to Cuba's national archives back in Havana. I wanted to find out more about what happened to Cuba's black leaders during the US occupation. Before the *Maine* sank, they were respected leaders of the revolution. What happened to them when the Americans showed up? I found a number of fascinating, disturbing stories. One stood out especially. After Maceo died, another general, named Quintín Bandera, became one of Cuba's most popular black leaders. He inspired Afro-Cubans and was a revered figure. People even wrote poems about the man. I searched the archives for his correspondence, and I was shocked by a letter that I found, dated after the United States had come to power. In it, Bandera wrote to a benefactor, a wealthy woman, begging her for money. He told her that he was looking for work as a janitor but that he couldn't find any jobs. He said he desperately needed her help. If he ever received any reply to this letter, it has not been preserved. And regardless, it made no difference. Four years later, Bandera was killed in the countryside by government forces during an uprising.

As I pored over the archives, I saw the same thing over and over. US segregationists and the white Cubans who welcomed them formalized racism into national policies, if not actual laws. And great Afro-Cubans like Bandera died impoverished and disowned by their own nation. Deeply disturbed, I then learned something even more shocking. On September 17, 1899, a patriotic commission exhumed the body of Antonio Maceo, the great black hero of the wars of independence, to bury the remains in a mausoleum built with subscriptions from the public, along with the remains of the son of Máximo Gómez, who was Maceo's assistant and was killed with him and then buried beside him. In the process, scientists decided to investigate the difference between Maceo's black ancestry and his white ancestry, to determine—rather, to ensure—that Maceo was really, in fact, far more white than black, a fact supposedly responsible for his noble qualities. (Since Gómez was white, there was no need to do this for him.)

Imagine if Ulysses S. Grant had died during the Civil War. And imagine if scientists then decided to cut him up like a frog in biology class to find out if his skeleton looked more English, say, or Irish. This was scandalous. How had Afro-Cubans reacted to this? And just what had European scientists hoped to accomplish? I thought of Mexico's *casta* paintings—created at the moment when racism was trying to become science. I had to wonder if the same thing happened in Cuba.

Armando Rangel of the University of Havana offered to show me some scholarly writings on Maceo's cranial structure, so I headed right over. Rangel met me in his lab room, filled with skulls and other bones. It was all a little strange, quite frankly. But his kind demeanor and matter-of-fact approach soon put me at ease. Rangel explained that a French scientist named Henri Dumont had set up shop in Cuba to prove the superiority of the white race by conducting so-called scientific experiments on corpses. Dumont and his team dismantled, weighed, and measured different bodies, trying to determine the exact traits that made the white race superior. Often, they did this by linking black characteristics to those of apes.

Sadly, I'd heard this all before. "Why do you think so many studies try to prove this connection?" I asked.

"That current of thought developed mainly during the nineteenth century," Rangel explained. "It appeared when Darwin stated that there was an evolution of the species. The relation was proposed because the black man was seen as inferior. Black people were seen by whites to be closer to orangutans and other hominids, so they classified them that way."

"So in other words, you're saying that if scientists could show that Africans were closer to apes by looking at their skulls, this could be used to justify discrimination," I said.

"Yes," he replied.

Rangel pulled out an article written about Maceo's examination. What fascinated him, he told me, was that Maceo's career influenced the study of his body. The researchers wrote that Maceo had a "perfect" skull, a skull more European than African, and that his body had been incredibly strong, like Hercules. The researchers didn't try to diminish his legacy, but they sought to valorize the European part of his genetic heritage. They explained that although his bone structure was that of an African, the measurements of his skull affirmed that his brain was that of a white man.

"If Maceo was a superior man, then he couldn't be black," Rangel explained. "A superior man would have to have European characteristics. That was really a mistake, a scientific mistake, made at the time. And it's a curious fact—the more these investigations went on, the whiter the images of Maceo became. His facial features were pictured as more and more European."

I'd seen all kinds of whitening on my journey. But this was something new. I soon found myself reaching out to another Cuban scholar, Tomás Fernández Robaina, an expert on Cuba's racial policies in the early twentieth century. We met up at Havana's National Library. He told me that after Cuba became independent, it launched an aggressive period of whitening in which oppressive practices became commonplace. In 1906, Fernández Robaina said, a new immigration law authorized one million dollars to be spent importing Europeans to Cuba. The same policies had been implemented in Brazil and in Mexico. Over the next twenty years, six hundred thousand white Europeans—mostly from Spain—arrived to add more corrective whiteness to the mixed Cuban gene pool.

This determination to "whiten" Maceo's body, even in death, had a curious precedent in colonial times: if wealthy, powerful whites had children who looked black, they didn't have to accept their status as black Cubans. *Gracias al sacar* allowed them to purchase legal recognition of "purity of blood," or a degree of "whiteness," for these children through the state. Class, in other words, could trump race.

"Cuba has been a very racist country," Fernández Robaina said, sighing. "There was a tradition that blacks could not enter certain areas within parks, because they were white areas. It was just like in the US, where, at this stage, black people were marginalized."

After nearly ten years of these policies, Afro-Cubans finally pushed back. In 1908, a man named Evaristo Estenoz and his companions (including a man named Pedro Yvonnet) formed the Independent Party of Color, one of the first black political parties anywhere in the New World. They lobbied for Afro-Cuban rights, reviving the dream of a color-blind Cuba. The response was severe. Whites, as before, feared a black takeover, and the government stoked these fears by falsely claiming that the Independent Party of Color identified itself as a black party, not a party that believed in a multiracial Cuba. They banned the party from even holding meetings. Estenoz tried to negotiate with the government, even throwing his support behind a presidential candidate who promised to legitimize the party if he got elected. But soon after, this same politician publicly characterized the arrangement as a bribe —and persecution of the party continued.

Fernández Robaina guided me through the library to show me some press clippings from this time. The Independent Party of Color's critics were vicious. In political cartoons and caricatures, I saw blacks pictured as cannibals, eager to eat the white government. Blacks were compared to rats, which had recently caused an outbreak of bubonic plague on the island, as Marial Iglesias had discovered. And of course, all the blacks looked like monkeys. The climate was so hostile, Fernández Robaina told me, that blacks hid in their homes at night, afraid of being attacked or even lynched.

Leafing through the cartoons, I was reminded of the racist caricatures appearing in United States at the time. Curiously enough, in US

The Independent Party of Color (Partido Independiente de Color) leadership in 1912, with founder Evaristo Estenoz in the center in white jacket and mustache. (A color version of this photo is in the Museo de la Revolución, Havana.) (Gloria Rolando)

papers, Cuba was often depicted as a black child, just as African Americans were often referred to by US anthropologists as "the child" or "the lady" of the races.

In 1912, Estenoz, Yvonnet, and their followers tried to stage a revolt and were crushed. A massacre followed in which the Cuban government killed three thousand Afro-Cubans, including both leaders. The official report states that they were shot while trying to escape capture, but most historians believe that they were simply executed. I asked Fernández Robaina how this slaughter could possibly have been justified by the government. After all, many of Estenoz's men fought in the wars for independence and helped free Cuba from Spain. Yvonnet served as a captain under the command of Maceo himself.

"It is possible that the massacre was carried out in order to satisfy the Americans," Fernández Robaina speculated. "There was a threat from Washington. If the Cuban government could not demonstrate that it had control and was in charge of the island, the US might intervene again and, this time, remain in Cuba."

In the wake of the party's defeat, Cuban efforts at whitening intensified. Blacks could vote, Fernández Robaina noted, and some black politicians were elected. But elite whites fought to re-create Europe

"The Sword of the Caudillo." *La Política Cómica*, July 28, 1912. (Marial Iglesias Utset)

in the Caribbean, with help from the United States' Jim Crow model. There could be no talk of African roots, much less black pride, as part of Cuba's official national identity. Black cultural practices were discouraged as primitive and vulgar. Black groups were prohibited from singing and dancing at public celebrations like Carnival. Afro-Cubans could only practice their religions and hold drumming sessions in secrecy. Cuba tried, with conviction, to exorcise or erase its own blackness.

But as in every other Latin American nation, suppressed African traditions found expression and evolved. They could not be eradicated, and they certainly could not be silenced. For decades after Cuba became independent, traditional African musical forms were rejected as "jungle music," Fernández Robaina explained. But instead of disappearing, they simply went underground—then reappeared. During the extremely repressive years of the early twentieth century (and right around the time jazz first appeared in New Orleans), a new kind of Cuban music emerged. It was called Son.

Son was born deep in Cuba's rural interior, on the eastern end of the island, around Santiago de Cuba in Oriente province. It made its way into Cuban cities around 1908, when the nation began organizing a new military. As people began to move from rural areas into urban ones to serve their country, they brought this exciting new music with them. Slowly, this new sound came to be heard in cafés and nightclubs, on street corners and in shabby neighborhood bars. Son was sexy—really sexy. And among Afro-Cubans, most of whom were illiterate and had no political voice, Son became wildly popular.

I managed to set up a meeting with a band called the Septeto Típico de Sones, one of the oldest Son bands in the world. They didn't have a lot of time to spare, but they told me I was welcome to attend a rehearsal. To me, that sounded just about perfect. I arrived at the home of one of the members of the band and sat with them in his backyard. I could hear immediately how Son combined Cuba's many cultures. The percussion evoked Bantu music, and there were call-and-response elements to the song. But the guitar playing was straight out

"Current Sport": playing football with the heads of Estenoz and Ivonet. *La Discusión*, June 8, 1912. (Marial Iglesias Utset)

of Spanish folk tradition. It was an intoxicating combination, and the air was filled with a seething, sensual energy. I couldn't stop grooving, off in my corner.

When they finished, I introduced myself. I told the musicians a little bit about my project, researching blacks in Latin America. And they told me about themselves.

"When were you born?" I asked one of them.

"In 1926," said Francisco Antonio Bacallao Villaverde. "I'm about to be eighty-four."

"Was Son music legal eighty-four years ago?" I wanted to know.

"No," he replied, laughing. "Back then, they said Son was black people's business. The police would come and arrest you. You couldn't play Son back then. You had to play Son in hiding. The police would come and take everyone to the police station."

As it turns out, Son wasn't technically illegal, but like other forms with recognizably African roots, no one could perform it at state-sponsored public events without causing trouble.

"How much of the music is African, and how much is Spanish?" I asked next. I only trusted my own ears so much.

"From Spain, it gets the string elements," said Angel Marrero, one of the younger band members. "But from Africa, it gets the drums and the backing vocals. The flavor with which the singer performs is much more African than Spanish, too."

As we talked, they told me that Son eventually came to mark an important turning point in Cuban culture: for the first time, black was cool. By the late 1920s, even wealthy whites wanted a piece of the action. They threw secret Son parties of their own. The forbidders themselves enjoyed the forbidden fruit. In 1925, President Gerardo Machado even gave special permission to a Son band to play at his own birthday party. He must have enjoyed it, because soon after, the government formally recognized Son as a valuable part of Cuban pop culture.

I've been to so many places on this journey, I thought—and always the same story. African cultures persist through an underground religion and through the arts, and through the arts, they emerge and begin to transform everything. The official acceptance of Son did more than just get my new favorite septet a few more plum gigs. According to the band, the acceptance of Son was part of a much wider movement—a movement in which the Cuban elite (and their government) stopped

The author with Septeto Típico de Sones. (George Hughes)

rejecting everything Afro-Cuban in favor of everything European. They accepted, even applauded, an expression of black roots. And by the 1940s, though Cuba was still in many ways a racist society—though, like Brazil, it was never legally segregated—Cubans were beginning to celebrate their mixed identity, quite unlike their US counterparts. How could a nation change its official ideology about blackness so quickly?

I had a lunch scheduled with the scholar Eduardo Torres Cuevas, the head of the National Library. I called him up to let him know I was on my way. On the phone, I told him about my journey—and how confused it had made me. He laughed. What he was cooking, he said, would explain everything.

I arrived to find Torres Cuevas's home filled with the most marvelous smells. He greeted me warmly and, wiping his hands with a dishcloth, led me into his kitchen. He told me he was preparing a stew called *ajiaco*. It's a mixture of meats, fruits, and vegetables—combining many, many flavors into one unique taste. He offered me a spoonful from the bubbling pot. "*Gracias, muchas gracias!*" I said, the spices dancing over my tongue. "It's very good!" I could taste tender bits of pork, and the sauce was robust and savory. It was delicious.

"This is one of the dishes that defines Cuba," he told me, as I helped myself to a little more. "*Ajiaco* is a Cuban word that signifies the connections that make up our cultural characteristics: our language, society, customs, and traditions."

Torres Cuevas told me that the dish was of particular interest to the great pioneer of Cuban social science Don Fernando Ortiz. He used the concept of *ajiaco* to define *cubanidad*—or "the essence of being Cuban." This concept had been kicked around since the 1920s as a way of explaining Cuban identity. But in 1943, Ortiz published a seminal article on *cubanidad*. Cuevas explained that by coining the term, Ortiz simply gave a name to the ideals of independence leaders Martí and Maceo. Ortiz criticized the whitening process and reminded Cuba of its unique racial history and destiny. He encouraged Cuba to embrace itself by celebrating its African cultural roots.

"What matters is that you were brought up here," Torres Cuevas went on. "You identify yourself with the traditions and customs invented here, the way of dressing, popular songs. It didn't matter that your ethnic roots were African or Spanish. What mattered was that you became part of the universal Cuban identity."

But wouldn't black roots get lost in the sauce, so to speak? I asked Torres Cuevas what he thought.

"Cuban identity is the result of multiple ingredients that lose some of their original flavor in order to acquire a new flavor," he acknowledged. "In North America, a black person is anyone who has a drop of black color. In Cuban society, this is very difficult to establish, because all of us have that drop. So racial differentiations are extraordinarily false. When you get to the heart of Cuban society, it is a society that is by its nature multicolored, but multicolored within the individual himself. All these elements are mixed inside each person."

We sat and ate the *ajiaco*, and I thought a lot about *cubanidad*. I couldn't help but be reminded of Vasconcelos's cosmic race and Freyre's theory of racial democracy in Brazil, and it made me think of Mexico's decision to remove information about race from birth certificates. The idea that national pride can supersede racial identity had spread all across Latin America. But it has rarely succeeded, at least in my view, because too many black people, to put it bluntly, had stayed visibly, identifiably "black." Too often, these well-meaning policies had led to blackness being forced to become invisible, or to brown-pride movements that buried black roots. I had to wonder what *cubanidad* really meant for Afro-Cubans.

I thanked Torres Cuevas for his hospitality and headed back to my hotel with a wonderfully full tummy. I had a big day ahead of me. In the morning, I was going to press my knowledge of Cuba into the modern era. More conflicts, more upheaval, more searching. I tiptoed past the scale in my bathroom and collapsed into bed.

In the morning, I felt refreshed and ready for my appointment with historian Graciela Chailloux. We met up at the historic Hotel Nacional. And over some delicious coffee and pastries, we got acquainted and starting talking about Cuba's race relations after the introduction of *cubanidad*. Chailloux told me that the idea really did inspire a new yearning for Cuban unity. Cubans increasingly embraced their mixed heritage. They appreciated Cuban identity as something new—like *ajiaco*, a mix of many flavors that combine to create one.

With a start, I realized I'd seen evidence of this on my trip. Whenever I asked Afro-Cubans to describe themselves, they usually replied, "I'm a Cuban who is black." They didn't say, "I'm black and also a Cuban." That's different from what I've heard in the United States, where black people tend to identify themselves as black first and American second. *Cubanidad* was, in a way, I supposed, partly responsible for this habit.

As Cuba was embracing its multicultural identity, I found out, its economy was surging. In the 1940s, as the United States rebounded from the Great Depression with a war economy, the Cuban tourism industry began to thrive. Tourists flooded in, and new hotels sprang up right and left. Havana became a tourist hotspot. And soon enough, all that glitz and glamour attracted a new kind of visitor. Famed mobster Meyer Lansky moved into a luxury suite at the Hotel Nacional. His associates set up huge gambling operations—casinos, lotteries, and horse-racing clubs—and the city came to be known as the "Latin Las Vegas."

While the party in Havana was raging, a new leader came to power in Cuba—Fulgencio Batista. He was a sergeant in Cuba's Republican Army, and in 1933, as part of a coalition with students and other progressive forces, Batista participated in a revolution that forced the ineffective and increasingly dictatorial President Gerardo Machado to resign. The United States did not recognize the revolutionary government that then came to power under the presidency of Ramón Grau San Martín, which did things like unilaterally abrogating the Platt Amendment, which had defined the terms of Cuban-US relations since 1901. But it remained in contact with Batista. And when Batista pushed Grau out in 1934, the United States granted the new regime recognition right away. Batista controlled Cuban politics as of that date and became elected president in 1940.

"Batista came to prominence in Cuban society and remained in power for twenty-six years, largely because he was the guardian of North American interests in Cuba," Chailloux explained, delicately placing her cup back in its saucer. "And he was a man with an extraordinary thirst for power."

I knew Batista was a mixture of European, African, Chinese, and Native American ancestry and that he was considered to be a mulatto in Cuban society, so I asked Chailloux about his policies toward black people. Was he a racist? Or was he proud of being black?

"I don't think Batista ever saw himself as a black person or that he ever felt the need to identify himself as a black man," she replied, shaking her head. "He thought of himself as a man of power within Cuban norms. He transgressed, because he managed to enter the domain of the white elite. But he didn't change the structure of segregation that existed in Cuba in any way."

As we have seen, Batista initially participated in the progressive coalition that brought Grau San Martín to power in 1933. But he was the main figure in Grau's deposal. In 1934, Batista was key in the repression of students and other progressive political figures. Once much of the opposition was neutralized (a process that involved forcing many of Batista's opponents into exile), Batista then engaged in policies that sought to expand his political base beyond the military. For a time, he faithfully pursued a social agenda as a populist leader. He created a national bank and reformed public programs in education and health. With the support of the Communist Party, he even held a constitutional convention in 1940, adding clauses that discouraged racism. He then helped the nation prepare for democratic elections, and he was legitimately elected president. Cuba's economy thrived; Cuba became one of the most prosperous countries in all of Latin America.

But much of what Batista did was to preserve his own position, Chailloux explained. After being voted out of office in 1944, he returned in 1952 via a military coup. Lansky, the mafia kingpin, soon became Batista's close friend and literal partner in crime. For the next seven years, Batista protected the mafia's cash flow through his country, and the mob protected Batista from increasing numbers of Cubans who wanted to stop him. Batista went so far as to allow some of Lansky's minions to serve in the Cuban senate—even though they weren't Cuban.

The economy continued to roar. By 1957, Cuba had the second-highest per-capita income anywhere in Latin America. But the country's prosperity was very lopsided. The rich kept getting richer, and richer and richer, while the poor suffered bitterly. There were two Cubas, Chailloux explained. One was wealthy, urban, and primarily white. The other was desperately poor, both urban and rural, and almost entirely black. In 1953, an estimated 15–20 percent of Cuba's population was unemployed. The average Cuban family earned six dollars per week. Only about a third of all homes had running water. And blacks still had far fewer opportunities than whites did.

Batista's policies, in the end, hadn't eased segregation or discrimination; while there were no laws mandating racial segregation, in practice, blacks were disproportionately represented in the lower classes and informally segregated in many public places. And as injustice and inequality in Cuba mounted, Batista became more and more ruthless in his efforts to quell dissent. His government became increasingly brutal, and some historians estimate that Batista's forces killed as many as twenty thousand men, black and white, who tried to rise up against him. Curiously enough, on the other hand, a vibrant and very critical press flourished, publishing things like political manifestoes and letters about the need for radical social change—including some written from the mountains by a young Fidel Castro. By 1955, riots began to erupt. Desperate Cubans started staging anti-Batista demonstrations and attacks on government forces. Batista's response? To torture and kill as many of these people as he could. This paved the way for a new war—a new revolution—led by Castro, then a twenty-nine-year-old attorney with a talent for guerrilla warfare and military strategy.

I explained to Chailloux that many Americans have an unfavorable view of Castro. He's widely viewed as a dictator, a man who aligned himself with the Soviet Union, then took a troubled country and made

Santa Ifigenia Cemetery. (George Hughes)

it much worse, leading to the ongoing embargo and travel restrictions that have alienated much of the United States from Cuba. Of course, many of us, myself included, also remember the Cuban Missile Crisis acutely and personally—as one of the most terrifying events of our lives. Chailloux listened patiently and then explained that Castro was viewed differently by many Cubans.

Cuba's socialist revolution was one of the most complex developments in its history. Batista was opposed by many different groups, all with different goals for their country. Many of these groups were passionately anti-Communist, and not all of them wanted to see blacks gain equality. But Castro's strong vision—and his knack for inspiring popular support—shaped the revolution. He used all his charisma, and he persuaded the nation that it was time for revolutionary change. But he did not embrace Communism initially; that came two years later.

When Castro finally came to power in 1959, Chailloux told me, he set out to transform Cuba into a place where the white, the black, the brown, the rich, and the poor were all equal. Castro declared racism illegal, and he eliminated the many informal policies that discriminated against Afro-Cubans. He desegregated social clubs, public parks, and beaches. He founded a new government agency to eliminate race discrimination in hiring. The government took over abandoned properties and homes, and it redistributed them to poor families—both white and black. Perhaps most significantly, Castro started providing education and health care to everyone in the country. This had a dramatic effect on the poorest people in Cuba—most of whom were black. He cast off elitist access to education, he made medical care free to everyone, and he seemed to be ushering in a promised era of *cubanidad*. Many Afro-Cubans, Chailloux told me, were euphoric.

"My family's life changed absolutely and radically," she told me. "My sister and I were in primary school, but we hadn't expected to study any further under Batista's regime. The revolution opened up possibilities for everyone."

"Did the lives of black people change for the better after the revolution?" I asked.

"The most important change was that they had new access to education, to better standards of living, better employment, and better health," she explained, "but it wasn't because Cuba prescribed specific treatment for the most deprived sectors in the society. These benefits were the result of an equality policy."

In 1961, Castro called on Cuban teens to be part of a new literacy program. He urged them to go to the countryside and teach reading and writing to the largely uneducated rural population, which included blacks and whites. About one hundred thousand kids participated—and Chailloux was one of them. She was eleven years old. She was away from her family for eight months.

When I was eleven, I could never have left my parents. Every summer, my brother and I would travel to my aunt's house for two weeks, and I would cry because I was so homesick. I assumed Chailloux must have been terrified. She shook her head. "There were loads of others like me who had also left home," she said. "The kids with a problem were the ones who couldn't get permission from their parents!"

I'm a parent, and I couldn't imagine giving that permission myself. I asked Chailloux if her own family tried to keep her at home. But she said they didn't. Chailloux's father was a well-educated man, graduating from law school in 1949. Everyone acknowledged that it was a special moment in Cuban history, she said, and many families encouraged their children to be part of it.

"On the twenty-second of December in 1961, Cuba was declared an illiteracy-free territory," Chailloux told me. "And all of the young people who had taken part paraded in Revolution Square."

I asked her if this was Cuba's finest moment.

"Yes, I think so," she answered tearfully.

Of course, Chailloux said, not everyone was happy about the revolution. Privileged whites were angry with Castro. They felt that by desegregating their favorite haunts, he was intruding on their private lives. So after making a strong initial push for equality, Castro backed off. Blacks, on paper, had all the same rights and privileges as whites. But they didn't get much political representation—and to stop tensions from escalating further, the government banned race-based political parties. It stated, firmly, that racism was finished in Cuba, so there was no need for Cubans to form such groups. In 1962, Castro even went so far as to officially declare that racism in Cuba had ended, and he closed the subject from further discussion. No one was allowed to talk about discrimination anymore, because that was criticizing the government—and criticizing the government would be punished as sedition. By doing this, I imagine, he hoped to mollify the white elites, while still being able to claim he'd done the right thing for Afro-Cubans.

I finished the last of my coffee and sat back. Chailloux had brought my knowledge of Cuban history into the Castro era, and she'd shared her personal experience of the revolution as a citizen. But I knew there were veterans of the war still living who were eager to tell their story. I thanked Chailloux warmly for all the time she'd taken with me, and I headed back to my hotel. I wanted to hear about Castro's revolution from the inside.

I managed to arrange an interview with a black member of Castro's army, Colonel Víctor Dreke. He lived nearby, and he agreed to meet me at Cuba's national museum for black culture, the Center for the Study of Africa and the Middle East, which he directs. Colonel Dreke was Che Guevara's second in command during the Cuban intervention in the Congo in 1965, on behalf of the followers of Patrice Lumumba, who was assassinated in 1961, shortly after assuming office. Dreke directed Cuba's military intervention in Guinea-Bissau between 1966 and 1968, helping Amilcar Cabral's forces to fight for independence from Portugal. He then headed Cuba's mission in the Republic of Guinea. Dreke earned a degree in politics from the Máximo Gómez Military

Academy and, in 1981, also a degree in law from the University of Santiago de Cuba. He returned to Guinea-Bissau and lived there between 1986 and 1989.

I met Colonel Dreke in the museum, and we talked surrounded by African art. His face is deeply lined. I knew, before we even started talking about the war, that this man had been a devoted soldier and an officer in Castro's army, from the time the revolution started in the mid-fifties. Dreke told me he joined Castro's rebel militia when he was just fifteen years old. Incredibly, he served under Che Guevara both in the revolution and in the dreadfully unsuccessful guerrilla war in the Congo. Now, Guevara's image has become oddly pervasive in US pop culture, particularly among young people who don't know who he was! But for men like Dreke, Guevara was a serious and inspiring leader. And he pursued the goals of the revolution with ruthless efficiency.

"They were very unforgettable days for us," Dreke said slowly, the memory of combat and death, but also their ultimate, unlikely victory, in his eyes. "For those of us who had the opportunity to be there, they were unforgettable days."

I sat rapt as he vividly recalled the experience to me. Dreke fought in Cuba's hills for seven years. As his unit neared Havana, they were outnumbered ten to one by government forces. The battles became bloodier and bloodier. But somehow, he survived. "The triumph of the revolution happened in the middle of war," he told me. "That is to say, we were fighting until the day that the last government troops surrendered. At about 6:00 a.m., we saw a white flag. And someone said to me, 'Look, Dreke, they are surrendering, they are surrendering!' I did not believe it. It was all a bit surreal. We cried with joy—and also with sorrow, because there were comrades who had died just a few days earlier, who had not lived to see our victory."

Guevara and his forces, exhausted but triumphant, entered Havana just as Batista fled (it's said that he was gone from the country in twelve hours, carrying over four hundred million US dollars and accompanied by 180 of his cronies). The revolutionaries received a hero's welcome. "We did not think we would live to see the triumph of the revolution," Dreke confided. "That was a wonderful moment, for all the fighters and for all the people of Cuba, who threw themselves into the streets, en masse: men, women, children, all clapping their hands, celebrating the victory of the revolution. Even some people who had not wanted the revolution went into the streets to support its triumph. Blacks and whites, they were all there."

I knew there were some Cubans who didn't support the revolution, and I was curious to know more about them. I asked Dreke if any black Cubans opposed it.

"Some black people teamed up with the enemy," he confirmed. "But they didn't understand the revolution. I told them, 'You cannot be against the revolution, because this revolution has given you what you have never had before. It has given you the possibility to be a human being, to be the same as the rest of society.' I also said the same thing to poor white people who opposed it."

Some Afro-Cubans felt a sense of solidarity with Batista because he was a mulatto. Dreke, needless to say, did not share their feelings. "But he was not for blacks," he told me. "Before the triumph of the revolution, black people in Cuba were exploited by the wealthy classes. They lived in the worst areas. They had no economic opportunities. There were places they couldn't even enter. Batista did nothing to stop any of this."

By contrast, Dreke said, Castro immediately passed laws condemning racism. He banned discrimination against women. And in Dreke's view, he permanently changed race relations in Cuba.

"In Cuba, everybody has the right to study," he said with great emotion. "Everybody has the right to work. Everybody has the right to fight to defend the principles of the revolution—whites and blacks. We cannot say that there is discrimination."

It was fascinating to hear Cubans describe their revolution with such pride. Both Chailloux and Dreke were passionate defenders of what Castro accomplished, even romantic about it. They truly believe their nation had been transformed for the better by it.

I told Dreke about my own experience with his revolution—that I was twelve years old during the Cuban Missile Crisis in October 1962 and that I had never been so scared in my life. We all thought that nuclear destruction was imminent—and that we were going to die. When I was in school, I could hardly pay attention. When I wasn't in school, I was on my knees praying. I started to laugh a little, telling my story. In retrospect, I can find humor in it, but it sure wasn't funny at the time. Dreke reached over and thumped me reassuringly on the shoulder. He smiled at this picture of me as a frightened child. And I realized that as a soldier, he'd long ago conquered his own fear of death.

"I was a military leader during the October Crisis, as we call it," he said. "We were practically being forced into a war, and we had two choices: either give in or defend Cuba's dignity. But luckily, there was no war."

"Did you, like me, think that you were going to die?" I asked.

"Yes, I thought I could die," he replied steadily. "I thought this many times. I fought in the revolution, and I was injured—I could have died then. I was also injured in the Bay of Pigs invasion—I could have died then. But it's not true that I'm brave. You just decide to die for the cause."

The cause. The words stuck with me as I thanked Colonel Dreke humbly for his time and took my leave. (Before I did, he asked me to thank Colin Powell for him for resisting the attempt of the Cuban community to prevent his visit on a book tour, because they accused him of being a murderer. I promised I would tell General Powell when next I saw him.) The cause was certainly admirable—social and economic equality, the end of racial and sexual discrimination, universal literacy, and access to health care. By ending segregation, outlawing racism, and reaching out to poor blacks and whites with health care and education, Castro's government did make an effort to transform the nation. But I didn't see a transformed Cuba as I drove through Havana. I saw poor blacks clustered in rough neighborhoods and sharply dressed whites in rich enclaves. Of course, there will always be rich and poor, I thought to myself. And there are certainly poor whites in Cuba too. I wanted to believe that the revolution's best hopes had been achieved and that racism had been eradicated. I just didn't see it.

It was time to get back out on the streets. I needed to talk to real Cubans and to find out what they thought about race and racism in their society. Soon enough, I was chatting away with our drivers, two men who were part of our film crew named Rafael and Yoxander. They were proud to be Cuban and happy to discuss race with me. I started by asking Rafael, who has a complexion like coffee, what color he is.

"I am mixed race," he replied. "I'm simply Cuban. It is a mixture of all the races."

"Sure, I know that," I replied. "But what does it say on your ID card?"

Fulgencio Batista y Zaldivar (1901–1973), soldier and dictator who ruled Cuba twice, first from 1933 to 1944, during which he produced a strong, efficient government, and then from 1952 to 1959 as a dictator fond of terrorist tactics. (Bettmann/Corbis UK)

"White," he said.

That was odd. The man isn't white. And he couldn't tell me why his ID card says he is. This sent our conversation in a different direction. Rafael might want to be just Cuban, and his ID card might officially categorize him as white. But what about unofficial Cuba? How do people think of themselves when they stop walking politically correct lines? I asked the two men to tell me about the people around us on the streets. They are Cuban, yes, but what else are they? I soon learned there are still categories of blackness within *cubanidad*.

That person over there? "*Moreno*." That one over there? "*Mulato*."
"What about me?" I asked.

"*Negro*," Rafael answered. That's all right with me. I'm happy to be black. But I then took the opportunity to ask them why there weren't more professors like me at the universities—and why the affluent neighborhoods didn't have more black residents.

"I think perhaps it is because white people like to study more," Yoxander said, surprising me with his frankness. "They keep on going and try to improve their life, day after day."

As you can imagine, I felt some strong emotions in that moment. But I wasn't talking to Yoxander to judge him.

"Why don't black people have the same values?" I asked.

"Perhaps it's because of their genes, their own mentality, the way they see life, the way they are," he answered. "Or perhaps, because of the context in which they grew up, they are happy the way they are and don't want anything else."

I asked him if he believes there is racial discrimination in Cuba.

Yvonnet and a rat, *La Discusión*, July 11, 1912. (Marial Iglesias Utset)

"Not really," he said, shaking his head, "not on a grand scale. We all grew up together—white, mestizo, black, mulatto. We were all educated to the same level."

"And there are black people with a low level of education and white people with a low level of education," Rafael piped in. "The problem is that black people sometimes have complexes. They discriminate against themselves. They call each other black. But they have the same rights."

Okay, I thought. The word on the street, among average Cubans, is that discrimination doesn't exist. But I wanted to get another perspective. So I ended my discussions about race with Rafael and Yoxander and decided to jump to the top of the income ladder. As in much of the world, successful blacks in Cuba are often athletes, not lawyers or doctors. I called Omar Linares, a famous baseball player—and an Afro-Cuban. I was curious how he feels. He invited me to a baseball game on a Sunday morning. For several minutes, we just chatted about baseball. Most Cubans love the sport, as do I. Then we turned to the matter at hand. I wanted to know why athletics are such a singular avenue for success for black Cubans.

"Black people here like to practice a lot of sport," Linares told me amiably.

"Why do you think there are more baseball players, proportionately, than black lawyers or doctors?" I asked.

"There's a tendency for black people to practice sports," he said, patiently. He was listening to my questions, but they weren't really engaging him. He told me he had never experienced discrimination in Cuba, and he assured me that ordinary Cubans don't either. The revolution got rid of racism, he said.

"Why didn't you come to the US?" I asked. "You could have been like Big Papi and made so much money."

"Because I was born here in Cuba," he replied, "and the revolution gave me the opportunity to study and play. I owe my success to Cuba."

After I said goodbye to Linares, I must confess that I was baffled. I saw segregation everywhere around me. But Cubans didn't seem to blame racism. I saw a wide gap between rich and poor, and so many poor seemed to have brown faces. But the black Cubans I had interviewed so far insisted that each individual's success (or lack thereof) was his or her own responsibility.

I told Tomás Fernández Robaina about my conversations with

Rafael Muñoz Portela, Yoxander Oritz Matos, and Omar Linares. It seemed like *cubanidad* supersedes race, I told him, and that even Afro-Cubans believe there is no racism.

"I class myself as an ordinary Cuban," he told me. "But speaking as a black Cuban, I also know, deep down, that the first thing people see is that I'm black, not that I'm Cuban. The police always remind me of that first and foremost."

"So you believe Afro-Cubans do face racism?" I asked.

"All Cubans, whether they are aware of it or not, have been a victim of racism," he responded, without skipping a beat. "Prejudice and humiliation make some people reject the fact that they are black. Here in Cuba, there are many different ways of referring to the racial category of black—there are forty-four different ways, in fact."

Forty-four categories of blackness! Considering that no one wanted to talk about it, that number was a lot bigger than I expected.

"What happens is that those with the lightest skin, who are almost white, straighten their hair so they can pass for white and become successful," he went on. "They just want to enjoy the same opportunities as white people."

This had the painful ring of truth. But I felt I still needed to learn more. I caught up in a black barbershop with another journalist, Tato Quiñones, who had lived in Cuba in 1989, when the Soviet Union collapsed. The Soviets were Cuba's biggest trading partner at that time, and when their empire fell apart, six billion dollars disappeared from Cuba's economy. The island descended into chaos. Quiñones covered the whole story.

I was looking forward to our talk with particular urgency because we were going to meet in a barber shop. In my haste to keep on schedule over the past two weeks, I hadn't had a chance to get my hair trimmed! Quiñones and I shook hands heartily and got comfortably settled in some grand, but fraying, old-school barber chairs, like the cars in Havana, refugees from the fifties. The hot towel around my neck felt lavishly wonderful, though the barbershop was in a poor section of town. Then I asked Quiñones how the Soviet Union's fall affected Cuba —and what it meant for Afro-Cubans. Quiñones told me that Cuba's economic landscape had been unequal for whites and blacks even while the Soviet Union was strong. And that was twenty years after the revolution.

"The majority of blacks still lived in the poorest neighborhoods," he explained. "And there was a remarkable disparity in terms of academic achievement. The percentage of black people in high-ranking positions, in political and governmental organizations, had no correlation with the percentage of the population that was black. The government took some measures to remedy this. But some, in my opinion, were naïve. There were new formations of social classes, but in these—as had always been the case in Cuba—the highest classes were made up of white families, and at the bottom of the pyramid were the black families."

When the Soviet Union collapsed, Cuba lost over 80 percent of its overseas trade. The country's gross domestic product was slashed in half. Cuban industry and agriculture essentially ceased to function. Malnutrition and famine spread quickly, and most Cubans found themselves in desperate straits. Many had to rely on support from Cuban exiles in the United States—and the Cuban community abroad is mostly white, even if it is getting more diverse all the time. Still, most blacks in Cuba had no lifeline, so their situation became markedly worse. Race relations became bitter.

"I went to the USA at the end of the nineties," Quiñones told me, "and I found out that, you know, 97 percent of Cubans living there considered themselves white. And so the hundreds or thousands of millions of dollars, some say, sent to Cuba every year ends up in the hands of those who consider themselves white." Many of the Cubans in Miami wouldn't think of themselves as black or as mulattoes.

Why, if there was no more racism in Cuba, would multiethnic Cubans who achieved success choose to whiten their own identity? That didn't sound like *cubanidad* to me.

"Thirty years after the triumph of the revolution, there were still some racist germs in Cuba," Quiñones explained, "and when the Soviet Union went away, they multiplied at an astounding rate. It was incredible. It was as if Cuba's immune system had failed, and this disease took hold of society."

Incredible, indeed. I asked Quiñones if he experienced racism. He didn't hesitate.

"Yes, of course I've experienced racism," he said. "There is racial discrimination in Cuba. It gets worse every day—more apparent and more shameless."

The race divide is exacerbated, he told me, by Cuba's monetary policy. Since 1994, following the fall of the Berlin Wall, the country has used a dual currency system. Today, Cubans are paid in pesos, but tourists use Cuban convertible pesos, also known as CUCs, which were introduced a few years ago. The difference? CUCs are worth about twenty-five times more than pesos. By using two currency systems, Quiñones explained, Cuba has rendered many of its well-intentioned reforms meaningless. After all, why should a Cuban go to school to become a doctor and get paid the equivalent of twenty dollars a month when a waiter serving tourists can make that amount in one day?

I found this notion deeply troubling. I remembered Graciela Chailloux's gleaming eyes as she told me about Castro's education initiative. I remembered Omar Linares's sincere expression of gratitude to his nation for providing him with an education and a chance to succeed. I understood immediately how such a currency system upended their conventional wisdom, and I wanted to know more about how it affected Afro-Cubans.

Quiñones helped me out by taking me to visit Roberto Zurbano, a writer and critic. Zurbano was happy to give me a few minutes in the restaurant in my hotel, introducing me to Cuban beer. But he didn't mince words—the two-currency system in Cuba has been a disaster for poor blacks.

I told him, "I've been in many places like Cuba, and as a black American, I always look for black people, always. But here, I see very few black people on airplanes, in the hotels, or in restaurants. Why?"

"Unfortunately, that's the way it is," Zurbano replied. "Maybe they clean the rooms, or they work in the kitchen or as performers. They are likely to be paid in pesos. In Cuba, there are just few black people in the strong economic sectors. Why? Because prejudice never went away. Prejudice never disappeared. It was simply concealed under the table. And silence allowed all the problems to grow, under the table."

By "silence," I took Zurbano to mean silence from the government, from the elites, and from black people, who were fearful of persecution. And I thought about his analysis as I sipped my beer. Silence is rarely a good response to injustice—and I feared that Afro-Cubans themselves had become silent. Of course, I don't accept that black people are lazy and that their poverty is their own fault. I think that is a racist justification of the effects of a history of racism. How is that different from saying blacks are poor because they're naturally inferior to whites? If you really think blacks are equal to whites and as capable as they are, don't you have to question what keeps them in poverty?

I decided to spend a little time with some Afro-Cubans who are making some noise about the state of race relations in contemporary Cuba. I headed to the home of a rapper known as Soandres. His proper name is Soandres Del Rio Ferrer, and his stage name is Soandry. He's the leader of one of Cuba's top hip-hop bands, Hermanos de Causa. I was very eager to meet him. I knew the Cuban government had banned two of his songs because they are about racism. I'd actually planned to record one of his concerts during my trip, but the government told me I couldn't attend. (We sneaked a camera crew in and recorded the concert anyway.) When I arrived, I realized Soandres hadn't just invited me to his home—this was also his underground recording studio. After a very thoughtful and long discussion while we waited for a tropical rain storm to pass, he agreed to perform one of his banned songs for me:

Hey, yo
The black Cuban wants to be just like the white man
Because he thinks that darkness is obsolete and that whiteness is
    progress
It's this way so much that he's always laughing loudly at racist jokes
The black Cuban discriminates against his brother and is violent to him
And even though he has no master, he crawls like a worm
He has nothing of his own because his self-esteem and pride are
    broken
The black Cuban is the rubbish of his island

Soandres told me that he grew up during the Soviet Union's collapse. He saw what it did to Afro-Cubans, and he began to wage his own personal war on the silence that followed. Listening to him, I started to feel inspired. Soandres wants to see social reform—to see the lives of Afro-Cubans get better, now. He wants all of Cuba to recognize a little reality and to join him in his personal war. "What we do is underground rap," he explained. "Underground rap informs the people of what is really going on. What is being shown to us on television is not really what is going on. On television, they tell us that everything's good, that everything's okay, that everything is going the way it should, that the economy is doing great, that the country is getting better. But in the poor areas, this is not true."

"We do everything in an independent way," he went on. "Our strategy is to get our music to people, because government institutions don't play us. We build our own recording studios, we burn our CDs, and we give them out at concerts. We decided not to wait for major Cuban labels to tell us what they want. We create our own possibilities."

I asked him about the two songs I'd been told he is not allowed to perform because they deal with racism. "Well, I'm kind of allowed to sing them," Soandres said, looking at me sideways and smiling, "but it puts the success of the concert and my colleagues at risk. The police could stop the concert right then and there. I could maybe sing that song, but the next person might not be allowed on stage, and that would be a loss for the rap movement. We want hip-hop to continue."

Soandres told me the government wants to censor artists of all kinds, but it also wants to avoid criticism for doing it. So punishments are not always direct. Soandres and his fellow musicians just keep making their music and testing their limits.

"Many of us have been put down for what we do," he told me. "But we haven't stopped doing it, because this is our reality. When you accept your reality, at least you have the courage to face what is happening. And you can begin working on how to fix it."

"So you believe there is real racism against black people in Cuban society?" I asked.

"Yes, yes it exists," he said emphatically. "The system feeds its existence, because the system does not speak of its existence. The system pretends that there is no racism toward black people in Cuba. All along Cuba's history, Cuba's future has been put first, and the black people's situation took a back seat. But we need to analyze this problem and face it up front and say that racism exists. Cuban soap operas show blacks almost like slaves. In the movies, the black man is always a thief, a criminal. This is what people are seeing. We need to say that we have a problem with racism, and we have to fight against it."

I loved Soandres's spirit. The boldness of his critique of contemporary Cuban race relations was so refreshing and invigorating—and I realized that while I respect Cubans' love for the idea of *cubanidad*, even more, I respect those who see how Cuba is falling short of its ambitions and are determined to do something about it, despite repression from the government.

I left Soandres and went to visit Miguel Barnet, Cuba's most successful living writer. Barnet is the author of the international bestseller *Biography of a Runaway Slave*. He works in Havana as the director of the Fernando Ortiz Foundation, a most fitting appointment since he was Ortiz's student. He believes passionately that only one thing can truly eradicate racism in Cuba: education.

"The knowledge that people have of their African legacy comes from the roots, comes from the family," he told me, as I sat down in his office. "But I want them to talk about it in universities, in secondary schools, in primary schools."

Barnet told me that he doesn't want black pride buried in brown pride. As much as Cuba is a mixed-race nation, he feels its black roots deserve attention. "We have to introduce more of the African mythology and African history in our schools," he said. "The legacy of blacks in this country is not only cultural or philosophical or artistic. They have also contributed strongly to the economy of this country."

We talked together, in great detail, about the tragic pitfalls inherent in *cubanidad*, racial democracy, and other Latin American ideals that have sought to bury blackness. It's never healthy for any country to deny or hide any of its cultural roots. And Cuba's revolution—well-meaning though it may have been at times—suppressed cultural elements that were black. No one was learning about Afro-Cuban history. Young people didn't understand the origins of Afro-Cuban culture. By insisting that racial lines didn't exist in Cuba, the nation also insisted that a separate black cultural tradition didn't exist, either. But simply by considering the development of Son, or the origins of Santería, one recognizes that that is obviously not true.

Barnet and I agreed that Cuba had successfully banned institutional racism against people based on the color of their skin. And this is an important first step in any fight for equality. But it takes more than that to root out the racism of the mind, to eliminate behavioral racism.

I left Barnet's office hoping that his foundation could take the lead in this sort of broad and deep educational reform. While I'd met some Cubans who don't think there is any racial problem here, I'd also met highly influential people who know that anti-black racism here is a major problem, something not eliminated by the revolution. And those voices, deep in passion, are growing louder. Over time, I believe they'll persuade all Cubans to face a difficult truth—that Cuba has racism in the very fabric of its cultural being, rooted in its long history of slavery, and that the next great step forward for this multiracial country is to eradicate it for real, and for good.

As I left the elegant offices of the Ortiz Foundation, I tried to assess what I'd seen in Cuba. At the height of his power, Fidel Castro famously declared that Communism had put an end to racism here. But recently, he seems to have changed his mind. In a speech delivered in New York in 2000, Castro admitted, "We discovered that marginality and racial discrimination with it are not something that one gets rid of with a law or even with ten laws, and we have not managed to eliminate them completely in forty years." Lately, other Cuban leaders have mentioned this with some frequency as well. But that apparently is all they have done. As the Cuban scholar Alejandro de la Fuente points out, no policies have been implemented to address the growing income gap between white and black Cubans, and no measures have been taken to punish those who publicly state that they don't want "*negros*" to work in their companies. They act, almost uniformly, as if racism were a legacy of the old order of slavery and capitalism, a historical legacy that hasn't disappeared yet, rather than admitting that anti-black racism in Cuba is an ongoing, living phenomenon with a life of its own. I hadn't found much evidence to confirm the government's official policies on racism. Instead, I'd found an informal racism that is pervasive, internalized by some white people and even by some black people. Racism is not something that merely is inherited from a remote past; rather, it is a set of social practices and ideas that are constantly being re-created and reproduced, with the most devastating social consequences. The Cuban government has the institutional means to address both structural and behavioral racism, but beyond at least acknowledging the problem, it has not yet begun to confront it squarely and meaningfully.

Cuba's is a culture in which blackness is still in battle for expression, for inclusion, and for true equality, for an equal place at the social and cultural table. Cuban history is filled with examples of heroic, patriotic freedom fighters—men and women, black and white and every imaginable shade of brown in between—people who have battled with such nobility, courage, and determination for social justice, generation after generation. Like those of us in the United States, these activists haven't won the battle for civil rights yet in Cuba, just as they haven't won the battle to end racism and economic discrimination in Brazil, the Dominican Republic, Haiti, Mexico, and Peru. But I had no doubt, as I prepared to return home, that this admirable fight will only grow in intensity in Cuba. And I have absolutely no doubt, either, that the spirit which Soandres embodies and to which his relentlessly dynamic music gives voice will prevail over time. The struggle will emerge, culturally, from hip-hop musicians and visual artists and eventually, as these young people age, will move into the center of Cuba's political life, a life after Castro and Communism. Then this will become the next Cuban revolution. I have to believe that similar movements for the full equality of persons of African descent will arise and sustain themselves throughout the Americas, assuring that the sacrifices of the eleven million slaves who survived both the insufferably dreadful Middle Passage from Africa to the New World and then their harsh day-to-day lives within the inhumane institution of American slavery would not have made in vain.

Appendix

Color Categories in Latin America

While developing this project, I was continually struck by the sheer number of terms and categories applied to blacks in Latin America. In some cases, these categorizations carried very specific sociopolitical weight and were used to define and constrict generations of people of African descent. In other cases, the terms reflect simply the most casual forms of racism. All were, in their own way, of interest to me.

What follows is a bare attempt to capture the volume and content of this discourse.

Brazil

The Brazilian terms for shades of blackness include the following, drawn from a 1995 article by Christina Grillo in the country's leading daily paper, *Folha de S. Paulo*, concerning a study by the Brazilian Institute of Geography and Statistics:

Acastanhada	Amarelosa	Branca-melada
Agalegada	Amorenada	Branca-morena
Alva	Avermelhada	Branca-pálida
Alva escura	Azul	Branca-queimada
Alva rosada	Azul-marinho	Branca-sardenta
Alvarenta	Baiano	Branca-suja
Alvarinta	Bem branca	Branquiça
Alvinha	Bem clara	Branquinha
Amarela	Bem morena	Bronze
Amarela-queimada	Branca	Bronzeada
Amarelada	Branca-avermelhada	Bugrezinha-escura

Burro quando foge

Cabo verde

Cabocla

Café

Café-com-leite

Canela

Canelada

Cardão

Castanha

Castanha-clara

Castanha-escura

Chocolate

Clara

Clarinha

Cobre

Cor firme

Cor-de-café

Cor-de-canela

Cor-de-cuia

Cor-de-leite

Cor-de-ouro

Cor-de-rosa

Corada

Crioula

Encerada

Enxofrada

Esbranquicento

Escura

Escurinha

Fogoio

Galega

Galegada

Jambo

Laranja

Lilás

Loira-clara

Loura

Lourinha

Malaia

Marinheira

Marrom

Meio amarela

Meio branca

Meio morena

Meio preta

Melada

Mestiça

Miscigenação

Mista

Morena

Morena bem chegada

Morena-bronzeada

Morena-canelada

Morena-castanha

Morena-clara

Morena cor-de-canela

Morenada

Morena-escura

Morena-fechada

Morena-jambo

Morenão

Morena-parda

Morena-roxa

Morena-ruiva

Morena-trigueira

Moreninha

Mulata

Mulatinha

Negra

Negrota

Pálida

Paraíba

Parda

Parda-clara

Polaca

Pouco clara

Pouco morena

Preta

Pretinha

Puxa para branca

Quase negra

Queimada

Queimada de praia

Queimada de sol

Regular

Retinta

Rosa

Rosada

Rosa-queimada

Roxa

Ruiva

Russo

Sarará

Saraúba

Specada

Tostada

Trigo

Trigo

Trigueira

Verde

Vermelha

Mexico

Mexican terms for shades of blackness were set down in Nicolás León's *Las castas del México Colonial o Nueva España* and Gonzalo Aguirre Beltrán's *Cuijla: Esbozo etnográfico de un pueblo negro*. They include the following:

Ahi te estás
Albarazado
Albino
Barcino
Cambujo
Calpamulato (or
  campamulato)
Cuarterón
Cuarterón de mulata
Chino
Genízaro
Galfarro

Gente blanca
Gíbaro
Grifo
Jarocho
Limpios
Lobo
Morisco
Mulato
Mulato obscuro
No te entiendo
Octavón
Puchuela de negro

Quinterón
Quinterón de mulato
Requinterón de
  mulata
Saltatrás
Saltatrás cuarterón
Saltatrás quinterón
Tercerón
Zambo
Zambo prieto

Peru

Peruvian terms for shades of blackness, as compiled for me by the scholar Carlos Aguirre, include the following:

Moreno
Moreno claro
Moreno oscuro
Negro
Negro retinto (very dark black, or "black as ink")
Negro tinto (as above)
Trigueño (the color of wheat)
Zambo (used less often, mostly to refer to somebody with curly
    hair, not necessarily as a color category)

There are also some pejorative terms that refer not to skin color but to other physical characteristics and that are applied to blacks. The most common, according to Aguirre, is probably *bembón* or *negro bembón*, which means somebody with thick lips (this comes from *bemba*, or "lips," and is a term also used in Cuba and other parts of Latin America).

In addition, although I heard the terms on occasion, very few Peruvians, I was told, would use the words *mulato* or *mulata* in daily life or to self-identify.

Dominican Republic

In the early 1970s, the sociologist Daysi Guzmán identified twelve skin colors as being common to the Dominican Republic:

Lechoso (too white, like milk)
Blanco (white)
Cenizo (ashen)
Descolorido (without color)
Pálido (so pale as to appear sick)
Desteñido (jaundiced)
Pecoso (freckled)
Pinto (mostly light but with large freckles or moles)
Trigueño (light with a very slight dark touch)
Manchado (dark with dark streaks)
Negro (very dark)
Morado (so black as to be almost purple)

In addition, Guzman noted ten facial structures, six physical types, five general racial types, and—strikingly—fifteen kinds of hair texture on a spectrum between *bueno* (good) for soft, Caucasian hair and *malo* (bad) for kinky, Negroid hair, including the following:

Lacio (straight and smooth)
Achinado (straight, stiff hair)
Espeso (thick, abundant, and very slightly wavy)
Macho (thick and strong, abundant, but without luster)
Rizado (thick and fine with small waves, but dull)
Muerto (thin and greasy)
Ondulado (wavy; vivo, thick, dry, and out of control; variable, of
    any type, indescribable)

Crespo (thick and frizzy)
De pimiento (peppery, growing slow and tight to the skull in small
    balls)
Motica (like peppery hair but thin, wavy)
Pega'ito (so close to the skull that it is impossible to comb)

Today, skin-color denominations in the Dominican Republic, as compiled for me by the scholar Frank Moya Pons, include the following, organized from white to black:

Blanco
Blanco colorado
Blanco leche
Blanco jojoto
Jabao
Grifo
Trigueño
Indio claro
Indio
Indio canela
Indio quemado
Indio oscuro
Mulatón
Prieto
Moreno
Negro
Negro haitiano

Other common denominations of blackness include the following:

Blanco fino
Blanco ordinario
Blanquito
Mulaton, mulatona
Chino, china
Negro fino
Negro ordinario
Negro bembón

Haiti

Racial categorizations in Haiti are, interestingly, perhaps best conveyed not by contemporary discourse but by the definitive book on the subject, which was written by the French historian Médéric Louis Élie Moreau de Saint-Méry, who was born to a Creole family in Martinique in 1750. I have reproduced the relevant material from Saint-Méry's work here:

I. Combinaisons du Blanc

D'un Blanc et d'une Négresse, vient	un Mulâtre
Mulâtresse	Quarteron
Quarteron	Métis
Métive	Mamelouque
Mamelouque	Quarteronné
Quarteronnée	Sang-mêlé
Sang-mêlée	Sang-mêlé, qui s'approche continuellment du Blanc
Marabou	Quarteron
Griffone	Quarteron
Sacatra	Quarteron

II. Combinaisons du Nègre

D'un nègre et d'une Blanche, vient	un Mulâtre
Sang-mêlée	Mulâtre
Quarteronnée	Mulâtre
Mamelouque	Mulâtre
Métive	Mulâtre
Quarteronne	Marabou
Mulâtresse	Griffe
Marabou	Griffe
Griffonne	Sacatra
Sacatra	Sacatra

III. Combinaisons du Mulâtre

D'un Mulâtre et d'une Blanche, vient	un Quarteron
Sang-mêlée	Quarteron

Quarteronnée	Quarteron
Mamelouque	Quarteron
Métive	Quarteron
Quarteronne	Quarteron
Marabou	Mulâtre
Griffonne	Marabou
Sacatra	Marabou
Négresse	Griffe

IV. Combinaisons du Quarteron

D'un Quarteron et d'une Blanche, vient	un Métis
Sang-mêlée	Métis
Quarteronnée	Métis
Mamelouque	Métis
Métive	Métis
Mulâtresse	Quarteron
Marabou	Quarteron
Griffonne	Mulâtre
Sacatra	Mulâtre
Négresse	Marabou

V. Combinaisons du Métis

D'un Métis et d'une Blanche, vient	un Mamelouc
Sang-mêlée	Mamelouc
Quarteronnée	Mamelouc
Mamelouque	Mamelouc
Quarteronne	Métis
Mulâtresse	Quarteron
Marabou	Quarteron
Griffonne	Quarteron
Sacatra	Mulâtre
Négresse	Mulâtre

VI. Combinaison du Mamelouc

D'un Mamelouc et d'une Blanche, vient	un Quarteronné
Sang-Mêlée	Quarteronné
Quarteronnée	Quarteronné
Métive	un Mamelouc

Quarteronne	Métis
Mulâtresse	Quarteron
Marabou	Quarteron
Griffonne	Quarteron
Sacatra	Mulâtre
Négresse	Mulâtre

VII. Combinaisons du Quarteronné

D'un Quarteronné et d'une Blanche, vient	un Sang-mêlé
Sang-Mêlée	Sang-Mêlé
Mamelouque	Quarteronné
Métive	Mamelouc
Quarteronne	Métis
Mulâtresse	Quarteron
Marabou	Quarteron
Griffonne	Quarteron
Sacatra	Mulâtre
Négresse	Mulâtre

VIII. Combinaisons du Sang-mêlé

D'un Sang-Mêlé et d'une Blanche, vient	un Sang-mêlé
Quarteronnée	Sang-mêlé
Mamelouque	Quarteronné
Métive	Mamelouc
Quarteronne	Métis
Mulâtresse	Quarteron
Marabou	Quarteron
Griffonne	Quarteron
Sacatra	Quarteron
Négresse	Mulâtre

IX. Combinaisons du Sacatra

D'un Sacatra et d'une Blanche, vient	un Quarteron
Sang-mêlée	Quarteron
Quarteronnée	Mulâtre
Mamelouque	Mulâtre
Métive	Mulâtre
Quarteronne	Mulâtre

Mulâtresse	Marabou
Marabou	Griffe
Griffonne	Griffe
Négresse	Sacatra

X. Combinaisons du Griffe

D'un Griffe et d'une Blanche, vient	un Quarteron
Sang-mêlée	Quarteron
Quarteronnée	Quarteron
Métive	Quarteron
Quarteronne	Mulâtre
Mulâtresse	Marabou
Marabou	Marabou
Sacatra	Griffe
Négresse	Sacatra

XI. Combinaisons du Marabou

D'un Marabou et d'une Blanche, vient	un Quarteron
Sang-mêlée	Quarteron
Quarteronnée	Quarteron
Mamelouque	Quarteron
Métive	Quarteron
Quarteronne	Quarteron
Mulâtresse	Mulâtre
Griffonne	Marabou
Sacatra	Griffe
Négresse	Griffe

Cuba

There are twenty types of blackness in Cuba's popular discourse that were catalogued in Jesús Guanche Pérez's 1996 essay "Etnicidad y racialidad en la Cuba actual." In order from black to white, they are the following:

Negro-azul
Negro color teléfono

Negro coco timba
Negro cabeza de puntilla
Negro
Moro
Mulato
Indio
Mulato chino
Mulato color cartucho
Mulato blanconazo
Trigueño
Jabao
Colorao
Chino
Blanco
Rubio
Blanco orillero
Blanco lechoso
Albino

The scholar Tomás Fernández Robaina sent me the following additions to this list:

Negro (or Negra)
Negro achinado
Negro moro
Negro azul
Moreno
Mulato
Mulato indiao o mulato indio
Mestizo
Jabao o java
Blanco capirro
Moro o mora
Afrocubano
Trigueño

Bibliography

Aguirre, Carlos. *Agentes de su propia libertad: Los esclavos de Lima y la desintegración de la esclavitud, 1821–1854*. Lima: Pontificia Universidad Católica del Perú, 1993.

———. *Breve historia de la esclavitud en el Perú: Una herida que no deja de sangrar*. Lima: Fondo Editorial del Congreso del Perú, 2005.

———. *Dénle duro que no siente: Poder y transgresión en el Perú republicano*. Lima: Fondo Editorial del Pedagógico San Marcos, 2008.

———. "La población de origen africano en el Perú: De la esclavitud a la libertad." In *Lo africano en la cultura criolla*. Lima: Fondo Editorial del Congreso del Perú, 2000.

Aguirre, Carlos, and Charles Walker, eds. *Bandoleros, abigeos y montoneros: Criminalidad y violencia en el Perú (siglos XVIII–XX)*. Lima: Instituto de Apoyo Agrario/Instituto Pasado & Presente, 1990.

Albuquerque, Wlamyra Ribeiro de. *Algazarra nas ruas: Comemorações da independência na Bahia (1889–1923)*. Campinas, Brazil: Unicamp, 1999.

———. *Uma história do Negro no Brasil*. Salvador, Brazil: Centro de Estudos Afro-Orientais, 2006.

Andrews, George Reid. *Afro-Latin America, 1800–2000*. Oxford: Oxford University Press, 2004.

———. *Blackness in the White Nation: A History of Afro-Uruguay*. Chapel Hill: University of North Carolina Press, 2010.

Arrelucea Barrantes, Maribel. "Conducta social de los esclavos de Lima a fines de la colonia." Tesis de Licenciatura, UNMSM, Lima, 1999.

———. *Poder masculino, esclavitud femenina y violencia doméstica en Lima, 1760–1820*. Congreso Internacional Mujeres, familia y sociedad en la historia de América Latina, siglos XVIII–XXI. Lima: PUCP, 2003.

———. *Replanteando la esclavitud: Estudios de etnicidad y género en Lima borbónica*. Lima: CEDET, Centro de Desarrollo Étnico, 2009.

Bacha, Edmar Lisboa, and Herbert S. Klein. *Social Change in Brazil, 1945–1985: The Incomplete Transition*. Albuquerque: University of New Mexico, 1989.

Bandelt, H. J., et al. "Phylogeography of the Human Mitochondrial Haplo-

group L 3e: A Snapshot of African Prehistory and Atlantic Slave Trade."
Annals of Human Genetics 65 (2001): 549–63.

Barnet, Miguel. *Afro-Cuban Religions*. Princeton, NJ: Wiener, 2001.

———. *Biography of a Runaway Slave*. Willimantic, CT: Curbstone, 1995.

———. *Rachel's Song*. Willimantic, CT: Curbstone, 1995.

———. *A True Story: A Cuban in New York*. Trans. Regina Galasso. New York: Jorge Pinto Books, 2010.

Beato, Lucila B. "Inequality and Human Rights of African Descendants in Brazil." *Journal of Black Studies* 34, no. 6 (July 2004): 766–86.

Beauvoir, Dominique Rachel, and Morrison Charles. *L'ancienne cathédrale de Port-au-Prince: Perspectives d'un vestige de carrefours*. Port-au-Prince, Haiti: Henri Deschamps, 1991.

Beltrán, Gonzalo Aguirre. *Cuijla: Esbozo etnográfico de un pueblo negro*. Mexico City: Secretaria de Educación Pública, 1958.

Bennett, Herman L. *Africans in Colonial Mexico: Absolutism, Christianity, and Afro-Creole Consciousness, 1570–1640*. Bloomington: Indiana University Press, 2003.

———. *Colonial Blackness: A History of Afro-Mexico*. Bloomington: Indiana University Press, 2009.

———. "Lovers, Family and Friends: The Formation of Afro-Mexico: 1580–1810." Ann Arbor, MI: UMI Diss. Services, 2001.

Bettelheim, Judith. "Negotiations of Power in Carnaval Culture in Santiago de Cuba." *African Arts* (UCLA James S. Coleman African Studies Center), April 1991, 68.

Brock, Lisa, and Digna Castañeda Fuertes. *Between Race and Empire: African-Americans and Cubans before the Cuban Revolution*. Philadelphia: Temple University Press, 1998.

Bronfman, Alejandra. *Measures of Equality: Social Science, Citizenship, and Race in Cuba, 1902–1940*. Chapel Hill: University of North Carolina, 2004.

———. *On the Move: The Caribbean since 1989*. Halifax, NS: Fernwood, 2007.

Brown, David H. *Santeria Enthroned: Art, Ritual, and Innovation in an Afro-Cuban Religion*. Chicago: University of Chicago, 2003

Brown, Karen McCarthy. *Mama Lola: A Vodou Priestess in Brooklyn*. Berkeley: University of California, 2001.

Burke, Peter, and Maria Lúcia G. Pallares-Burke. *Gilberto Freyre: Social Theory in the Tropics*. Witney, UK: Peter Lang, 2008.

Campos Dávila, José. *Las negras noches del dolor*. Lima: San Marcos, 2004.

Candelario, Ginetta E. B. *Black behind the Ears: Dominican Racial Identity from Museums to Beauty Shops*. Durham: Duke University Press, 2007.

Canino, Maria Josefa, and Silvio Torres-Saillant. *The Challenges of Public Higher Education in the Hispanic Caribbean*. Princeton, NJ: Wiener, 2004.

Carrillo Zegarra, Mónica. *Unicroma*. Lima: Santo X Oficio, 2007.

Cooper, Frederick, Thomas C. Holt, and Rebecca J. Scott. *Beyond Slavery: Explorations of Race, Labor, and Citizenship in Postemancipation Societies.* Chapel Hill: University of North Carolina Press, 2000.

Crahan, Margaret E., and Franklin W. Knight. *Africa and the Caribbean: The Legacies of a Link*. Baltimore: Johns Hopkins University Press, 1979.

Cruz-Carretero, Sagrario, Alfredo Martínez Maranto, and Angélica Santiago Silva. *El Carnaval en Yanga: Notas y comentarios sobre una fiesta de la negritud*. Consejo Nacional para la Cultura y las Artes, Dirección General de Culturas Populares, Unidad Regional Centro de Veracruz, 1990.

Davis, Darién J., ed. *Beyond Slavery: The Multilayered Legacy of Africans in Latin America and the Caribbean*. Lanham, MD: Rowman and Littlefield, 2007.

Davis, F. James. *Who Is Black: One Nation's Definition*. University Park: Penn State University Press, 2001.

Derby, Lauren. "Haitians, Magic, and Money: Raza and Society in the Haitian-Dominican Borderlands, 1900 to 1937." *Comparative Studies in Society and History* 36, no. 3 (1994): 488.

Domínguez, Jorge I. *Cuba: Order and Revolution*. Cambridge: Belknap Press of Harvard University Press, 1978.

———. *To Make a World Safe for Revolution: Cuba's Foreign Policy*. Cambridge: Harvard University Press, 1989.

Douglass, Frederick. "Address Written to Be Presented Louis Mondestin Florvil Hyppolite." Notes for public address, November 14, 1889.

———. "American Opinion of Haiti: An Address Delivered in Port-au-Prince." Public address, February 18, 1890.

———. "A Fervent Hope for the Success of Haiti." December 11, 1889.

———. "Haiti among the Foremost Civilized Nations of the Earth." Public address, January 2, 1893.

———. "Haiti and the Haitian People." Public address, January 2, 1893.

———. "Resignation but Not Retirement: An Interview Given in Washington." Interview, August 11, 1891.

———. "Self-Made Men: An Address Delivered in Carlisle, Penn." Public address, March 1893.

Douglass, Frederick, John W. Blassingame, John R. McKivigan, and Peter P. Hinks. *The Frederick Douglass Papers*. New Haven: Yale University Press, 2003.

Dubois, Laurent. *Avengers of the New World: The Story of the Haitian Revolution*. Cambridge: Belknap Press of Harvard University Press, 2004.

———. *A Colony of Citizens: Revolution and Slave Emancipation in the French Caribbean, 1787–1804*. Chapel Hill: University of North Carolina Press, 2004.

Dubois, Laurent. *Haiti in the Early Nineteenth Century*. Kingston: Jamaican Historical Society, 2007.

Dubois, Laurent, and John D. Garrigus. *Slave Revolution in the Caribbean, 1789–1804: A Brief History with Documents*. Boston: Bedford/St. Martin's, 2006.

Dubois, Laurent, and Julius Sherrard Scott. *Origins of the Black Atlantic*. New York: Routledge, 2010.

Du Bois, William Edward Burghardt. *The Correspondence of W. E. B. Du Bois*. Edited by Herbert Aptheker. Amherst: University of Massachusetts Press, 1976.

———. *The Negro*. 1915. Reprint, Philadelphia: University of Pennsylvania Press, 2001.

Dumesle, Hérard. *Voyage dans le nord d'Hayti*. Cayes: Imprimerie du Gouvernement, 1824.

Dumont, Henry. *Antropología y patología comparadas de los hombres de color africanos que viven en Cuba*. La Real Academia de Ciencias Médicas, Físicas y Naturales de la Habana, 1876.

Dzidzienyo, Anani, and Suzanne Oboler, eds. *Neither Enemies nor Friends: Latinos, Blacks, Afro-Latinos*. New York: Palgrave Macmillan, 2005.

Eltis, David, and David Richardson. *Atlas of the Transatlantic Slave Trade*. New Haven: Yale University Press, 2010.

———. *Extending the Frontiers: Essays on the New Transatlantic Slave Trade Database*. New Haven: Yale University Press, 2008.

———. *Voyages: The Trans-Atlantic Slave Trade Database*. http://www.slavevoyages.org/.

Fatton, Robert. *Haiti's Predatory Republic: The Unending Transition to Democracy*. Boulder, CO: Lynne Rienner, 2002.

Feldman, Heidi Carolyn. *Black Rhythms of Peru: Reviving African Musical Heritage in the Black Pacific*. Middletown, CT: Wesleyan University Press, 2006.

Fernández Robaina, Tomás. *Apuntes para la historia de la Biblioteca Nacional José Martí de Cuba: Cien años, 1901–2001*. Havana: Biblioteca Nacional José Martí, 2001.

———. *Cuba, personalidades en el debate racial: Conferencias y ensayos*. Havana: Editorial de Ciencias Sociales, 2007.

———. *Historias de mujeres públicas*. Havana: Editorial Letras Cubanas, 1998.

———. *Identidad afrocubana: Cultura y nacionalidad*. Santiago de Cuba: Editorial Oriente, 2009.

Ferrer, Ada. *Insurgent Cuba: Race, Nation, and Revolution, 1868–1898*. Chapel Hill: University of North Carolina Press, 1999.

———. "Rustic Men, Civilized Nation: Race, Culture, and Contention on the

Eve of Cuban Independence." *Hispanic American Historical Review* 78, no. 4 (November 1998): 663–86.

Fick, Carolyn E. "The Haitian Revolution and the Limits of Freedom: Defining Citizenship in the Revolutionary Era." *Social History* 32, no. 4 (2007): 394–414.

Font, Mauricio A., and Alfonso W. Quiroz. *Cuban Counterpoints: The Legacy of Fernando Ortiz.* Lanham, MD: Lexington, 2005.

Franco Pichardo, Franklin J. *Los negros, los mulatos y la nación dominicana.* Santo Domingo: Editora Nacional, 1970.

———. *Los problemas raciales en la Republica Dominicana y el Caribe.* Santo Domingo: Ayuntamiento del Distrito Nacional, 1998.

Freyre, Gilberto de Mello. *The Mansions and the Shanties: The Making of Modern Brazil.* São Paulo: Companhia Editora Nacional, 1936.

———. *The Masters and the Slaves.* Rio de Janeiro: Maia & Schmidt, 1933.

———. *Order and Progress: Brazil from Monarchy to Republic.* Rio de Janeiro: José Olympio, 1959.

Fuente, Alejandro de la. "A propósito de un curso sobre 'Racialidad en la Cuba actual': Diálogo virtual con mis colegas de la isla." *Espacio Laical* 7, no. 26 (April–June 2011): 35–39.

———. "Myths of Racial Democracy: Cuba, 1900–1912." *Latin American Research Review* 34, no. 3 (Fall 1999): 39–73.

———. *A Nation for All: Race, Inequality, and Politics in Twentieth-Century Cuba.* Chapel Hill: University of North Carolina Press, 2001.

———. "The New Afro-Cuban Cultural Movement and the Debate on Race in Contemporary Cuba." *Journal of Latin American Studies* 40, no. 4 (November 2008): 697–720.

———. "Race and Income Inequality in Contemporary Cuba." *NACLA Report on the Americas* 44, no. 4 (July–August 2011).

Fuente, Alejandro de la, and M. Casey. "Race and the Suffrage Controversy in Cuba, 1898–1901." In *Colonial Crucible: Empire in the Making of the American Modern State,* ed. Alfred McCoy and Francisco Scarano, 220–29. Madison: University of Wisconsin Press, 2009.

Fuente, Alejandro de la, Cesar Garcia Del Pino, and Delgado Bernardo Iglesias. *Havana and the Atlantic in the Sixteenth Century.* Chapel Hill: University of North Carolina Press, 2008.

Furtado, Júnia Ferreira. *Chica da Silva: A Brazilian Slave of the Eighteenth Century.* Cambridge: Cambridge University Press, 2009.

———. *O Livro da Capa Verde: O regimento diamantino de 1771 e a vida no Distrito Diamantino no periodo da real extraco.* São Paulo: Annablume, 1996.

Garraway, Doris Lorraine. *Tree of Liberty: Cultural Legacies of the Haitian*

Revolution in the Atlantic World. Charlottesville: University of Virginia Press, 2008.

Garrigus, John D., and Christopher Morris, eds. *Assumed Identities: The Meanings of Race in the Atlantic World*. College Station: Texas A&M University Press, 2010.

Geggus, David Patrick, and Norman Fiering. *The World of the Haitian Revolution*. Bloomington: Indiana University Press, 2009.

Goldschmidt, Henry, and Elizabeth A. McAlister. *Race, Nation, and Religion in the Americas*. New York: Oxford University Press, 2004.

González, Anita. *Afro-Mexico: Dancing between Myth and Reality*. Austin: University of Texas Press, 2010.

Grillo, Christina. "Brasil quer ser chamado de moreno e só 39% se autodefinem como broncos." *Folha de S. Paulo*, Especial 5 (June 25, 1995).

Guanche Pérez, Jesús. "Etnicidad y racialidad en la Cuba actual." *Temas* 7 (1996): 54.

Gudmundson, Lowell, and Justin Wolfe. *Blacks and Blackness in Central America: Between Race and Place*. Durham: Duke University Press, 2010.

Guridy, Frank Andre. "'Enemies of the White Race': The Machadista State and the UNIA in Cuba." *Caribbean Studies* 31, no. 1 (January–June 2003).

———. *Forging Diaspora: Afro-Cubans and African Americans in a World of Empire and Jim Crow*. Chapel Hill: University of North Carolina Press, 2010.

———. "Racial Knowledge in Cuba: The Production of a Social Fact, 1912–1944." Ph.D. dissertation, University of Michigan, 2002.

Gutmann, Matthew C. *Perspectives on Las Americas: A Reader in Culture, History, and Representation*. Malden, MA: Blackwell, 2003.

Haber, Stephen H. *Mexico since 1980*. Cambridge: Cambridge University Press, 2008.

Hanchard, Michael George. *Racial Politics in Contemporary Brazil*. Durham: Duke University Press, 1999.

Harris, Christopher. "Edwin F. Atkins and the Evolution of United States Cuba Policy, 1894–1902." *New England Quarterly* 78, no. 2 (June 2005): 202–31.

Helg, Aline. "Abolition and Afro-Latin Americans." In *A Companion to Latin American History*, ed. Thomas H. Holloway. Malden, MA: Blackwell, 2008.

Hernández, Cuevas Marco Polo, and Richard L. Jackson. *African Mexicans and the Discourse on Modern Nation*. Lanham, MD: University Press of America, 2004.

Herrera, Claudia. *The African Presence in Mexico: From Yanga to the Present*. Chicago: Mexican Fine Arts Center Museum, 2006.

Heywood, Linda M. "Angolan-Afro-Brazilian Cultural Connections." *Slavery and Abolition* 20, no. 1 (April 1999).

———. *Central Africans and Cultural Transformations in the American Diaspora.* Cambridge: Cambridge University Press, 2002.

Heywood, Linda M., and the African Diaspora Committee, eds. *The African Diaspora: Africans and Their Descendants in the Wider World to 1800.* Boston: Ginn, 1989.

Heywood, Linda M., and Oswaldo Faustino. *Diaspora negra no Brasil.* São Paulo: Editora Contexto, 2008.

Heywood, Linda M., and John K. Thornton. *Central Africans, Atlantic Creoles, and the Foundation of the Americas, 1585–1660.* New York: Cambridge University Press, 2007.

Hooker, Juliet. *Race and the Politics of Solidarity.* Oxford: Oxford University Press, 2009.

Htun, Mala. "From 'Racial Democracy' to Affirmative Action: Changing State Policy on Race in Brazil." *Latin American Research Review* 39, no. 1 (2004): 60–68.

Iglesias Utset, Marial. *A Cultural History of Cuba during the U.S. Occupation, 1898–1902.* Chapel Hill: University of North Carolina Press, 2011.

———. *Las metáforas del cambio en la vida cotidiana: Cuba, 1898–1902.* Havana: Ediciones Unión, 2003.

Jiménez Román, Miriam, and Juan Flores, eds. *The Afro-Latin Reader: History and Culture in the United States.* Durham: Duke University Press, 2010.

Jones, Marcus D., and Charles Henry Rowell, eds. "Yanga, Mata Clara y pueblos cercanos: África en México contemporánea." *Callaloo* 31, no. 1 (Winter 2008).

Klein, Herbert S. *The Atlantic Slave Trade.* Cambridge: Cambridge University Press, 1999.

———. *The Middle Passage: Comparative Studies in the Atlantic Slave Trade.* Princeton: Princeton University Press, 1978.

———. *Slavery in the Americas: A Comparative Study of Virginia and Cuba.* Chicago: University of Chicago Press, 1967.

Klein, Herbert S., and Francisco Vidal Luna. *Brazil since 1980.* Cambridge: Cambridge University Press, 2006.

———. *Slavery and the Economy of São Paulo, 1750–1850.* Stanford: Stanford University Press, 2003.

———. *Slavery in Brazil.* Cambridge: Cambridge University Press, 2010.

Klein, Herbert S., and Ben Vinson III. *African Slavery in Latin America and the Caribbean.* New York: Oxford University Press, 1986.

Knight, Franklin W. *The Caribbean: The Genesis of a Fragmented Nationalism.* New York: Oxford University Press, 1978.

Knight, Franklin W. *Slave Society in Cuba during the Nineteenth Century.* Madison: University of Wisconsin Press, 1970.

Knight, Franklin W., Gordon K. Lewis, and Frank Moya Pons. *Migration and Caribbean Cultural Identity: Selected Papers from Conference Celebrating the 50th Anniversary of the Center.* Gainesville: University of Florida, Center for Latin American Studies, 1982.

Knight, Franklin W., and Vergne Teresita Martinez. *Contemporary Caribbean Cultures and Societies in a Global Context.* Chapel Hill: University of North Carolina Press, 2005.

Knight, Franklin W., and Colin A. Palmer. *The Modern Caribbean.* Chapel Hill: University of North Carolina Press, 1989.

Landers, Jane, and Barry Robinson. *Slaves, Subjects, and Subversives: Blacks in Colonial Latin America.* Albuquerque: University of New Mexico Press, 2006.

"La pintura de castas/The Painting of Castas." *Artes de México y del Mundo* 8, no. 1 (1990): 79.

León, Nicolás. *Las castas de México colonial o Nueva España.* Talleres Gráficos del Museo Nacional de Arqueología, Historia, y Etnografía, 1924.

Libby, Douglas Cole, and Júnia Ferreira Furtado. *Trabalho livre, trabalho escravo: Brasil e Europa, séculos XVIII e XIX.* São Paulo: Annablume, 2006.

Lorini, Alessandra. *An Intimate and Contested Relation: The United States and Cuba in the Late Nineteenth and Early Twentieth Centuries.* Firenze: Firenze University Press, 2005.

Luria, Sarah. "Santo Domingo, or the Ambiguities: Frederick Douglass, Black Imperialism, and the 'Ku Klux War.'" Paper presented at the annual meeting of the American Studies Association, Philadelphia, October 11, 2007.

Martins, Sérgio Da Silva, Carlos Alberto Medeiros, and Elisa Larkin Nascimento. "Paving Paradise: The Road from 'Racial Democracy' to Affirmative Action in Brazil." *Journal of Black Studies* 34, no. 6 (July 2004): 787–816.

Matory, James Lorand. *Black Atlantic Religion: Tradition, Transnationalism, and Matriarchy in the Afro-Brazilian Candomblé.* Princeton: Princeton University Press, 2005.

———. "A Broken Calabash: Social Aspects of Worship among Brazilian and West African Yoruba." Unpublished thesis, 1982.

McKnight, Kathryn Joy, and Leo Garofalo. *Afro-Latino Voices: Narratives from the Early Modern Ibero-Atlantic World, 1550–1812.* Indianapolis: Hackett, 2009.

Minority Rights Group, ed. *No Longer Invisible: Afro-Latin Americans Today.* London: Minority Rights Publications, 1995.

Mintz, Sidney W. *Caribbean Transformations*. Piscataway, NJ: Transaction, 2007.

———, ed. *Slavery, Colonialism, and Racism*. New York: Norton, 1974.

———. *Sweetness and Power: The Place of Sugar in Modern History*. London: Penguin, 1986.

———. *Three Ancient Colonies: Caribbean Themes and Variations*. Cambridge: Harvard University Press, 2010.

Mintz, Sidney W., and Richard Price. *The Birth of African-American Culture: An Anthropological Perspective*. Boston: Beacon, 1992.

Mintz, Sidney W., and Sally Price, eds. *Caribbean Contours*. Baltimore: Johns Hopkins University Press, 1985.

Moore, Robin. *Nationalizing Blackness: Afrocubanismo and Artistic Revolution in Havana, 1920–1940*. Pittsburgh: University of Pittsburgh Press, 1997.

Moreno, Fraginals Manuel, Frank Moya Pons, and Stanley L. Engerman. *Between Slavery and Free Labor: The Spanish-Speaking Caribbean in the Nineteenth Century*. Baltimore: Johns Hopkins University Press, 1985.

Moya Pons, Frank. *Después de Colón: Trabajo, sociedad y política en la economía del oro*. Madrid: Alianza, 1987.

———. *The Dominican Republic: A National History*. Princeton, NJ: Wiener, 2010.

———. *History of the Caribbean: Plantations, Trade, and War in the Atlantic World*. Princeton, NJ: Wiener, 2007.

Nicholls, David. *From Dessalines to Duvalier: Race, Colour, and National Independence in Haiti*. New Brunswick: Rutgers University Press, 1996.

Olaniyan, Tejumola, and James H. Sweet. *The African Diaspora and the Disciplines*. Bloomington: Indiana University Press, 2010.

Ortiz, Fernando. *Contrapunteo cubano del tabaco y el azúcar*. 1940. Reprint, Madrid: Edito Cuba España, 1999.

———. *La africanía de la música folklórica de Cuba*. 1950. Reprint, Madrid: Música Mundana, 1998.

———. *Los instrumentos de la música afrocubana*. 2 vols. 1952–1955. Reprint, Madrid: Música Mundana, 1996.

———. *Los negros brujos*. 1906. Reprint, Miami, FL: Ediciones Universal, 1973.

Pallares-Burke, Maria Lúcia G. *Gilberto Freyre: Um vitoriano dos trópicos*. São Paulo: Editora UNESP, 2005.

Palmie, Stephan. *Africas of the Americas: Beyond the Search for Origins in the Study of Afro-Atlantic Religions*. Leiden: Brill, 2008.

Paterson, Thomas G. "U.S. Intervention in Cuba, 1898: Interpreting the Spanish-American-Cuban-Filipino War." *Magazine of History* 12, no. 3 (Spring 1998): 5–10.

Pena, Sérgio D. J., et al. "The Genomic Ancestry of Individuals from Different Geographical Regions of Brazil Is More Uniform Than Expected." *PLoS ONE* 6, no. 2 (February 2011): 1–9.

Pérez, Louis A., Jr. *Cuba in the American Imagination: Metaphor and the Imperial Ethos.* Chapel Hill: University of North Carolina Press, 2008.

Pérez, Sarduy Pedro, and Jean Stubbs. *Afro-Cuban Voices: On Race and Identity in Contemporary Cuba.* Gainesville: University Press of Florida, 2000.

Price, Richard. *First-Time: The Historical Vision of an African American People.* Chicago: University of Chicago Press, 2002.

———. *Making Empire: Colonial Encounters and the Creation of Imperial Rule in Nineteenth-Century Africa.* Cambridge: Cambridge University Press, 2008.

———. *Maroon Societies: Rebel Slave Communities in the Americas.* Baltimore: Johns Hopkins University Press, 1996.

Price-Mars, Jean. *Ainsi parla l'oncle: Essais d'ethnographie.* Port-au-Prince: Imprimerie de Compiegne, 1928.

———. *De Saint-Domingue à Haïti.* Paris: Présence Africaine, 1959.

———. *La République d'Haïti et la République Dominicaine.* Port-au-Prince, 1953.

———. *La vocation de l'elite.* Port-au-Prince: Impre. E. Chenet, 1919. .

———. *Silhouettes de nègres et de négrophiles.* Paris: Présence Africaine, 1960.

Reis, João José. *Death Is a Festival: Funeral Rites and Popular Rebellion in Nineteenth-Century Brazil.* Chapel Hill: University of North Carolina Press, 2003.

———. *Slave Rebellion in Brazil: The Muslim Uprising of 1835 in Bahia.* Baltimore: Johns Hopkins University Press, 1993.

Restall, Matthew. *Beyond Black and Red: African-Native Relations in Colonial Latin America.* Albuquerque: University of New Mexico Press, 2005.

Rothman, Adam. *Slave Country: American Expansion and the Origins of the Deep South.* Cambridge: Harvard University Press, 2005.

Salcedo-Mitrani, Lorry. *A la sombra del guarango* (In the Shade of the Guarango Tree). Lima: Fondo Editorial del Congreso del Peru, 2007.

Sawyer, Mark Q. "Du Bois' Double Consciousness versus Latin American Exceptionalism: Joe Arroyo, Salsa and Negritude." *SOULS* 7, nos. 3–4 (2004): 88–98.

———. "Racial Politics in Multi-ethnic America: Black and Latino Identities and Coalitions." In *Neither Enemies nor Friends: Latinos, Blacks, Afro-Latinos,* ed. Anani Dzidzienyo and Suzanne Oboler. New York: Palgrave Macmillan, 2005.

———. *Racial Politics in Post-revolutionary Cuba.* New York: Cambridge University Press, 2006.

———. "Unlocking the Official Story: Comparing the Cuban Revolution's

Approach to Race and Gender." *UCLA Journal of International Law and Foreign Affairs*, Winter 2001, 401–17.

Sawyer, Mark Q., and John Guidry. "Contentious Pluralism: The Public Sphere and Democracy." *Perspectives on Politics* 1, no. 2 (June 2003): 273–89.

Sawyer, Mark Q., and Tianna Paschel. "Contesting Politics as Usual: Black Social Movements, Globalization, and Race Policy in Latin America." *SOULS* 10, no. 3 (July 2008): 197–214.

Sawyer, Mark Q., and Yesilernis Peña. "Racial Cycles? A Dynamic Approach to the Study of Race in Post-Revolutionary Cuba and Beyond." *National Political Science Review* 9, no. 1 (2003): 138–55.

Sawyer, Mark Q., Yesilernis Peña, and James Sidanius. "Cuban Exceptionalism: Group-Based Hierarchy and the Dynamics of Patriotism in Puerto Rico, the Dominican Republic and Cuba." *Dubois Review* 1, no. 1 (2004): 93–114.

———. "Inclusionary Discrimination: Pigmentocracy and Patriotism in the Dominican Republic." *Journal of Political Psychology* 22, no. 4 (December 2001): 827–51.

———. " 'Racial Democracy' in the Americas: A Latin and North American Comparison." *Journal of Cross-Cultural Psychology* 35, no. 6 (2004): 749–62.

Schwartz, Stuart B. *Sugar Plantations in the Formation of Brazilian Society: Bahia, 1550–1835*. Cambridge: Cambridge University Press, 1985.

———. *Tropical Babylons: Sugar and the Making of the Atlantic World, 1450–1680*. Chapel Hill: University of North Carolina Press, 2004.

Scott, Rebecca J. *The Abolition of Slavery and the Aftermath of Emancipation in Brazil*. Durham: Duke University Press, 1988.

———. *Degrees of Freedom: Louisiana and Cuba after Slavery*. Cambridge: Belknap Press of Harvard University Press, 2005.

———. *Mobilizing Resistance among Slaves and Free People: Two Moments of Rural Rebellion in Cuba*. Ann Arbor, MI: S.n., 1988.

———. *Slave Emancipation in Cuba*. Pittsburgh: University of Pittsburgh Press, 2000.

Seed, Patricia. "Conquest of Mexico and Peru." In *A Companion to Latin American History*, ed. Thomas H. Holloway. Malden, MA: Blackwell, 2008.

Serna, Juan Manuel de la, ed. *De la libertad y la abolición: Africanos y afrodescendientes en Iberoamérica*. Mexico City: Universidad Nacional Autónoma de México, 2010.

———. *El Caribe en la encrucijada de su historia, 1780–1840*. Mexico City: Universidad Nacional Autónoma de México, Coordinación de Humanidades, Centro Coordinador y Difusor de Estudios Latinoamericanos, 1993.

Serna, Juan Manuel de la. *Ideas pedagógicas en el Caribe*. Mexico: SepCultura, Dirección General de Publicaciones, 1985.

———. *Los afronorteamericanos: Historia y destino*. Instituto de Investigaciones Dr. José María Luis Mora, Mexico, 1994.

Serna, Juan Manuel de la, ed. *Pautas de convivencia étnica en América Latina colonial: Negros, mulatos y esclavos*. Mexico City: Universidad Nacional Autónoma de México, 2005.

Sherwin, Martin J., and Winn, Peter. "The U.S. and Cuba." *Wilson Quarterly* 2, no. 1 (Winter 1978): 56–68.

Simmons, Kimberly Eison. *Reconstructing Racial Identity and the African Past in the Dominican Republic*. Gainesville: University Press of Florida, 2009.

Singleton, Theresa A. "Slavery and Spatial Dialectics on Cuban Coffee Plantations." *World Archaeology* 33, no. 1 (2001): 98–114.

Sommer, Doris. *Cultural Agency in the Americas*. Durham: Duke University Press, 2006.

———. *Foundational Fictions: The National Romances of Latin America*. Berkeley: University of California Press, 1991.

———. *One Master for Another: Populism as Patriarchal Rhetoric in Dominican Novels*. Lanham, MD: University Press of America, 1983.

———. *The Places of History: Regionalism Revisited in Latin America*. Durham: Duke University Press, 1999.

———. *Proceed with Caution When Engaged with Minority Writing in the Americas*. Cambridge: Harvard University Press, 1999.

Stavans, Ilan. *José Vasconcelos: The Prophet of Race*. New Brunswick: Rutgers University Press, 2011.

———, ed. *The Norton Anthology of Latino Literature*. New York: Norton, 2010.

Sweet, James H. *Domingos Alvares, African Healing, and the Intellectual History of the Atlantic World*. Chapel Hill: University of North Carolina Press, 2011.

———. *Recreating Africa: Culture, Kinship, and Religion in the African-Portuguese World, 1441–1770*. Chapel Hill: University of North Carolina Press, 2003.

Telles, Edward Eric. *Race in Another America: The Significance of Skin Color in Brazil*. Princeton: Princeton University Press, 2004.

Telles, Edward Eric, and Vilma Ortiz. *Generations of Exclusion: Mexican Americans, Assimilation, and Race*. New York: Russell Sage Foundation, 2008.

Thomas, Hugh. *The Conquest of Mexico*. London: Pimlico, 1994.

Thompson, Robert Farris. *Flash of the Spirit: African and Afro-American Art and Philosophy*. New York: Random House, 1983.

Thornton, John K. *Africa and Africans in the Making of the Atlantic World, 1400–1800*. Cambridge: Cambridge University Press, 1998.

———. "African Soldiers in the Haitian Revolution." *Journal of Caribbean History* 25 (1993): 59–80.

———. "As guerras civis no Congo e o tráfico de escravos: A história e a demografia de 1718 a 1844 revisitadas." *Estudos Afro-Asiaticos* (Rio de Janeiro) 32 (1997): 55–74.

———. "'I Am the Subject of the King of Congo': African Ideology in the Haitian Revolution." *Journal of World History* 4 (1993): 181–214.

———. "On the Trail of Voodoo: African Christianity in Africa and the Americas." *Americas* 44 (1988): 261–78.

Torres-Saillant, Silvio. *An Intellectual History of the Caribbean.* Basingstoke, UK: Palgrave Macmillan, 2006.

———. "The Tribulations of Blackness: Stages in Dominican Racial Identity. *Callaloo* 23, no. 3 (Summer 2000): 1086–1111.

Torroni, Antonio, et al. "Do the Four Clades of the mtDNA Haplogroup L2 Evolve at Different Rates?" *American Journal of Human Genetics* 69 (2001): 1384–56.

Trouillot, Michel-Rolph. "Abortive Rituals: Historical Apologies in the Global Era." *Interventions* 2, no. 2 (2000): 171–86.

———. "Alter-Native Modernities: Caribbean Lessons for the Savage Slot." In *Critically Modern,* ed. B. Knauft. Bloomington: Indiana University Press, 2002.

———. "The Caribbean Region: An Open Frontier in Anthropological Theory." *Annual Review of Anthropology* 21 (1992): 19–42.

———. "Coffee Planters and Coffee Slaves: From Saint-Domingue to Dominica." In *Cultivation and Culture: The Shaping of Slave Life in the Americas,* ed. I. Berlin and P. Morgan. Charlottesville: University of Virginia Press, 1993.

———. "Culture, Color and Politics in Haiti." In *Race,* ed. Steven Gregory and Roger Sanjek. New Brunswick: Rutgers University Press, 1994.

———. "Culture on the Edges: Creolization in the Plantation Context." *Plantation Society in the Americas* 5, no. 1 (1998): 8–28.

———. "Discourses of Rule and the Acknowledgment of the Peasantry in Dominica, W.I., 1838–1928." *American Ethnologist* 16, no. 4 (1989): 704–18.

———. *Haiti, State against Nation: The Origins and Legacy of Duvalierism.* New York: Monthly Review Press, 1990.

———. *Peasants and Capital: Dominica in the World Economy.* Baltimore: Johns Hopkins University Press, 1988.

———. "Silencing the Past: Layers of Meaning in the Haitian Revolution." In *Between History and Histories: The Making of Silences and Commemorations,* ed. G. Sider and G. Smith. Toronto: University of Toronto Press, 1997.

Trouillot, Michel-Rolph. *Silencing the Past: Power and the Production of History.* Boston: Beacon, 1995.

Turits, Richard Lee. *Foundations of Despotism: Peasants, the Trujillo Regime, and Modernity in Dominican History.* Stanford: Stanford University Press, 2003.

Turits, Richard Lee. "A World Destroyed, a Nation Imposed: The 1937 Haitian Massacre in the Dominican Republic." *American Historical Review* 82, no. 3 (August 2002): 589–635.

Vasconcelos, José. *The Cosmic Race.* 1925. Reprint, Baltimore: Johns Hopkins University Press, 1997.

Vaughn, Bobby. "Race and Nation: A Study of Blackness in Mexico." Ph.D. dissertation, Stanford University, 2001.

Vega, Bernardo, and José del Castillo Pichardo. *Dominican Cultures: The Making of a Caribbean Society.* Princeton, NJ: Wiener, 2007.

Velázquez Gutiérrez, María Elisa. *Juan Correa: "Mulato libre, maestro de pintor."* Mexico: Consejo Nacional para la Cultura y las Artes, 1998.

———. *La huella negra en Guanajuato: Retratos de afrodescendientes de los siglos XIX y XX.* Guanajuato, Gto.: Ediciones la Rana, 2007.

———. *Mujeres de origen africano en la capital novohispana, siglos XVII y XVIII.* Mexico City: Universidad Nacional Autónoma de México, 2006.

Velázquez Gutiérrez, María Elisa, and Ethel Correa Duró. *Poblaciones y culturas de origen africano en México.* Mexico: Instituto Nacional de Antropología e Historia, 2005.

Vinson, Ben. "African (Black) Diaspora History, Latin American History—A Comment." *Americas* 63, no. 1 (July 2006): 1–18.

———. *The African Diaspora in the Colonial Andes.* Washington, DC: Academy of American Franciscan History, 2006.

———. "Afro-Mexican History: Trends and Directions in Scholarship." *History Compass* 3, no. 1 (2005): 1–14.

———. "Articulating Space: The Free-Colored Military Establishment in Colonial Mexico from the Conquest to Independence." *Callaloo* 27, no. 1 (February 2004): 150–71.

———. *Bearing Arms for His Majesty: The Free-Colored Militia in Colonial Mexico.* Stanford: Stanford University Press, 2001.

———. "Fading from Memory: Historiographical Reflections on the Afro-Mexican Experience." *Review of Black Political Economy,* Summer 2005, 65–78.

———. "Free-Colored Voices: Issues of Representation and Racial Identity in the Colonial Mexican Militia." *Journal of Negro History* 80, no. 4 (Fall 1995): 170–82.

———. "La categorización racial de los afromexicanos durante la época colonial: Una revision basada en evidencia referente a las milicias." *Memorias de la academia Mexicana de la historia: Correspondiente de la real de Madrid* 44 (2001): 27–53.

———. "Los milicianos pardos y la construcción de la raza en el México colonial." *Signos Históricos* 2, no. 4 (July–December 2000): 87–106.

———. "Race and Badge: The Free-Colored Militia in Colonial Mexico." *Americas* 56, no. 4 (April 2000): 471–96.

———. "The Racial Profile of a Rural Mexican Province in the 'Costa Chica': Igualapa in 1791." *Americas* 57, no. 2 (October 2000): 269–82.

Vinson, Ben, and Stewart R. King. "Introducing the New African Diasporic Military History in Latin America." *Journal of Colonialism and Colonial History* 5, no. 2 (Fall 2004).

Vinson, Ben, and Cynthia Milton. "Counting Heads: Race and Non-native Tribute Policy in Colonial Spanish America." *Journal of Colonialism and Colonial History* 3, no. 3 (2002): 1–18.

Vinson, Ben, and Matthew Restall. *Black Mexico: Race and Society from Colonial to Modern Times.* Albuquerque: University of New Mexico, 2009.

Vinson, Ben, and Bobby Vaughn. *Afroméxico: El pulso de la población negra en México: Una historia recordada, olvidada y vuelta a recordar.* Mexico: Fondo de Cultura Económica, 2004.

Whitney, Robert. *State and Revolution in Cuba: Mass Mobilization and Political Change, 1920–1940.* Chapel Hill: University of North Carolina Press, 2001.

Wucker, Michele. *Why the Cocks Fight: Dominicans, Haitians, and the Struggle for Hispaniola.* New York: Hill and Wang, 1999.

Index

About the Author

HENRY LOUIS GATES, JR., is the director of the W. E. B. Du Bois Institute for African and African American Research and holder of the distinguished title of Alphonse Fletcher University Professor at Harvard University. He is the author of several award-winning works of literary criticism as well as the memoir *Colored People; The Future of the Race,* coauthored with Cornel West; and *Thirteen Ways of Looking at a Black Man.* Gates has hosted, written, and narrated eleven PBS television specials, including *Looking for Lincoln, Faces of America,* on which his book *Faces of America: How 12 Extraordinary People Discovered Their Pasts* (NYU Press, 2010) is based, and the two-part series *African American Lives,* on which another book, *In Search of Our Roots* (2009) was based. He is winner of the 2009 Ralph Lowell Award for Outstanding Contributions to Public Television and the 2010 NAACP Image Award for *In Search of Our Roots.*